The Lost Warfare o
An Illustrated Guide
By
Harjit Singh Sagoo & Antony Cummins

Copyright © 2016 by Harjit Singh Sagoo & Antony Cummins

Cover by Jay Kane

All rights reserved. No part of this document may be reproduced or transmitted in any form or by any means, electronic or mechanical, including photocopying, recording, or by an information storage and retrieval system without permission in writing from the authors.

WARNING AND DISCLAIMER: The information contained in this book can be dangerous and could result in serious injury and death. The author, publisher, and distributors disclaim any liability from any damage or injuries of any type that a reader or user of information contained in this book may incur from the use or misuse of said information. Always consult a qualified medical professional before beginning any nutritional program or exercise program. This book is presented for academic study only.

Dedication

Dedicated to our families for their continuous support and encouragement, and to the memory of Dr. Rudrapatnam Shamashastry, who discovered the *Arthashastra* and translated it into English. This book would not have been possible without them.

— Harjit Singh Sagoo & Antony Cummins

Acknowledgements

We wish to thank Rani Kaur for taking the photographs which were transformed into the silhouette graphics contained herein. We are also very grateful to Guru Piumal Edirisinghe, Gurumustuk Singh, Prasanna Revan, the Kaur Khalsa Gatka Group, Ranjeet Singh, Varun Kapur, Amrit Pal Singh 'Amrit', www.tripura4u.com, Arthur Mitchell Fraas, Abdul Qadir Memon, Linda De Volder, Sri E.S. Narayanan Embranthiri and Kiranjot Singh Malhotra for providing excellent photographs for use in this book.

CONTENTS

A History Of An Ancient Indian War Manual......... 1
Spies......... 18
Weapons......... 30
Weapons Of The Armoury......... 37
Battle......... 50
The Invasion......... 66
On The March......... 73
Treachery......... 80
Preparation......... 87
The Battlefield......... 94
The Array Of Troops......... 100
Different Formations......... 105
The Battle Of Intrigue......... 117
Slaying The Enemy Commander......... 121
Fire, Spies, Poison And Destruction......... 124
Remedies And Antidotes......... 137
Stratagems......... 142
Sowing The Seeds Of Dissension......... 148
Enticement Of Kings......... 152
Fortifications......... 161
Spies In A Siege......... 172
The Operation Of A Siege......... 181
Awards And Punishments......... 195
Assassination......... 203
Biological And Chemical Agents......... 218
Wonderful And Delusive Contrivances......... 228
The Application Of Mantras And Medicines......... 237
Assorted Sections......... 254
Roundup......... 291
The Collected Quick-Lessons......... 292
Glossary (Sanskrit-English)......... 307
Bibliography......... 313
Photo And Image Credits......... 316
About The Authors......... 317

A HISTORY OF AN ANCIENT INDIAN WAR MANUAL

The Original Text at a Glance

There exists an excellent ancient manual on warfare that was translated into the English Language over one hundred years ago; it is not Sun Tzu's *The Art of War*. This manual, while being available in not only English but as a Penguin Classic, is a manual that we rarely ever hear about and while there *are* scholars and enthusiasts who are not only aware of it but have studied the writing with depth, our aim is to make this manual known to a much wider audience, putting it in its correct place, on the shelf next to Sun Tzu and Machiavelli. The name of the manual is *Arthashastra*.

The following is pronounced as thus:

Arthashastra -- Ar-thah-shas-tar
Kautilya -- Koh-tell-lee-ah
Chanakya -- Chaa-nahk-kya

Around the year 350 BCE, there lived a man named Kautilya, who is also known as Chanakya (Fig. 1), and he was born in Northern India. It is thought that the authorship of the *Arthashastra* is attributed to Kautilya as this name is peppered throughout the text:

"But Kautilya holds that four and only four are the sciences; wherefore it is from these sciences that all that concerns righteousness and wealth is learnt, therefore they are so called."

It is believed that the name *Vishnu Gupta* is an alternative name of Kautilya as it is mentioned at the end of the text:

'Having seen discrepancies in many ways on the part of the writers of commentaries on the Sástras, Vishnu Gupta himself has made (this) Sútra and commentary.'

The two names – Kautilya and Vishnu Gupta – are generally considered by historians to be other names for Chanakya, the 3rd or 4th century BCE scholar and advisor to Chandragupta Maurya, founder of the Mauryan Empire. According to political economist and author, L. N. Rangarajan, the name Chanakya means 'son of Chanak' and that the name Vishnu Gupta is his personal name, while the name Kautilya indicates his clan name. Throughout this book, however, the author of the *Arthashastra* shall be referred to as Chanakya in both the text and commentary.

Tip list:
- *Arthashastra* is the name of the text and means 'science of governance'
- *Chanakya* is the name of the author and may mean 'son of Chanak'
- *Kautilya* is thought to be his clan name
- *Vishnu Gupta* is thought to be his personal name
- The manual was written in Sanskrit

Fig. 1

What is the Arthashastra?

The *Arthashastra* text is not solely concerned with warfare but is more of a total system of government, including military ways. The fifteen books of the text are as follows:

1. Concerning Discipline
2. The Duties of Government Superintendents
3. Concerning Law
4. The Removal of Thorns
5. The Conduct of Courtiers
6. The Source of Sovereign States
7. The End of the Six-Fold Policy

8. Concerning Vices and Calamities
9. The Work of an Invader
10. Relating to War
11. The Conduct of Corporations
12. Concerning a Powerful Enemy
13. Strategic Means to Capture a Fortress
14. Secret Means
15. The Plan of a Treatise

The subjects contained within include, but not limited to:
- deceiving enemies
- battle arrays
- battle injury remedies
- poisons
- spells
- flammable weapons
- encampment
- siege warfare
- assassination
- types of weapons
- armour
- training and uses of chariots, elephants, cavalry and infantry

Other subjects include seizing criminals, duties of a king, measurement of time and space, restoring peace and so much more.

Who Translated the Original Text?

The original 3rd/4th century BCE text has most likely withered away. In 1905, a Brahmin Sanskrit scholar named Dr. Rudrapatnam Shamashastry (1868 – 1944) (Fig. 2), who hailed from the state of Karnataka, South West India, discovered the *Arthashastra* among other old manuscripts sitting at the Oriental Research Institute in the city of Mysore, the third largest city of Karnataka. That text was a copy of a reproduction made centuries ago. By 1915, Dr. Shamashastry became the first person to publish the English translation.

Fig. 2

Dr. Shamashastry's version of the English text has become the property of Public Domain and can be read alongside the translation of L.N. Rangarajan from the Penguin Classics Collection among other translations. However, we felt that the reason for the text's relatively limited appeal was due to its length, complexity and use of old fashioned prose. Also, while many parts of the text are important, they hold little interest to the modern reader who simply wishes to delve into the ancient world. With this as a foundation, we set off to edit and extract the most exciting parts of the text, give commentary and open up a gateway for you, the reader, to enter into Dr. Shamashastry's translation and the wonderful world of the lost warfare of India.

The Aim of this Version

This book should *never* be considered as a replacement for the full text, quite the opposite. The pages that follow are designed to allow a casual reader to have access to the most compelling and enthroning parts of the original translation. Again, this is an edited and cut down version and should be seen as 'highlights from the *Arthashastra* with commentaries and visual explanations'. Therefore, while we have attempted to keep most teachings *in situ* and next to other lessons from the original, there has been some movement to keep a more fluid read. Because of the availability of such translations we feel that the key feature of this book should be *accessibility* and *ease*. Therefore, a new reader of Dr. Shamashastry's work should fully enjoy this book in the format and order it is presented in, moving on to the full manual at a later date, while an experienced reader, who is at ease with the teachings of the *Arthashastra*, will find the illustrations and commentaries stimulating.

The Set Up

Original Text and Translation:
All of Dr. Shamashastry's translation and text has been presented in *italics* so that it is easily identifiable. To the best of our ability, we have attempted to keep his text exactly how he presented it. However, at times, old fashioned and outdated words have been changed to a more modern version, but this has been kept to an absolute minimum.

Titles:
Each section of original text has been given an evocative title. These titles are our invention and are simply there to prep the reader's mind so that the text can be better understood and to be used as a marker for any study of the manual.

Quick-lessons:
Due to the nature of the text and the era of the translation, an instant or full understanding is sometimes difficult to arrive at with speed. Therefore, after most sections of the text we have given our brief commentary which highlights the main principle of the teaching. A list of the Quick-lessons is given at the end of the book to be used as a guideline to the main principles of Indian Warfare.

Speech Bubbles:
In addition to the above, we have included speech bubbles with information pertaining to difficult words or points of interest. Some book and chapter numbers from the original text are also provided in speech bubbles for reference.

The Illustrations:
Today we live more and more in a visual world. Our generation of readers prefer a visual guide to writing – another reason why the original text is not as widespread as it may be – therefore we have inserted as many visual aids as practical to help guide the reader through the complex world of ancient India. However, these are just interpretations and should not be taken as totally literal. They are there to give the reader a glimpse at the world that would have been and should be treated as such and should be considered as triggers for the imagination.

India, Culture and War

Many are familiar with Sun Tzu's *The Art of War*, Miyamoto Musashi's *A Book of Five Rings*, Niccolo Machiavelli's *The Prince* and other great works on strategy. Unfortunately, Chanakya's *Arthashastra* does not seem to share this familiarity. We want to change that by introducing this legendary strategist and his great work to the wider audience. Firstly, however, we have to understand the land from where this work came.

India, which is perhaps best known for its spiritual practices and spicy cuisines, has a very rich martial culture, but before we discuss warfare it is best to understand the political situation in which the author, Chanakya, was brought up in.

Chanakya, who was a university teacher in the city of Taxila (Fig. 3), lived in turbulent times. India was divided and it particularly suffered under the tyrannical rule of the cruel emperor Dhana Anand (reigned between 329 – 321 BCE) of the Nanda Dynasty. After suffering great humiliation in the court of this hated ruler, a furious and vengeful Chanakya untied his Orthodox Hindu hair lock and declared the vow that he would only tie his lock once the Nanda Dynasty had fallen. He would one day fulfil his promise after finding an ideal pupil, Chandragupta Maurya, who, with Chanakya's words of wisdom, became a formidable warrior, defeated the Nanda forces and established the Mauryan Empire.

> The year in which Chanakya was born and died as well the location of his birthplace is debated among researchers. However, S. K. Agarwal in his book, *Towards Improving Governanace*, and V. K. Subramaniam in his book, *Maxims of Chanakya*, both mention Chanakya being born circa 350 BCE. and dying circa 275 BCE.

> Chanakya was educated at the prestigious Takshila (also Taxila) University in ancient India, later becoming a teacher there.

Under Chanakya's direct guidance, Chandragupta rose from a mere boy to a powerful emperor who held power over vast areas. Chandragupta was akin to Alexander the Great. Greek historian, biographer and essayist, Plutarch (46 – 120 CE), writes in his *Parallel Lives*, a book of biographies, that a young Chandragupta (known as Androcottus to the Greeks) even saw the Macedonian warrior king himself (as Alexander had managed to force his way into India in 326 BCE). Chandragupta's grandson, Ashoka, followed in his grandfather's footsteps and went onto become even more powerful and famous. It may be interesting to note that in 250 BCE, Ashoka had several pillars erected, on top of which was placed sandstone sculptures of lions, which today has become the National Emblem of India. That emblem appears in Indian currency, and the 24-spoked wheel symbol from the emblem appears in the centre of India's national flag. An image of both the emblem and flag even appeared on a rocket launched by India in September 2014 to place the country's first satellite into orbit around the planet Mars. Would any of this have been possible without the advice and strategies of the great scholar and teacher, Chanakya, and his epic war manual?

Fig. 3. An excavated site at ancient India's Taxila (now in Pakistan), the city where Chanakya was a teacher.

Set in an age of oppression, we see how the author came to study warfare. Therefore, to get a better understanding of the types of fighting, it is best to look at the martial traditions of India. Contrary to popular belief, martial arts are not exclusively a Far Eastern tradition. They have long existed far beyond the borders of China, Japan and Korea. Greece has its *Pankration*, France has its *Savate*, Hawaii has its *Lua*, Nigeria has its *Dambe*, New Zealand has its *Mau Rakau*, and Europe had its various medieval traditions, such as *Liechtenauer*, etc. India is not without its indigenous martial arts.

Many of India's native martial arts and combat sports have survived to the present day. There may have been many others, but have met extinction. The following are some of the more well-known forms of Indian fighting arts and combat sports, almost all of which still exist and are currently practised:

Shastar Vidya (Northern India)
Complete battlefield art covering all aspects of combat

Vajramushti (Karnataka, South West India)
Boxing and grappling sport with knuckle-dusters

Aki-kiti (Nagaland, North East India)
Low-line kicks-only fighting sport

Mardani khel (Maharashtra, West India)
Sword- and stick-wielding, single or double

Paika Akhada (Odisha, East India)
Weapons-based fighting system and martial exercises

Cheibi Gad-Ga (Manipur, North East India)
Sword and shield fighting art

Thang-Ta (Manipur, North East India)
Spear and sword fighting, also unarmed combat (i.e. *Sarit-sarak*)

Pari-khanda (Bihar, North India)
Sword and shield combat

Inbuan wrestling (Mizoram, North East India)
Wrestling with the aim of lifting the opponent

Kabbadi (All over India)
Tag-wrestling game designed for battle preparation

Mukna (Manipur, North East India)
Pin-back-to-ground wrestling form

Thoda (Himachal Pradesh, North India)
Archery game with round wooden-headed arrows

Kirip wrestling (Nicobar Islands, East of India)
Takedown wrestling game

Silambam (Tamil Nadu, South India)
Primarily a bamboo staff-fighting system

Phansi (Various Indian states)
Strangulation methods of the murderous Thuggee cult

Kushti (Northern India)
Wrestling with the aim to get the opponent on their back (Fig. 4)

Kalaripayattu (Kerala, South West India)
Yoga-like battlefield art covering combat, massage and medicine (Fig. 5)

Gatka (Punjab, North West India)
Dance-like, weapons-based combat art (Fig. 6)

Fig. 4. *Kushti* fighters locking limb

Fig. 5. *Kalaripayattu* practitioners fighting with axes

Fig. 6. *Gatka* players fighting with swords and shields

Similarities between techniques in several of the aforementioned arts can be found, especially when it comes to weapon-twirling and wrestling, the most well-known and commonly practised Indian combat arts. Arts such as *Kushti*, *Vajramushti*, *Gatka* etc. are displayed on Hindu and Sikh holidays such as Vaisakhi, Dasara, Hola Mohalla, etc.

Heroic Indian warriors such as Arjuna (lived over 5,000 years ago according to astrological calculations), Chandragupta Maurya (340 – 298 BCE), King Porus (died 317 BCE), Prithviraj Chauhan (1149 – 1192 CE), Shivaji Bhosale (1627 – 1680 CE) and Guru Gobind Singh Ji (1666 – 1708 CE), all would have undergone formal training in some form of Indian martial arts because studying the arts of combat was a warrior duty. Without knowledge of the use of arms, a warrior would not be permitted, and obviously be unable, to fight in the field of battle.

Fig. 7. Baba Deep Singh (1682 – 1757 CE) was a great Sikh warrior, renowned for his courage, fighting skills and martyrdom. Like his fellow Sikh warriors, he was skilled in the ancient combat art of *Shastar Vidya*. In both old and contemporary art, he is usually portrayed holding a double-edged sword (i.e. *khanda*), which appears to have been his favourite weapon.

Indian martial culture even had an influence upon cultures of other countries, particularly where Hinduism was imported. Hinduism was introduced to Indonesia in the first century and so the four-fold Hindu caste system was also embraced. There, the Kshatriya (warrior caste) are called Kesatria or Satria. China and Japan, like Vedic India, similarly divided society into four classes and they had their equivalent of the Kshatriya class, i.e. Wu Shi and Samurai. Thailand's traditional combat art, *Muay Thai,* contains fighting techniques and martial dance moves based on Hindu warriors such as Rama, the ancient North Indian warrior prince (protagonist of the *Ramayana*, one of India's ancient epics) and his humanoid monkey general, Hanuman. These include *Hanuman thayarn* (flying knee kick). There is a style of Malay *Silat* called *Silat Harimau Seri Rama* and it is based on the actions of Rama.

Fig. 8. Rama with bow and arrow at Prambanan, a ninth century Hindu temple compound, Central Java, Indonesia. Rama is shown performing the Ūrdhvasandhāna (higher draw).

The 6th/7th century CE Indian monk, Bodhidharma, is *believed* to have taught Dhyana Buddhism and exercises to the monks of the Shaolin Temple, China, which may possibly have led to the development of Shaolin *Kung fu*, starting with the 18 Hands of the Lohan style. Indian warrior skills reached the Philippines via the ancient Hindu-Buddhist Malay Srivijaya Empire. The *mudras* (hand gestures) and *mantras* (incantations) of Hinduism/Buddhism, which were transmitted to Japan via China have found their way into samurai tradition and are known as *Kuji-in*. The indigenous martial art of Sri Lanka, known as *Angampora* (literally, limb-fighting) (Fig. 9), belongs to the Sinhalese people and its style is quite similar to Southern Indian *Kalaripayattu* and *Silambam*. Considering the close proximity between southern India and Sri Lanka, there may be a link between these arts. It is thanks to Indian merchants and missionaries that knowledge of Indian spirituality, medicine, martial arts, etc. passed across India's borders and into neighbouring nations.

Fig. 9. Angampora master applying a knife technique

So little has been written on Indian martial culture. Centuries of Mughal rule overshadowed the ancient Dharmic faiths and traditions of India. It was because of this cultural takeover that ancient Indian Vedic martial culture almost became extinct. Even today, there are many natives of India who are fascinated by *Kung fu, Karate* and *Taekwondo*, but unaware of their own ancestral martial heritage; this is even more so with the treasure that is the text of the *Arthashastra*.

This book has been written to promote awareness of India's rich martial culture. The focus of the contents is the *Arthashastra*, an ancient Indian treatise which contains a wealth of information concerning covert and overt warfare. Several books based on the *Arthashastra* have been published by various scholars. However, the focus of *those* books is the *Arthashastra's* advice on politics and financial management, while we have decided to concentrate solely on the military aspects.

Buddhism, an Indian religion, which became widely practiced in China, Japan, Thailand, Sri Lanka, Afghanistan, Vietnam and other nations, was founded by Siddhartha Gautama (lived 6th/5th century BCE), a prince born into a Hindu Kshatriya (warrior) family. Hindus believe Buddha to be the ninth incarnation of the god, Vishnu, who rescues the world whenever great evil arises.

It is our greatest hope that more research is done on Indian martial culture and information made available to people worldwide so that one day the popularity of Indian martial culture stands, at least, shoulder-to-shoulder with the martial cultures of China, Japan and Korea.

Crime

The world of ancient India is a complex system and it is understood that the reader may not have access to a visual idea of the society. To understand the world in which someone lives, it is often better to know what society deems a crime. Here is a table of crimes from the time of the manual:

CRIME	PENALTY
Catching hold of a man by his legs, clothes, hands or hair	Fine ranging above 6 panas (coins used in ancient India)
Striking a man with the hand	Fine below 3 panas
Causing a bloodless wound with a stick, mud, a stone, an iron bar, or a rope	Fine of 24 panas
Hurting a man's tongue or nose	Severing of fingers
Wantonly murdering another man, or stealing a herd of cattle	Beheading
Hurting a man with a weapon under intoxication	Severing of hand
Non-soldier stealing weapons or armour	Shot down by arrows
Castrating a man	Severing of generative organ
Man poisoning another man or a woman murdering a man	Drowning
A man or woman under sinful passions committing suicide by means of rope, arms, or poison	Dragged by rope along public roads

Measurements

The following are some of the ancient Indian measurements given in the *Arthashastra* and their modern English equivalent. An entire chapter is devoted to measurements of time and space in Book 2 (Chapter 20) of the original manual. However, the following selection has been placed here so that it can be used as a quick guide when reading the original measurements in the text.

- 1 *angula* = 0.75 inches
- 1 *dhanurgraha* = 3 inches
- 1 *dhanurmushti* = 6 inches
- 1 *vitasti* or 1 *chháyápaurusha* = 9 inches
- 1 *sama, sala, pariraya* or *pada* = 10.5 inches
- 1 *aratni* or 1 *hasta* = 18 inches
- 1 *kishku* = 31 inches
- 1 *vyáma* = 63 inches
- 1 *danda*, 1 *dhanus*, 1 *nálika* or 1 *purusha* = 6 foot
- 1 *rajju* = 60 foot
- 1 *yojana* = 8 miles

The Lost Warfare of India

SPIES

A spy's primary objective is to obtain information behind enemy lines. The purpose of this intelligence-gathering is to gain an advantage over an opponent. The use of spies can be found in India's ancient epics, such as the *Ramayana*, in which Ravan, the demon king of Lanka (ancient Sri Lanka), sent a loyal spy on a reconnaissance mission in the camp of his rival, Rama, the righteous North Indian prince and seventh avatar (incarnation) of the Hindu god Vishnu. According to Book 6, Canto 20: The Spies:

"Sárdúla, Rávan's spy, surveyed, the legions on the strand arrayed... First let each wiser art be tried; bribe them, or win them, or divide. Such was the counsel of the spy..."

Hindu epics tell of Devas (gods) and Asuras (demons) shape-shifting for various purposes. One notable event that takes place in the *Ramayana* is the kidnapping of Rama's wife, Sita, by Ravan. As Sita would not have trusted Ravan in his true form, he takes on the appearance of a holy man to lure and abduct her (Book 3, Canto 47).

In several chapters of his manual, Chanakya emphasises spying in matters of monitoring a king's subjects, defeating enemies in war as well as capturing criminals. He lists the numerous forms and roles a spy can assume. These would enable spies to operate without arousing suspicions.

The Institution of Spies

The following section is from Book 1, Chapter 11 of the original text.

Assisted by the council of his ministers tried under espionage, the king shall proceed to create spies: Spies under the guise of:

- *a fraudulent disciple*
- *a recluse*
- *a householder* (Fig. 10)
- *a merchant* (Fig. 11)
- *an ascetic practising austerities* (Fig.12)
- *a class-mate or a colleague*
- *an assassin* (*tíkshna*)
- *a poisoner* (Fig. 13)
- *a mendicant woman*

Fig. 10

Fig. 11

Fig. 12

Fig. 13

The Fraudulent Disciple
A skilful person capable of guessing the mind of others is a fraudulent disciple. Having encouraged such a spy with rewards of honour and wealth, the minister shall tell him, "sworn to the king and myself, you shall inform us of whatever treachery you find in others."

> The term tikshna was originally translated as fire-brand but should be understood to mean assassin.

Quick-lesson
Have intelligent people search the land for plots and rebellions.

The Recluse
One who is initiated in asceticism and is possessed of foresight and pure character is a recluse. This spy, provided with much money and many disciples, shall carry on agriculture, cattle-rearing, and trade on the lands allotted to him for the purpose. Out of the produce and profits thus acquired, he shall provide all ascetics with subsistence, clothing and lodging, and send on espionage such among those under his protection as are desirous to earn a livelihood, ordering each of them to detect a particular kind of crime committed in connection with the king's wealth and to report of it when they come to receive their subsistence and wages. All the ascetics (under the recluse) shall severally send their followers on similar errands.

Quick-lesson
Land is given to a trusted person, land which yields profit, the profit is then used to feed and provide for spies who venture out into the lands around to gather information and discover who is against the ruler.

The Cultivator
Fallen from his profession, but possessed of foresight and pure character is termed a householder spy. This spy shall carry on the cultivation of lands allotted to him for the purpose, and maintain cultivators.

Quick-lesson
Take those who have fallen on hard times (but not through their own fault) and provide for them so that they can become spies.

The Trader
Fallen from his profession, but possessed of foresight and pure character, he is a merchant spy. This spy shall carry on the manufacture of merchandise on lands allotted to him for the purpose.

Quick-lesson
Any merchant who has fallen on hard times (but not through their own fault) shall be given land so that they can continue their trade but with the aim of espionage.

The Priest
A man with a shaved head or braided hair and who desires to earn a livelihood is a spy under the guise of an ascetic practising austerities. Such a spy surrounded by a host of disciples with shaved head or braided hair may take his abode in the suburbs of a city, and pretend to be a person barely living on a handful of vegetables or meadow grass taken once in the interval of a month or two, but he may take in secret his favourite foodstuffs.

Quick-lesson
Bogus holy men are set up with a residence; word of their austere living should be made public. The pilgrims who come to see the holy man will bring information to the spy as they gather. In secret, the bogus holy man eats anything they wish.

Aides to the Above
Merchant spies pretending to be his disciples may worship him as one possessed of otherworldly powers. His other disciples may widely proclaim that:
 "This ascetic is an accomplished expert of otherworldly powers."
Those who desire the knowing of their future, throng to him, he may, through palmistry, foretell such future events as he can ascertain by the nods and signs of his disciples concerning the works of high-born people of the country – for example:
- *small profits*
- *destruction by fire*
- *fear from robbers*
- *the execution of the seditious*
- *rewards for the good*

- *forecast of foreign affairs*

saying:
"This will happen today, that tomorrow, and that this king will do such."
Such assertions of the ascetic his disciples shall corroborate (by presenting facts and figures).
He shall also foretell not only the rewards which persons possessed of foresight, eloquence, and bravery are likely to receive at the hands of the king, but also probable changes in the appointments of ministers.
The king's minister shall direct his affairs in conformity to the forecast made by the ascetic. He shall appease with offer of wealth and honour those who have had some well-known cause to be disaffected, and impose punishments in secret on those who are for no reason disaffected or who are plotting against the king.

Quick-lesson
Once set in position, informants bring information to the bogus holy man, who then appears to predict the truth of a target's situation. Upon making a prediction, agents of the ruler bring the outcome about. Through this, movement and aims in society can be monitored. Powerful people will trust in this 'holy man' and secrets will come fourth. Thus, gather information on a person, predict a future for that person, have the ruler bring about such a predicted future. As a result, the 'holy man' will have a solid reputation and will become a centre point for gathering where news will be gathered.

The Five Institutes of Espionage
Honoured by the king with awards of money and titles, these five institutes of espionage shall ascertain the purity of character of the king's servants.

Quick-lesson
Using people of all backgrounds and professions to gather intelligence will give a king eyes and ears everywhere. Those with the ability to calculate likely future events are most ideal.
The five institutes of espionage are:
1. The Fraudulent Disciple
2. The Recluse
3. The Cultivator
4. The Trader/merchant
5. The Priest

Present-day India's intelligence agencies are no less dedicated than Chanakya's institution of spies were. These agencies include the Research and Analysis Wing (RAW), the country's external intelligence agency; Intelligence Bureau (IB), the country's internal intelligence agency; Defence Intelligence Agency (DIA), providers of intelligence to the armed forces; All India Radio Monitoring Service (AIRMS), monitors of national and international radio broadcasts, and several others.

> One of RAW's major operations was named Operation Chanakya, which involved infiltrating separatist groups in Kashmir in order to expose their funding and backing.

While the infamous Chinese general, Sun Tzu (circa 544 – 496 BCE) devotes only one chapter on espionage in his 13-chapter treatise, *The Art of War*, Chanakya writes extensively on this subject throughout his text. It is quite clear from his advice that he felt a ruler must have eyes and ears everywhere in order to have the upper hand and eliminate potential threats against him.

"Thus, what enables the wise sovereign and the good general to strike and conquer, and achieve things beyond the reach of ordinary men, is foreknowledge... Knowledge of the enemy's dispositions can only be obtained from other men. Hence the use of spies, of whom there are five classes:
1. *local spies*
2. *inward spies*
3. *converted spies*
4. *doomed spies*
5. *surviving spies"*

The Art of War, Section 13: The Use of Spies:

> The following section is from Book 1, Chapter 12 of the original text.

Classmate Spies
Those orphans who are to be necessarily fed by the state and are put to study science, palmistry, sorcery, the duties of the various orders of religious life, legerdemain, and the reading of omens and augury, are classmate spies or spies learning by social intercourse.

Quick-lesson
Orphanages are to be funded and orphans trained up as agents.

Fire-brand Spies or Assassins
Such brave desperados of the country who, reckless of their own life, confront elephants or tigers in fight mainly for the purpose of earning money are termed fire-brands or fiery spies (Fig. 14).

Fig. 14

Quick-lesson
Fire-brand spies are considered as assassins and 'dare-devil commandos'.

Poisoners
Those who have no trace of filial affection left in them and who are very cruel and indolent are poisoners.

Quick-lesson
Assassination via poison is a suitable method for heartless persons.

The Female Spy
A poor widow of Bráhmin caste, very clever, and desirous to earn her livelihood is a woman ascetic. Honoured in the king's harem, such a woman shall frequent the residences of the king's prime ministers.

Quick-lesson
Destitute but beautiful and intelligent women should be used as spies.

The Religious Female
The same rule shall apply to women with shaved head, as well as to those of Shúdra caste.

Quick-lesson
Send out 'nuns' and women who live religious lives to gather information.

All these above are Wandering Spies.
Of these spies, those who are of good family, loyal, reliable, well-trained in the art of putting on disguises appropriate to countries and trades, and possessed of knowledge of many languages and arts shall be sent by the king to observe in his own country the movements of:

- *ministers*
- *priests*
- *commanders of the army*
- *the heir-apparent*
- *the door-keepers*
- *the officer in charge of the harem*
- *the magistrate*
- *the collector-general*
- *the chamberlain*
- *the commissioner*
- *the city constable*
- *the officer in charge of the city*
- *the superintendent of transactions*
- *the superintendent of manufactories*
- *the assembly of councillors*
- *heads of departments*
- *the commissary-general*
- *the officers in charge of fortifications*

Also, boundaries, and wild areas.

Quick-lesson:
A king must keep an eye on his inner circle, which is as vital as knowing his enemy's intentions and movements. The various forms of wandering spy should observe all of the

above to build a correct picture and form an understanding of the land, its people and those in positions of power.

The Use of Spy Types
Fiery spies, such as are employed to hold the royal umbrella, vase, fan, and shoes, or to attend at the throne, chariot, and conveyance shall espy the public character of these officers.

Classmate spies shall convey this information (i.e., that gathered by the fiery spies) to the institutes of espionage.

Poisoners such as a sauce-maker, a cook, procurer of water for bathing shampooer, the spreader of beds, a barber, toilet-maker, a water-servant; servants such as have taken the appearance of a hump-backed person, a dwarf, a pigmy, the dumb, the deaf, the idiot, the blind; artisans such as actors, dancers, singers, players on musical instruments, buffoons, and a bard; as well as women shall also study the private character of these officers.

Vagabond women shall convey this information to the institute of espionage.

The immediate officers of the institutes of espionage shall by making use of signs or writing set their own spies in motion (to ascertain the validity of the information).

Neither the institutes of espionage nor they (the wandering spies) shall know each other.

Quick-lesson
The gathering of information needs a central hub. The separate parts should not know of the existence of the other sections. This is done to validate the information which is streaming in from different channels. Have a network of spies that reaches out to the edges of the 'world' and have the information sent back to the central hub.

Validation of Information
When the information thus received from these different sources is exactly of the same version, it shall be held reliable. If they (the sources) frequently differ, the spies concerned shall either be punished in secret or dismissed.

Quick-lesson:
Spies who gather bad intelligence must face dire consequences. Often spies may simply forecast their own ideas of a situation, instead of actually doing the reconnaissance themselves, leading to a supply of bad information.

A Spy in the Enemy Camp
Those spies who are referred to in Book 4, "Removal of Thorns," (of the Arthashastra) shall receive their salaries from those foreign kings with whom they live as servants; but when they aid both the states in the work of catching hold of robbers, they shall become recipients of salaries from both the states.

Quick-lesson
Those in the employ of the enemy who are also spies shall receive income from both the enemy and the lord who has retained them as spies.

The Hostage Spy
Those whose sons and wives are kept (as hostages) shall be made recipients of salaries from two states and considered as under the mission of enemies. Purity of character of such persons shall be ascertained through persons of similar profession.

Quick-lesson
Keeping a spy's family as hostage will encourage their loyalty.

The Deformed and Accomplished
The hump-backed, the dwarf, the eunuch, women of accomplishments, the dumb, and various grades of Mlechcha caste shall be spies inside their houses (Fig. 15).

Mlechchha (variously spelt) is a term describing people considered non-Vedic, foreign, barbaric.

Fig. 15

Outposts
Merchant spies inside forts; saints and ascetics in the suburbs of forts; the cultivator and the recluse in country parts; herdsmen in the boundaries of the country; in forests, forest-dwellers, ascetics, and chiefs of wild tribes shall be stationed to ascertain the movements of enemies. All these spies shall be very quick in the dispatch of their work.

Quick-lesson
Set up outposts in strategic places to gather information on traffic in the land.

Fig. 16. A group of spear-grasping Yimchunger tribal warriors of Nagaland, north eastern India. In several places in his text, Chanakya mentions using tribal warriors for war and assassination. Perhaps he considered them ideal for use in overt and covert war due to their familiarity with terrains, hunting, etc.

Spy Hunter
Spies set up by foreign kings shall also be found out by local spies; spies by spies of like profession. It is the institutes of espionage, secret or avowed, that set spies in motion.

Quick-lesson
Spies sent by the enemy must be sought out and discovered.

Chanakya says:
"None of his enemies shall know his secret, but he shall know the weak points of his enemy."

Chapter 15 of Book 1

The advice above is a little reminiscent of one of Sun Tzu's most famous maxims. *The Art of War* states:

"...If you know the enemy and know yourself, you need not fear the result of a hundred battles."

Section 3: Attack by Stratagem

In the same chapter, Chanakya emphasises secrecy throughout. He says:

"Hence no outside person shall know anything of the work which the king has in view. Only those who are employed to carry it out shall know it either when it is begun or when accomplished."

And warns: *"Whoever discloses counsels shall be torn to pieces."*

Quick-lesson
Secrecy in espionage was a serious matter. The *Bansenshukai* shinobi manual and the shinobi teachings of a warrior known as Chikamatsu Shigenori both build on teachings from Chinese classics, stating that any spy who gives away any information, shall be, along with the person who is informed of any plan, put to death. This is used as a deterrent, stopping spies from leaking any information out, especially to those close to them.

Roundup
Spying is always considered as an auxiliary branch of any military force and while it is an additional department, it is also integrated throughout, having its 'eyes' everywhere and being 'present' through many threads which stretch from their own side, all the way to the enemy. This makes the department of spying not simply an additional force but a saturation that seeps into all facets of military life, and while the spy cannot exist without a military force, a military force would be hard-pressed to survive without its spies.

WEAPONS

Weapons can be found throughout the Hindu faith. Idols of the countless Hindu deities can be seen holding a variety of weapons in the hands of their many arms. The number of arms and types of weapons which each particular idol bears are created according to specific instructions in texts such as the *Agni Purana*, a collection of stories and scripture which contains a section devoted to building temples and idols. Weapons even find themselves in prayers, not just the epics. For example, the *Rig Veda*, one of the four oldest and holiest scriptures of Hinduism, contains a hymn dedicated to weapons:

"With Bow let us win cows, with Bow the battle, with Bow be victors in our hot encounters... Loosed from the Bowstring fly away, thou Arrow, sharpened by our prayer. Go to the foemen, strike them home, and let not one be left alive..."

Hymn 75, Weapons of War

In Hinduism, weapons are sacred instruments of divine origins, created to protect Dharma (righteousness) from Adharma (unrighteousness). According to the ancient Indian epic, the *Mahabharata*, Grandsire Bhishma, an elderly, wise and skilful war leader, narrates to Nakula – one of the five Pandava brothers – of how the creator-god caused the sword to exist (Fig. 17):

"...a creature sprang (from the sacrificial fire) scattering the flames around him, and whose splendour equalled that of the Moon himself when he rises in the firmament spangled with stars. His complexion was dark like that of the petals of the blue lotus. His teeth were keen. His stomach was lean. His stature was tall. He seemed to be irresistible and possessed of exceeding energy... Possessed of great energy, his name is Asi (sword or scimitar). For the protection of the world and the destruction of the enemies of the gods, I have created him. That being then, abandoning the form he had first assumed, took the shape of a sword of great splendour, highly polished, sharp-edged."
Book 12: Santi Parva, Apaddharmanusasana Parva, Section 166

Fig. 17

All categories of weapons according to ancient Indian texts are as follows:
1. those which are kept in the hand – e.g. sword
2. those thrown by the hand – e.g. bladed discus
3. those launched by a device – e.g. bow and arrow
4. those thrown, but retrieved – e.g. lasso
5. the limbs of the body – e.g. grappling
6. those powered by secret mantras – e.g. *Brahmastra* – the Brahma missile (Fig. 18)

Fig. 18

The last category of weapons refers to the *divyastra* (divine missiles). The effects and after-effects of these described in Hindu scriptures and epics are akin to the effects and after-effects of modern nuclear weapons. Such divine missiles are mentioned considerably in ancient Indian epics such as the *Mahabharata* and *Ramayana*. The *Dhanurveda Samhita* (authored by Sage Vasistha) is an ancient Indian text that deals primarily with archery, and it reveals several secret mantras, one of which is for the *Agni-astra* (fire missile) which is as follows:

"Oṁ agnistyatā hṛdañca śivaṁ vanāśvāviṇi hagādaśarūpanaḥ sad ve ti tataḥ hādati, toyati, rāma, thathā maso hitvā vān susedavedayā."

> Present-day India's first long-range nuclear-capable ballistic missile was named Agni-I.

After this, one should utter the name of their enemy. To withdraw this blazing weapon, one must recite the mantra in reverse.

The hierarchy of weaponry
1. the bow and arrow
2. the spear
3. the sword
4. the limbs of one's own body

Unarmed combat in ancient India was well-developed and covered all ranges. When weapons of wood and metal were unavailable to a warrior in a brawl or battle, they would resort to using their own limbs as tools of harm. In the *Mahabharata*, there are numerous detailed accounts of both armed and unarmed combat. One account describes a duel between Jarasandha, a villainous warrior king, and Bhima, one of the five Pandava brothers (and half-brother of Hanuman, the monkey general and patron deity of Indian wrestling). The following is a short excerpt from their lengthy bout consisting of seizing, head-butting, kicking, grappling, boxing and kneeing:

"And frequently seizing each other's necks with their hands and dragging and pushing it with violence... And striking neck against neck and forehead against forehead... and kicking each other with such violence as to affect the innermost nerves... The heroes then performed those grandest of all feats in wrestling called Prishtabhanga, which consisted in throwing each other down with face towards the earth and maintaining the one knocked down in that position as long as possible... And with clenched fists they struck each other at times, pretending to aim at particular limbs while the blows descended upon other parts of the body... And at times they struck each other with their knee-joints."

Book 2: Sabha Parva: Jarasandha-vadha Parva: Section 23

The *Dhanurveda Samhita* also advises that a martial guru should train his disciples in weapons that match their personality. For example:

- Brahmin (priest class) personality – projectiles, etc.
- Kshatriya (warrior class) personality – swords, etc.
- Vaishya (merchant class) personality – spears, etc.
- Shudra (labour class) personality – maces, etc.

Shastar puja – weapon worship is a ritual that takes place on ninth night of Navratri – a nine-night goddess-worshipping festival – in which weapons – and sometimes other tools and implements – are prayed over and anointed by a priest (Fig. 19).

Fig. 19. The weapons involved in this ritual are normally the traditional weapons of war, but in present-day India, modern firearms are sometimes placed next to them by Hindu police officers and soldiers seeking to have their weapons purified and blessed.

The Sikhs, who adopted the combat arts and several weapons of the Hindu Kshatriya, too have great reverence for weapons because they are considered sacred tools which, in the right hands, help to uphold justice. Guru Gobind Singh Ji, the tenth Sikh guru, authored the Shastar Naam Mala (Rosary of Weapon Names), one of his many martial-themed poetic compositions that were collected into one volume, the *Dasam Granth* (Tenth Master's Book). In 1,318 verses, he praises a variety of weapons as well as God in a martial manner. According to the guru:

"Curved sword, double-edged sword, scimitar,
Gun, axe and arrow,
Rapier, long sword, spear,
These are our masters."
        Dasam Granth, Shastar Naam Mala, The Praise of the Primal Power, 3

Sikhs have their own intriguing weapon-worshipping traditions. Weapons are prayed over and also anointed according to traditional customs. Exponents of the Sikh combat art, *Gatka*, always perform the *Shastar namaskar,* a ritualistic salutation to the weapons before they are used in training or displayed for audiences. Such is the great respect given to weapons by Sikhs. In Sikh temples, a several weapons are beautifully laid out in front of the Sri Guru Granth Sahib Ji, which is the scripture and eternal guru of the Sikhs.

The tenth Sikh guru founded the Khalsa Panth (pure community) in 1699 CE. The initiation ceremony involved using a *khanda* (double-edged sword) to stir and mix sugar crystals into a large iron bowl of water. This sweet water, referred to as Amrit (ambrosia), was then administered to devotees. Among the rules and regulations laid out that day, Khalsa Sikhs were instructed to wear five symbols at all times, including the *kirpan* (dagger/sword, a symbol of justice), *kara* (an iron bracelet, a reminder to do good deeds), *kesh* (uncut hair, which affirms a Sikh's commitment to his/her faith), *kangha* (a comb to keep uncut hair neat and tidy), and *kachera* (shorts, a sign of chastity). According to Nidar Singh Nihang, 9th Gurudev (master) of the 'Akali Nihang Baba Darbara Singh Sanatan Suraj Bansia Shastar Vidiya Shiv Akhara', the *kara* was also used as a knuckle-duster for self-defence as well as for settling disputes between rivals. A *kara* can have an edge that is blunt, bladed or spiked. Combat with such a weapon is known as *Loh-mushti* – iron fist (Fig. 20).

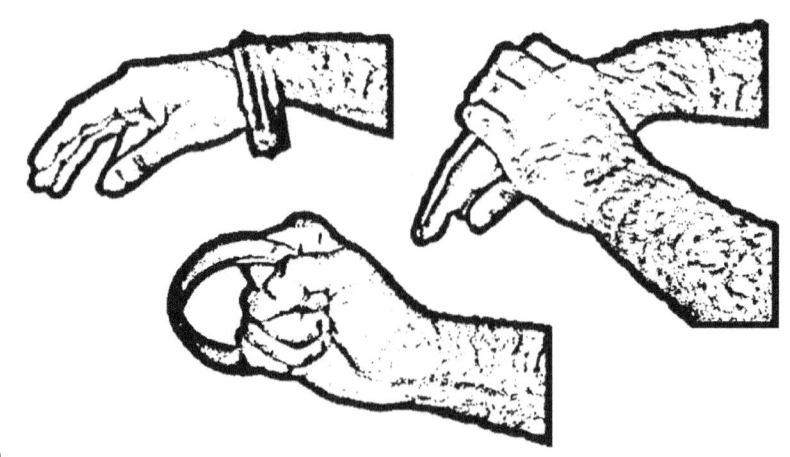

Fig. 20

Sikhs of the very martial Nihang Order always carry a variety of arms as well as adorn their conical turbans with several weapons, including small-sized double-edged swords, flat steel rings, metal claws, daggers, etc.

The battle standard of the tenth Sikh guru is known as the Ashtbhuja (Sanskrit: eight arms). This intriguing battle standard (Fig. 21), also referred to as a *shastar* (weapon), is believed to represent the eight arms of the Hindu Goddess Chandi who, according to Hindu texts, slew countless ultra-violent demons that could not be defeated by other deities. Since the ancient times, her name and deeds have been invoked by warriors seeking to 'psych themselves up' before battle to prepare for the horrors that would ensue.

Fig. 21

WEAPONS OF THE ARMOURY

The following selection deals with not only the weapons required to be kept in the armoury but also the duties of a superintendent who looks after the weapon stores. Here the practicality of keeping weapons and the imagining of life in the armoury come together, giving a clear picture of the costs and effort required.

> The following section is from Book 2, Chapter 18 of the original text.

The Superintendent of the Armoury shall employ experienced workmen of tried ability to manufacture in a given time and for fixed wages, wheels, weapons, mail armour, and other accessory instruments for use in battles, in the construction or defence of forts, or in destroying the cities or strongholds of enemies.

All these weapons and instruments shall be kept in places suitably prepared for them. They shall not only be frequently dusted and transferred from one place to another, but also be exposed to the sun. Such weapons as are likely to be affected by heat and vapour and to be eaten by worms shall be kept in safe localities. They shall also be examined now and then with reference to the class to which they belong, their forms, their characteristics, their size, their source, their value, and their total quantity.

Quick-lesson:
Weapon care is a high priority, and all weapons must be understood and maintained, down to the smallest details.

Weapon Typology
The following lists show the various weapon typologies and varied ways of defence. Some weapons which were designed for hand-to-hand combat, such as the mace, were also flung from chariots and even launched by ballistic devices.

The Immoveable Machines
(Fig. 22)
1. *wheeled stone-hurler*
2. *arrow-shooter*
3. *arrow-shooting turret*
4. *log*
5. *fire-thrower*
6. *log-thrower*
7. *fire-extinguisher*
8. *crushing-pillar*
9. *half-sized crushing-pillar*

Fig. 22

The Moveable Machines
(Fig. 23)
1. *spiked plank*
2. *dropping-log/beam*
3. *padded bag*
4. *pestle/club*
5. *cudgel*
6. *pronged-pole*
7. *dust-blower*

8. *hammer/mallet*
9. *mace*
10. *spiked club*
11. *spade*
12. *catapult*
13. *battering ram*
14. *wheeled spiked-pillar*
15. *trident*
16. *flat bladed ring*

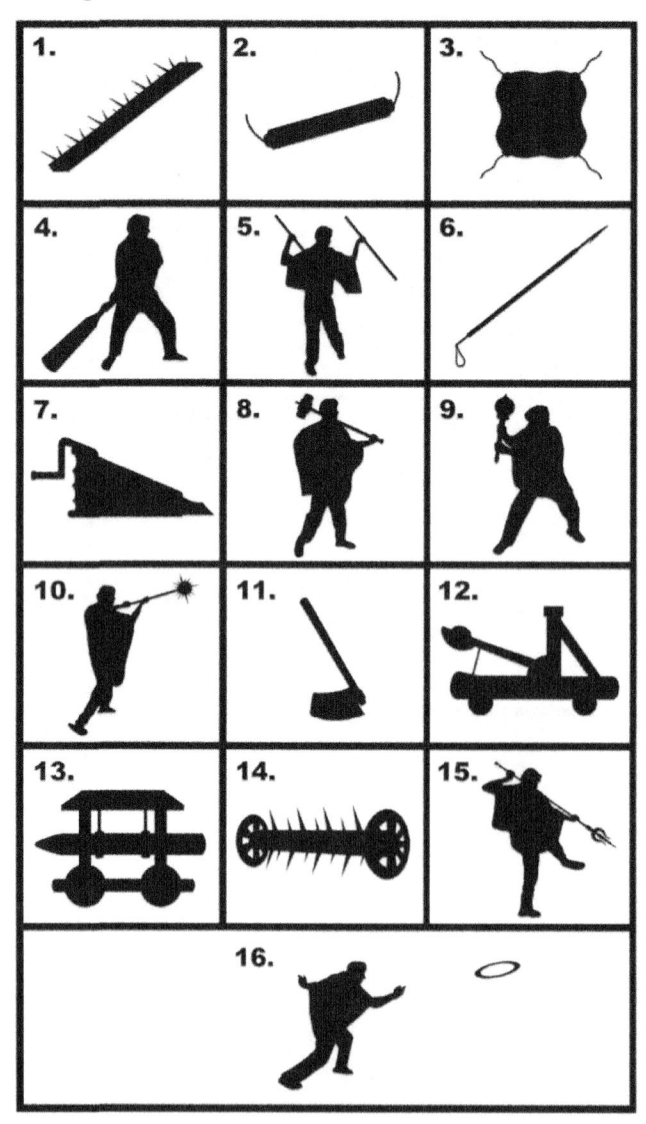

Fig. 23

Ploughshare Edged Weapons
(Fig. 24)
1. *dart*
2. *barbed dart*
3. *lance*
4. *multi-pointed lance*
5. *broad-tipped rod*
6. *spike-tipped rod*
7. *arrow-tipped rod*
8. *boar ear-shaped spear*
9. *double-ended trident*
10. *javelin*
11. *bladed rod*

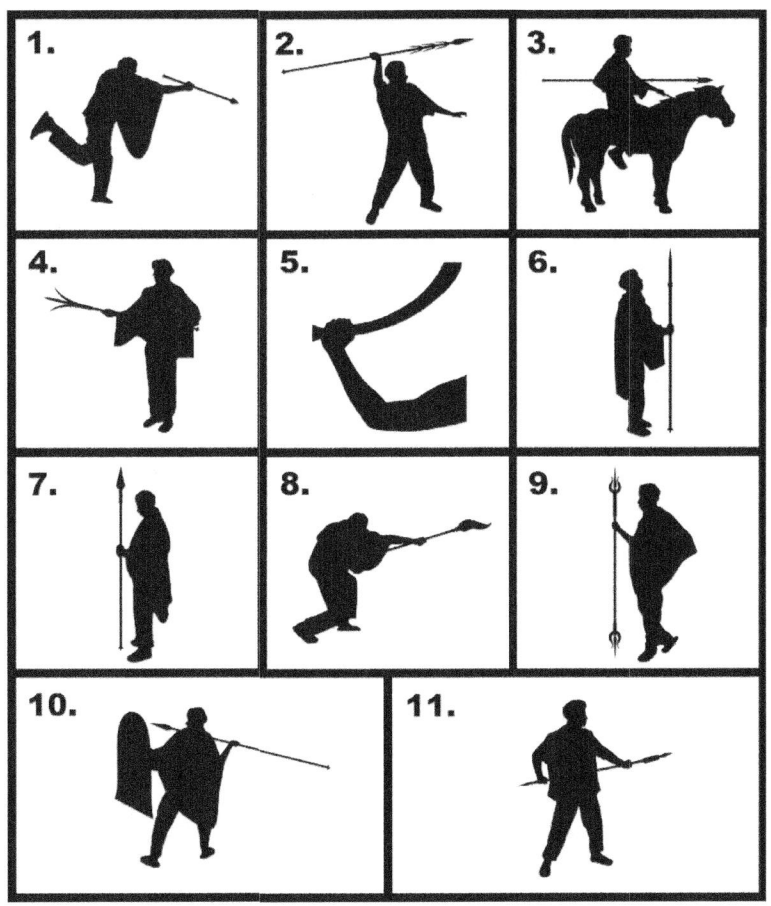

Fig. 24

Bows Typology:
1. *bows made of palmyra are named kármuka*
2. *bows made of bamboo are named kodanda*
3. *bows made of wood are named druna*
4. *bows made of bone or horn are named dhanus* (Fig. 25)

Fig. 25

Bow-string Types:
1. *Sansevieria roxburghiana*
2. *Calotropis gigantean*
3. *hemp*
4. *Coix barbata*
5. *bamboo bark*
6. *sinew*

Arrow Types:
(Fig. 26)
1. *bamboo arrow*
2. *reed arrow*
3. *wooden arrow*
4. *rod arrow*
5. *iron arrow*

The edges of arrows shall be so made of iron, bone or wood as to cut, rip or pierce.

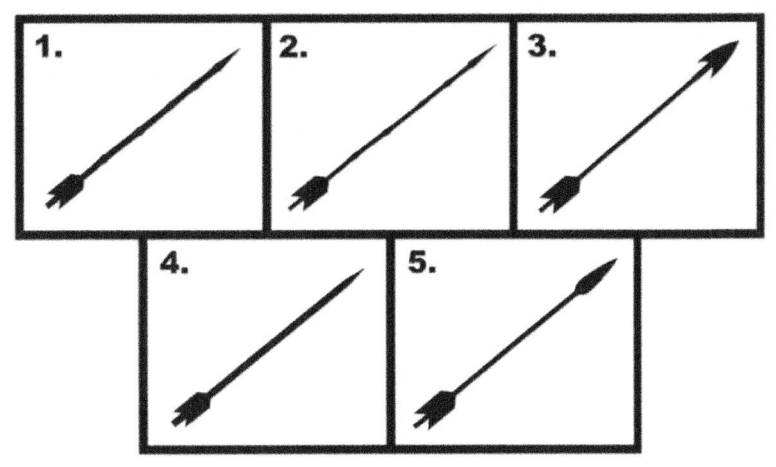

Fig. 26

Sword Typology:
(Fig. 27)
1. *long, curved sword*
2. *straight sword*
3. *thin, long sword*

The handles of swords are made of the horn of rhinoceros, buffalo, of the tusk of elephants, of wood, or of the root of bamboo.

Fig. 27

Razor-like Weapons:
(Fig. 28)
1. *battle axe*
2. *hatchet*
3. *double-ended trident axe*
4. *pick axe*
5. *spade*
6. *flat bladed ring*
7. *large axe*

The flat bladed metal ring comes in various sizes with either a smooth or serrated edge. They can either be held by the flat of the ring using the forefinger and thumb and then thrown at a target, or placed over the forefinger, twirled around and hurled forward at a target. These are similar to the shuriken and shaken (throwing blades) of the Japanese Ninja.

Fig. 28

Miscellaneous Weapons:
1. *stone devices*
2. *stone-gusher*
3. *stone fist*
4. *mill-stone* (Fig. 29)

Fig. 29

Armour:
(Fig. 30)
Armour can be made of iron or of skins of the hoofs and horns of porpoise, rhinoceros, bison, elephant or cow.
1. *helmet*
2. *neck cover*
3. *torso guard*
4. *knee-length coat*
5. *heel-length coat*
6. *sleeveless coat*
7. *gloves*

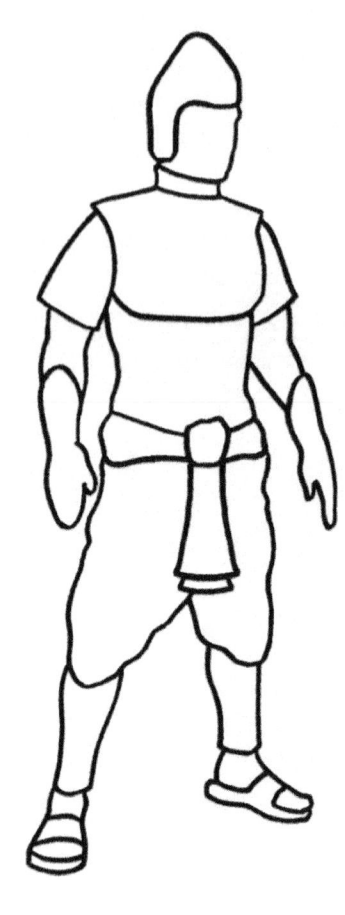

Fig. 30

Shields and Self-defence Equipment:
1. *wooden box cover*
2. *leather shield*
3. *large body shield* (Fig. 31)
4. *large flat shield*
5. *inflatable leather bag*
6. *wooden board/door*
7. *cane and leather shield*
8. *elephant-repeller*
9. *metal-tipped elephant-repeller*

Fig. 31

Additional Equipment
1. *ornaments for elephants*
2. *chariots*
3. *horses*
4. *goads* (Fig. 32)
5. *hooks to lead animals on battlefields*

Fig. 32

In this section, Chanakya has provided an extensive list of body armour, fort protectants, hand-to-hand combat weapons and anti-siege devices used in his time, such as the trident, bladed discus, dust-blower, etc., which are traditional, ancient weapons of India. Nowadays, museums in India display an array of historical weapons and armour, such as the *shamshir* (radically curved sword), *pesh-kabz* (curved knife), *char-ainah* (cuirass), etc. but the majority of these are of Persian origin and were brought to India by Mughal invaders who reigned between 1526 – 1857 CE. Therefore, they are not traditionally Indian. Chanakya's list, however, gives an insight into those which are.

> Weight training is an essential part of Indian wrestling training and wrestlers would regularly swing around a version of this mace (stone head, bamboo handle) to build muscle in the upper body.

The Indian mace (*gada*) has a large metal spherical head and a thick handle. It is generally heavy and wielded with two hands. This impact weapon was best suited to warriors who had a strong build. It is widely associated with the Hindu warrior deity, Hanuman, whose primary weapon it was.

The Persian mace (*gurz* in Persian but pronounced '*gurj*' by Indian people), however, which was brought to India by the Mughals, is generally a slim metal bar with a variety of metal head shapes, like the bull head, demon head, but commonly the flanged head (Fig. 33). Some have a typical Persian style hilt. In combat, it would be held in one hand and usually be paired with a round shield (*dhal*).

Fig. 33. A comparison between traditional Indian and Persian maces. On the left, an Indian *gada*. On the right, a Persian *gurz*.

In the Shastar Naam Mala, the tenth Sikh guru makes mention of both the Indian and Persian mace:

"You (referring to God) are Gurj, You are Gada (mace), You are Teer (arrow) and Tufang (rifle); protect me ever considering me as Your slave."
Dasam Granth, Shastar Naam Mala, The Praise of the Primal Power, 13

Despite the mention of so many weapons, Chanakya does not provide a description of their use. There are, however, other old Hindu texts which do. For example, the use of the *bhindivala* – the bladed rod, numbered among the weapons in Chanakya's list – is described in the *Nitiprakasika*:

"The bhindivala has a crooked body; its head, which is bent and broad, is a cubit long, and it is a hand in circumference. It is first whirled thrice and then thrown against the foot of the enemy. When throwing the bhindivala, the left foot should be placed in front."

The handling of weapons was no small matter, especially when theft was involved. In the *Arthashastra*, Chanakya lays downs several laws concerning weapons:

"When a man other than a soldier steals weapons or armour, he shall be shot down by arrows; if he is a soldier, he shall pay the highest amercement."
Book 4, Chapter 11

One intriguing weapon mentioned is the spiked-wheel pillar, known as *sataghni* in Sanskrit, and translated as the "hundred-killer". Chanakya lists this weapon of mass fatality as one of the "movable machines":

"...and such weapons as can destroy a hundred persons at once (sataghni)"
Book 2, Chapter 3

The following is a reference to it from the *Mahabharata*:

"Then a sataghni equipped with wheels, hurled by Ghatotkacha, slew the four steeds of Karna simultaneously."
Book 7: Drona Parva, Ghatotkacha-vadha Parva, Section 8

The *Arthashastra* lays down some strict rules concerning weapon care and weapon control:

"Weapons and armour shall be entered into the armoury only after they are marked with the king's seal." And: *"Persons with weapons shall not be allowed to move anywhere unless they are permitted by a passport."* Then: *"When weapons are either lost or spoilt, the superintendent shall pay double their value; an account of the weapons that are destroyed shall be kept up."*
Also:
"Boundary-guards shall take away the weapons and armour possessed by caravans unless the latter are provided with a passport to travel with weapons."

Book 5, Chapter 3

Roundup

Weapons and armour are without doubt the primary items required for a warrior on the ground. Ancient India had a sophisticated array of weaponry including machines and contraptions which may appear to us as exotic or strange. Information on some have been lost to us while others are well known. What must be understood is that India has a complex and long history of martial arts which can be as impressive as both their western and eastern counterparts. Therefore, be aware that Indian fighting skills have a long history and deserve a more serious level of research.

BATTLE

Warfare has significantly changed since the ancient and medieval era, but modern warfare does share some similarities. Nowadays, instead of spears, bayonet-fixed assault rifles are fought with; instead of chariots, armoured cars are ridden; instead of elephants, tanks are driven; instead of cannons, mortars are fired; instead of metal armour, poly-paraphenylene terephthalamide vests are worn, etc. Horses, however, still retain their battle-like uses and are used by law enforcers in several parts of the world today such as Canada. Rebels and insurgents are known to have used them in impoverished war-torn countries like Sudan i.e., the militia, Janjaweed (Arabic for "man with gun and horse". Also translated as "devils on horseback".).

Many people are aware that chariots and elephants were used in ancient warfare because of depictions in art and film, but how many know exactly how they were used in battle? In this section, Chanakya offers a rare insight into the methods employed by ancient Indians. Ancient textual evidence on the training and uses of chariots and elephants for warfare is very rarely found, especially in detail.

The Training of horses

Here the text gives details on the superintendent of horses and his tasks, the training and also maintenance of the animals and equipment.

The following section is from Book 2, Chapter 30 of the original text.

Horse Classification
The Superintendent of Horses shall register the breed, age, colour, marks, group or classes, and the native place of horses, and classify them as:
- *those that are kept in sale-houses for sale*
- *those that are recently purchased*
- *those that have been captured in wars*
- *those that are of local breed*
- *those that are sent thither for help*
- *those that are mortgaged*
- *those that are temporarily kept in stables*

He shall make a report (to the king) of such animals as are inauspicious, crippled, or diseased.

Quick-lesson
Keep an accurate record of the origin, history and current location of 'vehicles'.

Waste Not Want Not
Every horseman shall know how to make an economic use of whatever he has received from the king's treasury and storehouse.

Quick-lesson
Make sure each individual can maintain their equipment with the resources given to them.

The Stables
The superintendent shall have a stable constructed as spacious as required by the number of horses to be kept therein twice as broad as the length of a horse, with four doors facing the four quarters, with its central floor suited for the rolling of horses, with projected front provided with wooden seats at the entrance, and containing monkeys, peacocks, red spotted deer, mongoose, partridges, parrots, and maina birds; the room for every horse shall be four times as broad or long as the length of a horse, with its central floor paved with smoothened wooden planks, with separate compartments for fodder, with passages for the removal of urine and dung, and with a door facing either the north or the east. The distinction of quarters may be made as a matter of fact or relatively to the situation of the building.
Steeds, stallions and colts shall be separately kept.

Quick-lesson
Animals must be kept in good living conditions for them to remain healthy.

Birth
A steed that has just given birth to a colt shall be provided for the first three days with a drink of 1 prastha of clarified butter; afterwards it shall be fed with a prastha of flour and made to drink oil mixed with medicine for ten nights; after that time, it shall have cooked grains, meadow grass, and other things suited to the season of the day.

A colt, ten days old, shall be given a kudumba of flour mixed with ¼th kudumba of clarified butter, and 1 prastha of milk till it becomes six months old; then the above rations shall be increased half as much during each succeeding month, with the addition of 1 prastha of barley till it becomes three years old, then one drona of barley till it grows four years old; at the age of four or five, it attains its full development and becomes serviceable.

Grading Horses
The face of the best horse measures 32 angulas; its length is 5 times its face; its shank is 20 angulas; and its height is 4 times its shank.
Horses of medium and lower sizes fall short of the above measurement by two and three angulas respectively.
The circumference of the best horse measures 100 angulas, and horses of medium and lower sizes fall short of the above measurement by five parts.

Feed
For the best horse (the diet shall be):
- *2 dronas of any one of the grains*
- *rice*
- *barley*
- *panic seeds soaked or cooked*
- *cooked Phaseolus mungo or Phaseolus radiatus*
- *one prastha of oil*
- *5 palas of salt*
- *50 palas of flesh*
- *1 ádhaka of broth*
- *2 ádhakas of curd*
- *5 palas of sugar*

To make their diet relishing add 1 prastha of súrá (wine), liquor, or 2 prasthas of milk.

The same quantity of drink shall be specially given to those horses which are tired after a long journey or from carrying loads.

One prastha of oil for giving an enema, 1 kudumba of oil for rubbing over the nose, 1,000 palas of meadow grass, twice as much of ordinary grass; and hay-stalk or grass shall be spread over an area of 6 aratnis.

The same quantity of rations less by one-quarter is given to horses of medium and lower size.

A draught horse or stallion of medium size shall be given the same quantity as the best horse; and similar horses of lower size shall receive the same quantity as a horse of medium size.

Steeds shall have one quarter less of rations.

Half of the rations given to steeds shall be given to colts.

Thus is the distribution of ration dealt with.

Those who cook the food of horses, grooms, and veterinary surgeons shall have a share in the rations.

Breeding
Stallions which are incapacitated owing to old age, disease or hardships of war, and, being therefore rendered unfit for use in war live only to consume food shall in the interests of citizens and country people be allowed to cross steeds.

The breeds of Kámbhoja, Sindhu, Aratta, and Vanáyu countries are the best; those of Báhlíka, Pápeya, Sauvira, and Taitala, are of middle quality; and the rest ordinary.

Quick-lesson:
The ancient countries Chanakya refers to in his text may be the following present-day locations:
- Kámbhoja – present-day northern Pakistan and north-eastern Afghanistan
- Sindhu – present-day Sindh, southern Pakistan
- Aratta – area in present-day northern Pakistan
- Vanáyu – possibly present-day Iran
- Báhlíka – present-day Balkh, northern Afghanistan
- Pápeya – (unknown)
- Sauvira – present-day Multan, north-eastern Pakistan
- Taitala – area in present-day Odisha, eastern India

These three sorts may be trained either for war or for riding according as they are furious, mild, or stupid or slow.

Quick-lesson:
A good horse must be raised and maintained well and given the correct duties in accordance with its temperament.

Uses of the Horse
The regular training of a horse is its preparation for war. The following section takes us into the realm of the mounted warrior, the types of training and the complex movements of the horse.

Forms of Riding:
- *circular movement*
- *slow movement*
- *jumping* (Fig. 34)
- *gallop*
- *response to signals*

Fig. 34

The Types of Circular Movement
- *circular turning with diameter cubit*
- *advancing but circle turning*
- *figure of eight running*
- *simultaneous running and jumping*
- *forepart body movements*
- *back leg movements*

The same kind of movements with the head and ear kept erect are called slow movements.

Forms of Horse Jumping:
- *jumping like a monkey*
- *jumping like a frog*
- *sudden jump*
- *jumping with one leg*
- *leaping like a cuckoo*
- *dashing with its breast almost touching the ground*
- *leaping like a crane*

Forms of Gallop:
- *flying like a vulture*
- *dashing like a water-duck*
- *running like a peacock*
- *halt the speed of a peacock*
- *dashing like a mongoose*
- *half the speed of a mongoose*
- *running like a hog*
- *half the speed of a hog*

Movement following a signal is termed *nároshtra*.

Distances
Six, nine, and twelve yojanas (a day) are the distances (to be traversed) by carriage-horses.
Five, eight, and ten yojanas are the distances (to be traversed) by riding horses.

Quick-lesson
This means that carriages can move 48, 72 or 96 miles per day and riding horses can move 40, 64 and 80 miles per day.

Kinds of Trot:
- *trotting according to its strength*
- *trotting with good breathing*
- *pacing with a load on its back are the three kinds of trot*
- *trotting combined with circular movement*

- *ordinary trot*
- *middlemost speed*
- *ordinary speed*

Horse Husbandry

Qualified teachers shall give instructions as to the manufacture of proper ropes with which to tether the horses.

Charioteers shall see to the manufacture of necessary war equipment and accessories of horses.

Veterinary surgeons shall apply requisite remedies against undue growth or diminution in the body of horses and also change the diet of horses according to changes in seasons.

Duties:
- *those who move the horses*
- *those whose business is to tether them in stables*
- *those who supply meadow-grass*
- *those who cook the grains for the horses*
- *those who keep watch in the stables*
- *those who groom them*
- *those who apply remedies against poison*

The above shall satisfactorily discharge their specified duties and shall, in default of it, forfeit their daily wages.

Fines

When, owing to defects in medicine or carelessness in the treatment, the disease (from which a horse is suffering) becomes intense, a fine of twice the cost of the treatment shall be imposed; and when, owing to defects in medicine, or not administering it, the result becomes quite the reverse, a fine equal to the value of the animal shall be imposed.

Ashwayuja is the name of the seventh month of the traditional Hindu lunar calendar and is considered auspicious.

The same rule shall apply to the treatment of cows, buffaloes, goats, and sheep.

Washing Horses
Horses shall be washed, bedaubed with sandal powder, and garlanded twice a day. On new moon days sacrifice to spirits, and on full moon days the chanting of auspicious hymns shall be performed. Not only on the ninth day of the month of Ashwayuja, but also both at the commencement and close of journeys as well as in the time of disease shall a priest wave lights invoking blessings on the horses (New fig. 35).

Fig. 35

Quick-lesson:
Good horses should be cared for by both natural and supernatural means. People failing in their duty shall be fined accordingly.

A Word on Horses
In the ancient era, horses were 'man's best friend'. One animal with several uses. They not only provided civilians with a means of transport, but played a major role in warfare i.e., the cavalry and chariot division of an army.

The *Mahabharata* tells that horses were used in large numbers in battle:
"... and ten thousand horses, and two thousand elephants, and ten thousand foot-soldiers, and five hundred chariots, constituting the first irresistible division of his army..."
                        Book 5: Udyoga Parva, Uluka Dutagamana Parva, Section 199

The *Mahabharata* also tells of Nakula, one of the renowned five Pandava princes, specialising in all things horses. In one section, the epic details the Pandava brothers' thirteen-year exile which they accepted after losing a game of dice to their rivals, the Kauravas (whose victory was obtained by cheating). In the final year, the Pandavas were required to remain anonymous as per the conditions set. Therefore, to avoid being recognised, each of the Pandavas disguised themselves. Knowing the A to Z's of horsemanship and horse breeding, Nakula took on the role of a stableman who cared for the royal horses of King Viraata, in whose court the brothers stayed.

In ancient India, there was a royal martial tradition called *Ashwamedha* (horse sacrifice) which is prescribed in the *Vedas*, Hinduism's holiest books, and also detailed in the epics, the *Mahabharata* and *Ramayana*. Warrior kings would sacrifice a horse but not before undergoing a series of rituals performed by a priest and combatively challenging the kings of territories upon which the horse tread while it was free to roam. This tradition was carried out in order to ensure the prosperity of a king and his kingdom.

Even today, various law enforcement agencies value the efficient use of horses in their line of work, such as the Mounted Branch of Britain's Metropolitan Police Service and the Royal Canadian Mounted Police, a.k.a. Mounties. According to the Metropolitan Police website: "*From a vantage point 8 feet high the Mounted Officer is afforded a view that is invaluable at crowded venues. From this position the officer can spot possible potentially violent confrontations or crush situations and alleviate the problem with crowd management tactics. It is estimated that a trained Mounted Officer on a trained horse can be as effective as a dozen officers on foot in such situations.*"

The Training of Elephants

Elephants are classified into four kinds in accordance with the training they are given:

1. *tameable*
2. *trained for war*
3. *trained for riding*
4. *rogue elephants*

(The following section is from Book 2, Chapter 32 of the original text.)

Those which are Tameable Fall under Five Groups:
1. *those which suffers a man to sit on its withers*
2. *those which allows itself to be tethered to a post*
3. *those which can be taken to water*
4. *those which lies in pits*
5. *those which are attached to its herd*

All these elephants shall be treated with as much care as a young elephant.

Military Training is of Seven Kinds:
1. *drill*
2. *turning*
3. *advancing*
4. *trampling down and killing*
5. *fighting with other elephants*
6. *assailing forts and cities*
7. *warfare* (Fig. 36)

Binding the elephants with girths, putting on collars and making them work in company with their herds are the first steps of the above training.

Fig. 36

Elephants Trained for Riding Fall Under Eight Groups:
1. *those which suffer a man to mount over them when in company with other elephants*
2. *those which suffers riding when led by a warlike elephant*
3. *those which are taught trotting*
4. *those which are taught various kinds of movements*
5. *those which can be made to move by using a staff*
6. *those which can be made to move by using an iron hook*
7. *those which can be made to move without whips*
8. *those which are of help in hunting*

Autumnal work, mean or rough work, and training to respond to signals are the first steps for the above training.

Rogue and Bad Tempered Elephants
Rogue elephants can be trained only in one way. The only means to keep them under control is punishment. It has a suspicious dislike to work, is stubborn, of perverse nature, unsteady, wilful, or of infatuated temper under the influence of rut.

Rogue elephants whose training proves a failure may be purely roguish, clever in roguery, perverse, or possessed of all kinds of vice.

The form of shackles and other necessary means to keep them under control shall be ascertained from the doctor of elephants.

Binding Instruments:
- *tether posts*
- *collars*
- *girths*
- *bridles*
- *leg chains*
- *frontal shackles*

War-accessories:
- *mail-armour*
- *clubs*
- *arrow-bags*
- *machines*

People Who Attend the Elephants
Elephant doctors, trainers, expert riders, as well as those who groom them, those who prepare their food, those who procure grass for them, those who tether them to posts, those who sweep elephant stables, and those who keep watch in the stables at night (Fig. 37).

Fig. 37

Payment
Elephant doctors, watchmen, sweepers, cooks and others shall receive (from the storehouse):
- *1 prastha of cooked rice*
- *a handful of oil*
- *2 palas of sugar and of salt*

Fines Given
- *elephant doctors shall apply necessary medicines to elephants which, while making a journey, happen to suffer from disease, overwork, rut, or old age*
- *accumulation of dirt in stables*
- *failure to supply grass*
- *causing an elephant to lie down on hard and unprepared ground*
- *striking on vital parts of its body*
- *permission to a stranger to ride it*
- *untimely riding*
- *leading it to water through impassable places*
- *allowing it to enter into thick forests*

These are offences punishable with fines. Such fines shall be deducted from the rations and wages due to the offenders.

Ritual for Elephants
During the period of Cháturmásya (the months of July, August, September and October) and at the time when two seasons meet, waving of lights shall be performed thrice. Also on new-moon and full-moon days, commanders shall perform sacrifices to spirits for the safety of elephants.

Tusk Removal
Leaving as much as is equal to twice the circumference of the tusk near its root, the rest of the tusks shall be cut off once in 2½ years in the case of elephants born in countries irrigated by rivers, and once in 5 years in the case of mountain elephants.

Regarding elephants, the 'tanks' of the ancient world, Chanakya even goes as far as saying:

"The victory of kings (in battles) depends mainly upon elephants; for elephants, being of large bodily frame, are capable not only to destroy the arrayed army of an enemy, his fortifications, and encampments, but also to undertake works that are dangerous to life."

Book 2, Chapter 2

They were clearly protected:
"Whoever kills an elephant shall be put to death."

Book 2, Chapter 3

Chariots

Chariots were vehicles of war reserved only for the superior classes of warriors. Pulled by horses and driven by a charioteer, such a vehicle of war allowed the warrior to launch speedy, forceful assaults against the enemy. Whilst being driven, the warrior would shoot arrows and hurl a variety of weapons, such as the spear and even mace.

It was on a chariot that Krishna imparted his wisdom (i.e. Bhagavad Gita – translation: God song – contained within the *Mahabharata*, Book 6, Chapters 25-42) to the warrior, Arjuna. Krishna had taken on the role of being Arjuna's charioteer in the large-scale Kurukshetra War, which was fought between the Pandavas and Kauravas.

The duty of a commander-in-chief is to command and control his forces. In the past, the commander-in-chief was usually an experienced military tactician and warrior who physically led his troops into battle, while in the modern era, presidents and monarchs usually assume that position.

> The following section is from Book 2, Chapter 33 of the original text.

Construction of Chariots
The Superintendent of chariots shall attend to the construction of chariots.
The best chariot shall measure:
- *10 purushas in height (7 ½ feet)*
- *12 purushas in width (9 feet)* (Fig. 38)

After this model, seven more chariots with width decreasing by one purusha successively down to a chariot of 6 purushas (4.5 feet) in width shall be constructed.

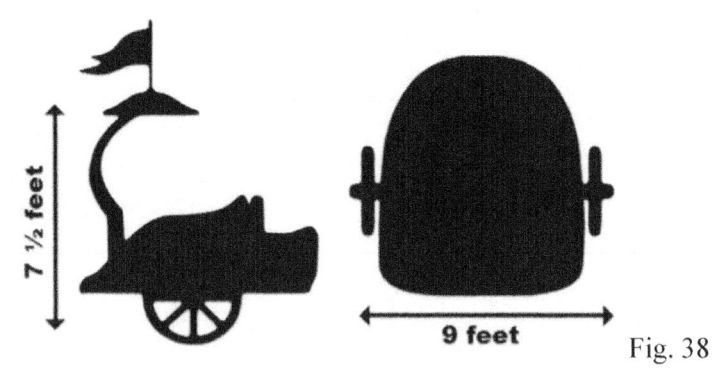

Fig. 38

He shall also construct:
- *chariots of gods*
- *festal chariots*
- *battle chariots*
- *travelling chariots*
- *chariots used in attacking enemy strong-holds*
- *training chariots*

Regarding festal chariots: a religious procession known as Ratha yatra (chariot festival/pilgrimage) sees many thousands of Hindus in various parts of India pull a large, decorated chariot upon which is a light-weight temple through the streets in celebration of various deities, such as Jagannath, while traditional energetic music is played.

Troop Training
He shall also examine the efficiency in the training of troops in shooting arrows, in hurling clubs and cudgels, in wearing mail armour, in equipment, in charioteering, in fighting seated on a chariot, and in controlling chariot horses (Fig. 39).

Fig. 39

Troop Quality
The latter shall know the exact strength or weakness of hereditary troops, hired troops, the corporate body of troops, as well as that of the army of friendly or unfriendly kings and of wild tribes.

Quick-lesson
Constant monitoring of troop training will lead to a better-trained army.

Training
He shall be thoroughly familiar with the nature of:
- *fighting in low grounds*
- *of open battle*
- *of fraudulent attack*
- *of fighting under the cover of entrenchment*
- *or from heights*
- *of fighting during the day and night*

Including the drill necessary for such warfare.

He shall also know the fitness or unfitness of troops on emergent occasions.

Tactics

With an eye to the position which the entire army trained in the skilful handling of all kinds of weapons and in leading elephants, horses, and chariots have occupied and to the emergent call for which they ought to be ready, the commander-in-chief shall be so capable as to order either advance or retreat.

He shall also know:
- *what kind of ground is more advantageous to his own army*
- *what time is more favourable*
- *what the strength of the enemy is*
- *how to sow dissension in an enemy's army of united mind*
- *how to collect his own scattered forces*
- *how to scatter the compact body of an enemy's army*
- *how to assail a fortress*
- *when to make a general advance*

Signals
Being ever mindful of the discipline which his army has to maintain not merely in camping and marching, but in the thick of battle, he shall designate the regiments by the names of trumpets, boards, banners, or flags.

Quick-lesson:
A good leader must know his men and the art of war thoroughly and understand terrain, timing, the control of men and how to maintain discipline both on and off the battlefield.

Roundup
Battle is the primary function of the warrior or soldier. The above was an eclectic mix of information from the original manual, edited to provide highlights. It shows that Indian warfare was complex and ingenious and that a reliance on animals such as horses and elephants is comparable to a modern reliance on tanks, four-wheeled vehicles and bikes. An army is only a good army when mobile and when trained to move to command.

THE INVASION

A strategist must have the ability to predict with fair accuracy the outcome of a war depending on the factors involved. This must be done without bias and should reflect the truth of any hostile situation. A leader that skews the facts in their favour and without a control of truth will fall into disaster. In this chapter, the text outlines the pre-planning needed to defeat an enemy and to form a good judgement on the actions needed.

Sun Tzu states:
"He will win who knows when to fight and when not to fight."
The Art of War, 3:17

The *Shukraniti*, a compendium of knowledge attributed to the ancient guru of the demons, Shukra (also Shukracharya) (Fig. 40) – whose school of thought Chanakya refers to in his *Arthashastra* – states:

"Having considered the time, place, the hostile army and also his own, the four expedients (i.e. negotiation, bribery, dissention, attack), and six principles of policy, he should think of war."

Fig. 40

> In the original text, Chanakya begins with the words: *"Om. Salutations to Shukra and Brihaspati."* Shukra is the guru of the demons and Brihaspati is the guru of the gods. Their schools of thought are referred to by Chanakya in various parts of his text.

Proper Preparation

> The following section is from Book 9, Chapter 1 of the original text.

The conqueror should know the comparative strength and weakness of himself and of his enemy; and having ascertained the power, place, time, the time of marching and of recruiting the army, the consequences, the loss of men and money, and profits and danger, he should march with his full force; otherwise, he should keep quiet.

Quick-lesson

Project the outcome of any action of war beforehand and ascertain if it is a positive move or not. If not, do not make a move.

Enthusiasm Versus Power

Others say:

My teacher says that of enthusiasm and power, enthusiasm is better: a king, himself energetic, brave, strong, free from disease, skilful in wielding weapons, is able with his army as a secondary power to subdue a powerful king; his army, though small, will, when led by him, be, capable of turning out any work. But a king who has no enthusiasm in himself, will perish though possessed of a strong army.

Chanakya disagrees and states:
No, he who is possessed of power overreaches, by the sheer force of his power, another who is merely enthusiastic. Having acquired, captured, or bought another enthusiastic king as well as brave soldiers, he can make his enthusiastic army of horses, elephants, chariots, and others to move anywhere without obstruction. Powerful kings, whether women, young men, lame or blind, conquered the earth by winning over or purchasing the aid of enthusiastic persons.

Quick-lesson:
Know the difference between *enthusiasm for power* and *power*.

Money and Power Versus Intrigue
Others say:
My teacher says that of power (money and army) and skill in intrigue, power is better; for a king, though possessed of skill for intrigue becomes a man of barren mind if he has no power; for the work of intrigue is well defined. He who has no power loses his kingdom as sprouts of seeds in drought vomit their sap.

Chanakya disagrees and states:
No, skill for intrigue is better; he who has the eye of knowledge and is acquainted with the science of polity can with little effort make use of his skill for intrigue and can succeed by means of conciliation and other strategic means and by spies and chemical appliances in over-reaching even those kings who are possessed of enthusiasm and power. Thus of the three acquirements, viz., enthusiasm, power and skill for intrigue, he who possesses more of the quality mentioned later than the one mentioned first in the order of enumeration will be successful in over-reaching others.

Quick-lesson
Master the following three; they are in order of importance:
1. skill for intrigue
2. power
3. enthusiasm

Types of Ground
'Country' means the earth; in it the thousand yojanas of the northern portion of the country that stretches between the Himalayas and the ocean form the dominion of no insignificant emperor; in it there are such varieties of land as:
- *forests*
- *villages*
- *waterfalls*
- *level plains*
- *uneven grounds*

In such lands, he should undertake such works he considers to be conducive to his power and prosperity. That part of the country, in which his army finds a convenient place for its manoeuvre and which proves unfavourable to his enemy, is the best; that part of the country which is of the reverse nature, is the worst; and that which partakes of both the characteristics, is a country of middling quality.

Quick-lesson
Land that is best suited to the army, aides that army.

Time
Time consists of cold, hot, and rainy periods. The divisions of time are:
- *the night*
- *the day*
- *the fortnight*
- *the month*
- *the season*
- *solstices*
- *the year*
- *the Yuga – cycle of five years*

In these divisions of time he should undertake such works as are conducive to the growth of his power and prosperity. That time which is congenial for the manoeuvre of his Army, but which is of the reverse nature for his enemy is the best; that which is of the reverse nature is the worst; and that which possesses both the characteristics is of middling quality.

Quick-lesson
The time that is best suited to an army, aides that army.

Of Strength, Place and Time

Others say:

My teacher says that of strength, place, and time, strength is the best; for a man who is possessed of strength can overcome the difficulties due either to the unevenness of the ground (Fig. 41) or to the cold, hot, or rainy periods of time. Some say that place is the best for the reason that a dog, seated in a convenient place, can drag a crocodile and that a crocodile in low ground can drag a dog. Others say that time is the best for the reason that during the day-time, the crow kills the owl, and that at night the owl the crow.

Fig. 41

Chanakya disagrees and states:

No, of strength, place, and time, each is helpful to the other;

- *Whoever is possessed of these three things should, after having placed one-third or one fourth of his army to protect his base of operations against his rear-enemy and wild tribes in his vicinity and after having taken with him as much army and treasure as is sufficient to accomplish his work, march during the month of December against his enemy whose collection of food-stuffs is old and insipid and who has not only not gathered fresh food-stuffs, but also not repaired his fortifications, in order to destroy the enemy's rainy crops and autumnal handfuls.*

- *He should march during the month of March, if he means to destroy the enemy's autumnal crops and vernal handfuls. He should march during the month of Jyestha (May-June) against one whose storage of fodder, firewood and water has diminished and who has not repaired his fortifications, if he means to destroy the enemy's vernal crops and handfuls of the rainy season.*
- *Or he may march during the dewy season against a country which is of hot climate and in which fodder and water are obtained in little quantities.*
- *Or he may march during the summer against a country in which the sun is enshrouded by mist and which is full of deep valleys and thickets of trees and grass*
- *Or he may march during the rains against a country which is suitable for the manoeuvre of his own army and which is of the reverse nature for his enemy's army.*
- *He has to undertake a long march between the months of December and January, a march of mean length between March and April, and a short march between May and June; and one, afflicted with troubles, should keep quiet.*

Quick-lesson:
Know the different seasons and fight accordingly because each has their advantages and disadvantages.

Time to March
Others say:
My teacher says that one should almost invariably march against an enemy in troubles.

Chanakya disagrees and states:
When one's resources are sufficient one should march, since the troubles of an enemy cannot be properly recognised; or whenever one finds it possible to reduce or destroy an enemy by marching against him, then one may undertake a march.

Quick-lesson:
Do not simply attack an enemy because they appear to be in period of internal trouble. The truth of their situation may not be fully apparent. Only march to war when you are prepared, especially when you are prepared and the enemy are in trouble.

Elephants in the Rain
When the weather is free from heat, one should march with an army mostly composed of elephants. Elephants with profuse sweat in hot weather are attacked by leprosy; and

when they have no water for bathing and drinking, they lose their quickness and become stubborn. Hence, against a country containing plenty of water and during the rainy season, one should march with an army mostly composed of elephants. Against a country of the reverse description, i.e., which as little rain and muddy water, one should march with an army mostly composed of asses, camels, and horses.

Quick-lesson:
A military vehicle should be suited to the environment.

Route Planning
Against a desert, one should march during the rainy season with all the four constituents of the army (elephants, horses, chariots, and men). One should prepare a programme of short and long distances to be marched in accordance with the nature of the ground to be traversed, viz., even ground, uneven ground, valleys and plains.

Quick-lesson:
The stages of a route and the waypoints of any military operation must be properly planned.

Be Quick or Be Dead
When the work to be accomplished is small, march against all kinds of enemies should be of short duration; and when it is great, it should also be of long duration; during the rains, encampment should be made abroad.

Quick-lesson:
Know the difference between what *should* be a short campaign and what *will* be a long one.

Roundup
- To be a commander, make preparations based on the forces at hand, the terrain, the weather, military equipment and the minds of men.
- Consider external and internal conditions and plan with an honest mind.
- Know when the enemy is in a state of weakness but also understand if your own forces are prepared.

ON THE MARCH

An army on the move is a vulnerable machine. Proper discipline should be maintained and knowledge of the road ahead is required. The commander should know the differences between troops on the move and troops stationed within fortifications. Here, this chapter deals with the requirements of the army on the march and some of the issues that accompany vast forces on the move.

The Route

The following section is from Book 10, Chapter 2 of the original text.

Having prepared a list of the villages and forests situated on the road with reference to their capacity to supply grass, firewood and water, the march of the army should be regulated according to the programme of short and long halts. Food-stuffs and provisions should be carried in double the quantity that may be required in any emergency. In the absence of separate means to carry food-stuffs, the army itself should be entrusted with the business of carrying them; or they may be stored in a central place (Fig. 42).

Fig. 42

73

Quick-lesson:
When moving an army, keep to the following:
1. Plan a route
2. Know what resources are along the route
3. Know the distances
4. Carry extra food in case of emergencies
5. If food cannot be carried, use the troops to carry it. If the troops cannot carry it, position it in storage areas.

Marching Order
(Fig. 43)
At the front:
- *the leader*

In the centre:
- *the harem*
- *the master (the king)*

To the side:
- *horses*
- *bodyguards*

At the extremity of the (marching) circular-array
- *elephants*
- *the surplus army*

On all sides
- *the army habituated to forest-life*
- *other troops following the camp*
- *the commissariat*
- *the army of an ally (whose followers should select their own road)*

Armies who have secured suitable positions will prove superior in fight to those who are in bad positions.

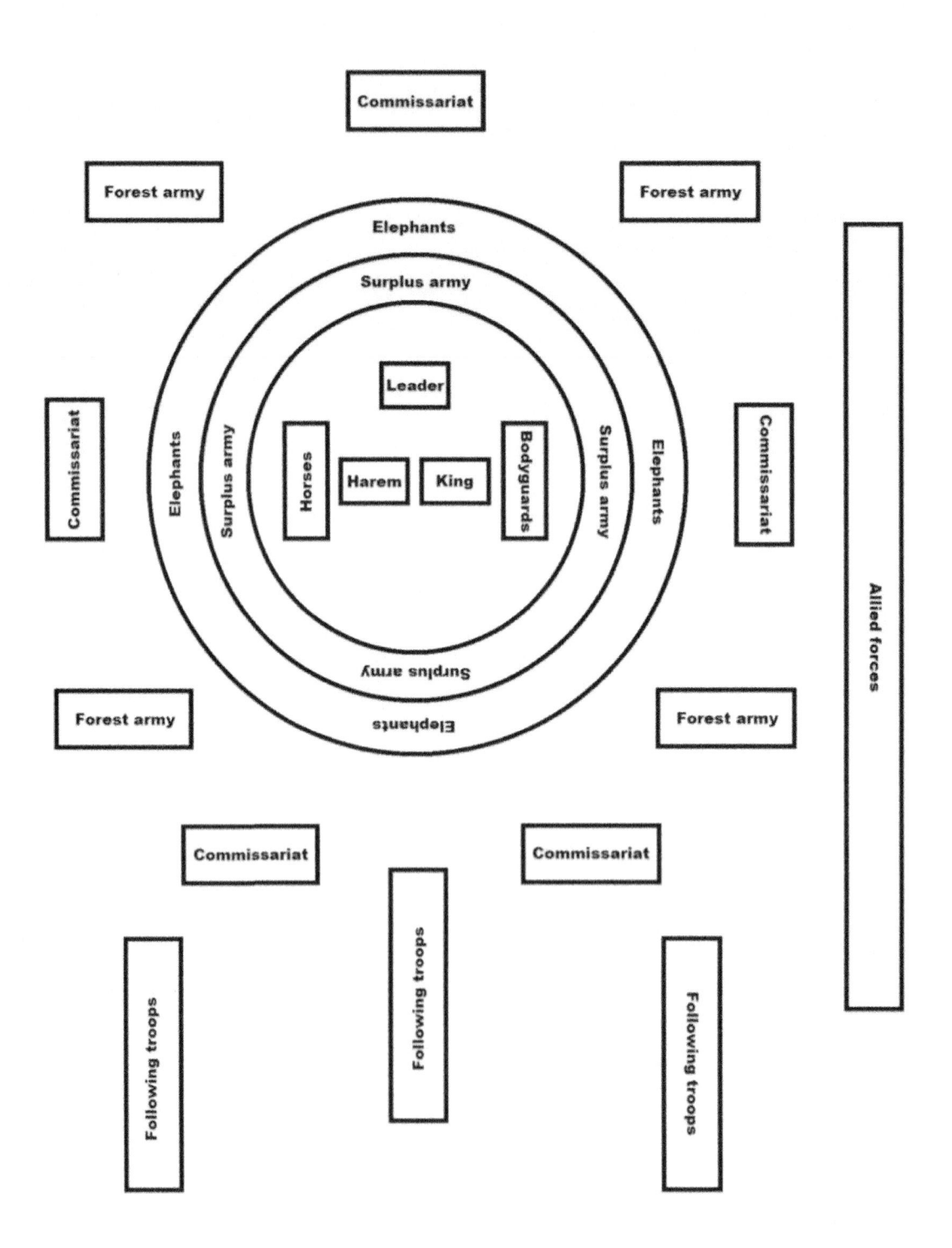

Fig. 43

Quick-lesson:
Have a structured set-up to ensure security and order.

Length of March
- *the army of the lowest quality can march a yojana (about 8 miles a day)*
- *the army of the middle quality can march a yojana and a half (about 12 miles a day)*
- *the best army can march two yojanas (about 16 miles a day)*

It is easy to ascertain the rate of march. The commander should march behind and put up his camp in the front.

Obstructions
In case of any obstruction, the army should march as follows:
- *in crocodile array at the front*
- *in cart-like array behind*
- *in diamond-like array at the sides (i.e., in four or five rows, each having its front, rear and sides) and in a compact array on all sides*

When the army is marching on a path passable by a single man, it should march in pin-like array.

Roads with obstructions should be examined and cleared.

Forecast
- *finance*
- *the army*
- *the strength of the armies of friends*
- *enemies*
- *wild tribes*
- *the prospect of rains*
- *the seasons*

These should be thoroughly examined.

Crossing Water
Waters may be crossed by means of:
- *elephants*
- *planks spread over pillars erected*
- *bridges*
- *boats*

- *timber and mass of bamboos*
- *as well as by means of dry sour gourds*
- *big baskets covered with skins* (Fig. 44)
- *rafts*

Fig. 44

Quick-lesson:
Water crossing has to be done by individuals and by masses of troops. The above covers both, from bridges for the masses down to floatation devices such as rafts and gourds. Interestingly, the baskets covered with skins also appear in the ninja manual, *Bansenshukai*.

Cross Water Away from the Enemy
When the crossing of a river is obstructed by the enemy, the invader may cross it elsewhere together with his elephants and horses, and entangle the enemy in an ambush.

Quick-lesson:
Do not cross bodies of water without a clear exit strategy.

A shinobi or ninja was a covert agent of medieval Japan who was skilled in espionage, sabotage and assassination.

Times to Protect and Times to Destroy
He should protect his army:
- *when it has to pass a long desert without water*
- *when it is without grass, firewood and water*
- *when it has to traverse a difficult road*
- *when it is harassed by enemy attacks*
- *when it is suffering from hunger and thirst after a journey*
- *when it is ascending or descending a mountainous country full of mire water-pools, rivers and waterfalls*
- *when it finds itself crowded in a narrow and difficult path*
- *when it is halting, starting or eating*
- *when it is tired from a long march*
- *when it is sleepy*
- *when it is suffering from a disease, pestilence or famine*
- *when a great portion of its infantry, cavalry and elephants is diseased*
- *when it is not sufficiently strong*
- *when it is under troubles*

He should destroy the enemy's army under such circumstances.

Quick-lesson:
At any point where an army is at more of a risk than other times, insert extra effort into defending the troops, whether on the move on in camp.

Observing the Enemy on the Road
When the enemy's army is marching through a path passable by a single man, the commander should ascertain its strength by estimating the quantity of food-stuffs, grass, bedding, and other requisites, fire pots, flags and weapons. He should also conceal those of his own army.

Quick-lesson:
Set up scouts at points where an enemy army will pass. It is performed in this manner because the army has to break up into single file, thus the scouts can easily count the troop numbers, troop types, weapons and size of the baggage train.

Roundup
Maintain discipline, have scouts move ahead and get a lay of the land, know the terrain ahead and understand the needs of an army on the march. Here Chanakya

talked about these elements and the forecasting of problems that may arise for a leader moving vast troops for long distances.

TREACHERY

Much of Chanakya's battle advice contradicts the ancient fair laws of engagement as laid down in Hindu law books and epics. He clearly discards rules of chivalry for the sake of attaining a decisive victory in war. The *Manusmriti*, the laws of Manu – the Hindu progenitor of mankind – states:

"When he fights with his foes in battle, let him not:
- *strike with weapons concealed (in wood)*
- *nor with (such as are) barbed, poisoned*
- *the points of which are blazing with fire*

Let him not strike one who (in flight) has:
- *climbed on an eminence*
- *nor a eunuch*
- *nor one who joins the palms of his hands (in supplication)*
- *nor one who (flees) with flying hair*
- *nor one who sits down*
- *nor one who says 'I am thine'*
- *nor one who sleeps*
- *nor one who has lost his coat of mail*
- *nor one who is naked*
- *nor one who is disarmed*
- *nor one who looks on without taking part in the fight*
- *nor one who is fighting with another (foe)*
- *nor one whose weapons are broken*
- *nor one afflicted (with sorrow)*
- *nor one who has been grievously wounded*
- *nor one who is in fear*
- *nor one who has turned to flight*

In all these cases let him remember the duty (of honourable warriors)."

Chapter 7

This list also shows that stealthy methods of attack were known of in ancient India and perhaps so common that rules of engagement based on respect and honour had to be written up.

It may be interesting to note that among the chivalrous laws that Manu lists, a warrior must not use weapons concealed in wood. This may be referring to weapons such as the *gupti*, a thin, straight sword and sheath disguised as a crutch/walking cane. Such a weapon was fit for an assassin who could take it past security whilst not arousing suspicions of danger.

The *Mahabharata* also records the rules of fair combat:
"Guided by considerations of fitness, willingness, daring and might, one should strike another, giving notice. No one should strike another that is unprepared or panic-struck. One engaged with another, one seeking quarter, one retreating, one whose weapon is rendered unfit, uncased in mail, should never be struck..."
Book 6: Bhishma Parva, Jamvu-khanda Nirmana Parva, Section 1

Chanakya, however, emphasises deception, striking unprepared enemies, overpowering a weak enemy, spreading disinformation, creating panic and chaos, using flammable weapons, etc.

Sun Tzu said: *"All warfare is based on deception."* (*The Art of War*, 1:17). However, thousands of years before the wise Chinese general stated that in his infamous treatise, Krishna had on numerous occasions stressed the importance of deception in battle. According to the *Mahabharata*, Krishna offered the Pandava warrior Bhima some strategic advice as he engaged his nemesis Duryodhana in a bloody and brutal one-on-one mace bout:

"Krishna said, 'The instruction received by them hath been equal. Bhima, however, is possessed of greater might, while Duryodhana is possessed of greater skill and hath laboured more. If he were to fight fairly, Bhima will never succeed in winning the victory. If, however, he fights unfairly he will be surely able to slay Duryodhana'."
Book 9: Shalya Parva: Section 59

After a prolonged fight, executing a variety of mace combat manoeuvres called *Mandala, Kausika, Yomaka, Gomutraka and Avasthana*, Bhima then, after seeing Krishna make signals indicating where to strike, finally smashed Duryodhana's thighs with his mace, breaking not only his adversary's thighs but also the rule of 'no strikes below the navel in a mace duel'. Duryodhana was defeated.

The ancient epic also tells in length the events of a surprise night attack, a tactic prohibited by the ancient Hindu rules of war. Ashvatthama, a warrior of the unrighteous

Kaurava army and son of the renowned Brahmin military guru Drona, reminds Kripa, his warrior uncle, about some of the dirty fighting methods employed by the righteous Pandava brothers (the protagonists of the epic) during the course of the Kurukshetra War (mostly on the incitement of Krishna, who was acting as the charioteer of Pandava brother, Arjuna).

"Ashvatthama said, '... The Pandavas, however, have before this broken the bridge of righteousness into a hundred fragments. In the very sight of all the kings, before thy eyes also, my sire, after he had laid down his weapons, was slain by Dhrishtadyumna. Karna also, that foremost of chariot-warriors, after the wheel of his chariot had sunk and he had been plunged into great distress, was slain by Arjuna. Similarly, Shantanu's son Bhishma, after he had laid aside his weapons and become disarmed, was slain by Arjuna with Shikhandi placed in his van. So also, the mighty bowman Bhurishrava, while observant of the praya vow on the field of battle, was slain by Yuyudhana in total disregard of the cries of all the kings! Duryodhana too, having encountered Bhima in battle with the mace, hath been slain unrighteously by the former in the very sight of all the lords of earth... When my sire, having slain hundreds and thousands of warriors with keen shafts, had laid aside his weapons, he was then slain by Dhrishtadyumna. I shall slay that slayer today in a similar condition that is, when he will have laid aside his armour.'"

Book 10: Sauptika Parva, Section 5

After trying to justify his vengeful intentions, Ashvatthama then proceeded to the Pandava camp and began slaying sleeping warriors indiscriminately with the frenzied blows of his sword and feet. Later it was found that his victims were not the Pandava brothers, his intended targets, but their sons.

According to the *Ramayana*, even the warrior prince, Rama, who was renowned for his righteousness, heroism and martial skills, killed the powerful Vali, warrior king of the forest kingdom, Kishkindha, by unfair means. While Vali was engaged in vicious hand-to-hand combat with his younger brother, Sugriva, Rama shot Vali with an arrow from behind a tree.

To be Deceptive or Not
He who is possessed of a strong army, who has succeeded in his intrigues, and who has applied remedies against dangers may undertake an open fight, if he has secured a position favourable to himself; otherwise a treacherous fight (Fig 45).

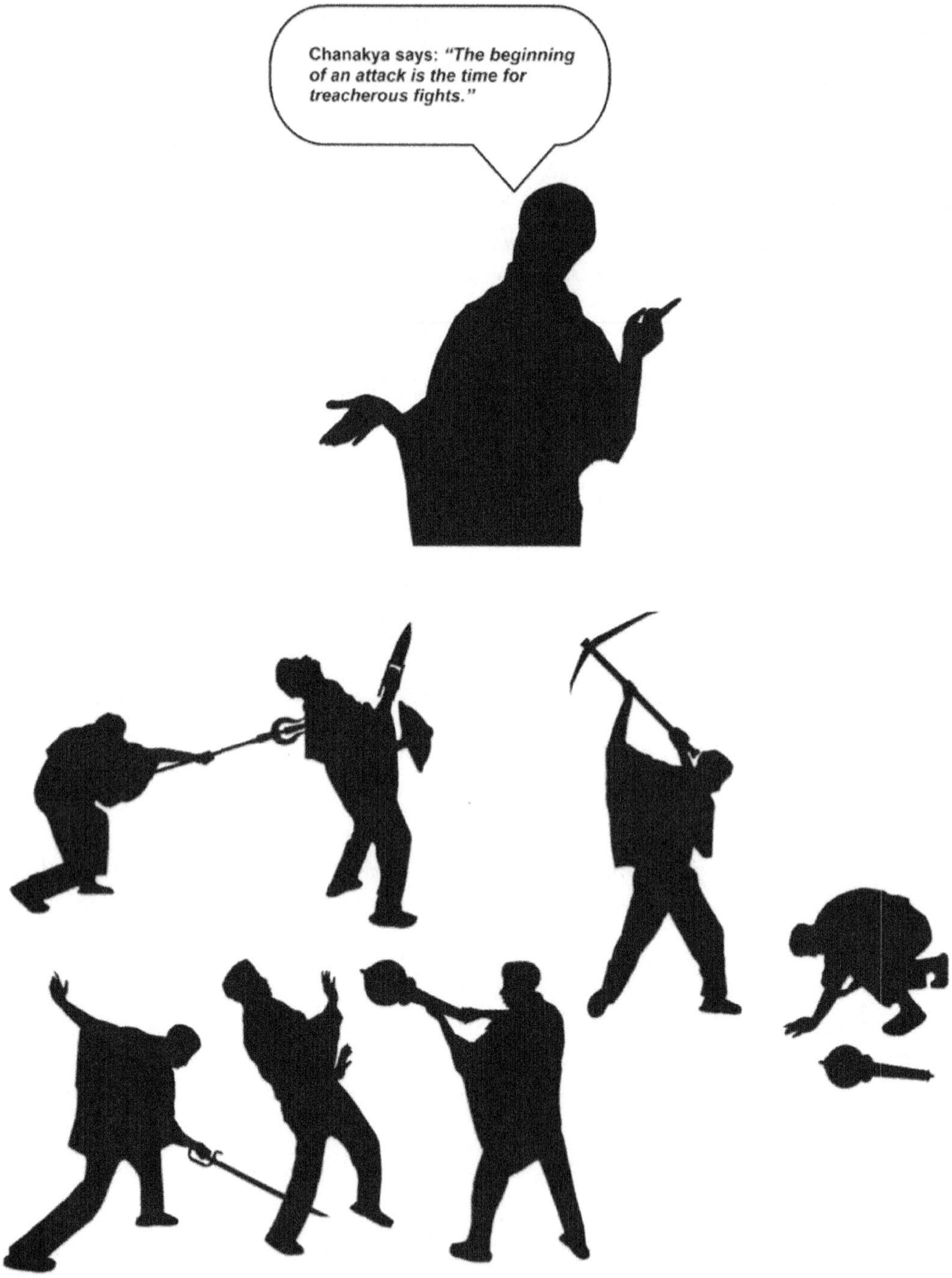

Fig. 45

Ways to Strike the Enemy with Treachery

The following section is from Book 10, Chapter 3 of the original text.

- *He should strike the enemy when the latter's army is under troubles or is furiously attacked*
- *he who has secured a favourable position may strike the enemy entangled in an unfavourable position*
- *he who possesses control over the elements of his own state may, through the aid of the enemy's traitors, enemies and inimical wild tribes, make a false impression of his own defeat on the mind of the enemy who is entrenched in a favourable position, and having thus dragged the enemy into an unfavourable position, he may strike the latter*
- *when the enemy's army is in a compact body, he should break it by means of his elephants*
- *when the enemy has come down from its favourable position, following the false impression of the invader's defeat, the invader may turn back and strike the enemy's army, broken or unbroken*
- *having struck the front of the enemy's army, he may strike it again by means of his elephants and horses when it has shown its back and is running away*
- *when frontal attack is unfavourable, he should strike it from behind*
- *when attack on the rear is unfavourable, he should strike it in front*
- *when attack on one side is unfavourable, he should strike it on the other*
- *having caused the enemy to fight with his own army of traitors, enemies and wild tribes, the invader should with his fresh army strike the enemy when tired*
- *having through the aid of the army of traitors given to the enemy the impression of defeat, the invader with full confidence in his own strength may allure and strike the over-confident enemy*
- *the invader, if he is vigilant, may strike the careless enemy when the latter is deluded with the thought that the invader's merchants, camp and carriers have been destroyed*
- *having made his strong force look like a weak force, he may strike the enemy's brave men when falling against him*

- *having captured the enemy's cattle or having destroyed the enemy's dogs, he may induce the enemy's brave men to come out and may slay them*
- *having made the enemy's men sleepless by harassing them at night, he may strike them during the day, when they are weary from want of sleep and are parched by heat, himself being under the shade*
- *with his army of elephants enshrouded with cotton and leather dress, he may offer a night-battle to his enemy*
- *he may strike the enemy's men during the afternoon when they are tired by making preparations during the forenoon*
- *he may strike the whole of the enemy's army when it is facing the sun*

Quick-lesson:
Deception before a strike gives an advantage. False retreats, feints and unexpected attacks all tip the balance and give favour to an army using such tactics. Notice the use of leather and cotton to silence the enemy on night attacks and the concept of attacking when facing the sun.

Temptation
- *a desert*
- *a dangerous spot*
- *marshy places*
- *mountains*
- *valleys*
- *uneven boats*
- *cows*
- *cart-like array of the army*
- *mist*
- *night*

These are temptations alluring the enemy against the invader.

Quick-lesson:
Know that an enemy will show interest in the above points.

Roundup
Treachery and deception are generally frowned upon in military manuals yet are often used and recorded. It appears that an enemy who attacks in an underhanded manner is deemed as impolite while an allied leader is deemed as ingenious if they use the same

tricks. Therefore, the lesson behind treachery is that a good defence against the unorthodox is required while a good mind for the construction of unconventional plans is obligatory.

PREPARATION

Preparation in war can allude to a vast number of different situations from preparation on a grand scale with the positioning of armies and the fortification of castles to the basics of reinforcing the morale of the men, making sure the leader is well-defended and to have prepared speeches before battle. Here are a few examples of the way Chanakya shows the ways of preparation.

Battle Speeches

The following section is from Book 9, Chapter 6 of the original text.

As to an open or fair fight, a virtuous king should call his army together, and, specifying the place and time of battle, address them thus:

"I am a paid servant like yourselves; this country is to be enjoyed (by me) together with you; you have to strike the enemy specified by me."

His minister and priest should encourage the army by saying thus:

"It is declared in the Vedas that the goal which is reached by sacrificers after performing the final ablutions in sacrifices in which the priests have been duly paid for is the very goal which brave men are destined to attain."

About this there are the two verses:

"Beyond those places which Bráhmins, desirous of getting into heaven, attain together with their sacrificial instruments by performing a number of sacrifices, or by practising penance are the places which brave men, losing life in good battles, are destined to attain immediately.

Let not a new vessel filled with water, consecrated and covered over with darbha grass be the acquisition of that man who does not fight in return for the subsistence received by him from his master, and who is therefore destined to go to hell."

> Darbha grass is considered sacred by Hindus and is used in rituals. Its Latin name is Desmostachya bipinnata.

Quick-lesson:
Men who die in battle will ascend to the place where preachers and men of the cloth spend their lives trying to be. The general is saying here: *"Fight for me and gain entrance to heaven"*. Likewise, the general is also saying: *"Do not fight for me and go to hell"*.

The King's Preparation
Astrologers and other followers of the king should infuse spirit into his army by pointing out:
- *the impregnable nature of the array of his army*
- *his power to associate with gods*
- *his power to know all*

They should at the same time frighten the enemy.

Prepare the king!
The day before the battle, the king should:
- *fast and lie down on his chariot with weapons*
- *make oblations into the fire pronouncing the mantras of the Atharvaveda*
- *cause prayers to be offered for the good of the victors as well as of those who attain to heaven by dying in the battle-field*
- *submit his person to Bráhmins*

Positioning Within the Army
The king should make the central portion of his army consist of such men as are noted for their bravery, skill, high birth, and loyalty and as are not displeased with the rewards and honours bestowed on them.

Position the King
The place that is to be occupied by the king is that portion of the army which is composed of his father, sons, brothers, and other men, skilled in using weapons, and having no flags and head-dress. He should mount an elephant or a chariot, if the army consists mostly of horses; or he may mount that kind of animal, of which the army is mostly composed or which is the most skilfully trained. One who is disguised like the king should attend to the work of arraying the army.

Quick-lesson:
Surround the leader with loyal men. Hide him in the ranks of normal men and have his doppelganger assume his place. From here, the leader can command while the other becomes a target.

Prowess and Reward
Soothsayers and court bards should describe heaven as the goal for the brave and hell for the timid; and also extol the caste, corporation, family, deeds, and character of his men. The followers of the priest should proclaim the auspicious aspects of the witchcraft performed. Spies, carpenters and astrologers should also declare the success of their own operations and the failure of those of the enemy.

After having pleased the army with rewards and honours, the commander-in-chief should address it and say:
- *A hundred thousand panas for slaying the king (of the enemy)*
- *fifty thousand for slaying the commander-in-chief, and the heir-apparent*
- *ten thousand for slaying the chief of the brave*
- *five thousand for destroying an elephant, or a chariot*
- *a thousand for killing a horse*
- *a hundred for slaying the chief of the infantry*

> Pana means punched-marked coins.

> Take note how each group of ten men has a leader.

- *twenty for bringing a head*

This information should be made known to the leaders of every group of ten (men).

Quick-lesson:
Supply the army with a feeling of ease before a battle to gain a confident feel in the forces and be clear on rewards to be given for specific actions.

Support
Physicians with surgical instruments, machines, remedial oils, and cloth in their hands; and women with prepared food and beverage should stand behind, uttering encouraging words to fighting men.

Favourable positions
- *The army should be arrayed on a favourable position, facing other than the south quarter, with its back turned to the sun, and capable to rush as it stands* (Fig. 46)
- *If the array is made on an unfavourable spot, horses should be run*
- *If the army arrayed on an unfavourable position is confined or is made to run away from it (by the enemy), it will be subjugated either as standing or running away; otherwise it will conquer the enemy when standing or running away.*
- *The even, uneven, and complex nature of the ground in the front or on the sides or in the rear should be examined*
- *On an even site, staff-like or circular array should be made; and on an uneven ground, arrays of compact movement or of detached bodies should be made*

Fig. 46

When to Give Peace

Having broken the whole army (of the enemy), (the invader) should seek for peace.

- *If the armies are of equal strength, he should make peace when requested for it*
- *and if the enemy's army is inferior, he should attempt to destroy it*
- *When a broken army, reckless of life, resumes its attack, its fury becomes irresistible; hence he should not harass a broken army (of the enemy)*

Quick-lesson:
To come to terms and give peace should only be done in certain circumstances, likewise, a broken enemy should only be destroyed at certain times. An army may be broken up but if it faces utter destruction it will gain resolve and the fight will be hard. Totally destroy an army when success is guaranteed, but if not, then bring about peace on your own terms.

Roundup
In the West, those familiar with the life and teachings of Chanakya often compare him to Nicollo Machiavelli (1469 – 1527 CE), a renowned Italian political theorist. The similarities between their thought is interesting. Towards the end of this section, Chanakya advises favourable positions for an army. In his 26-chapter treatise, Machiavelli makes a similar remark to Chanakya's:

"...by observing how the mountains slope, the valleys open, and the plains spread; acquainting himself with the characters of rivers and marshes, and giving the greatest attention to this subject. Such knowledge is useful to him in two ways; for first, he learns thereby to know his own country, and to understand better how it may be defended..."
The Prince, Chapter 14: Of the Duty of a Prince In Respect of Military Affairs

Chanakya also talked high morale and motivation. To appeal to the religious/superstitious side of soldiers, he advises that soothsayers, astrologers, etc., should tempt soldiers to lust for heavenly rewards and fear hellish punishment, something which has usually been the primary driving force of religious persons, causing them to commit daring and rare acts with immense determination and courage.

According to the *Mahabharata,* before the commencing of the Kurukshetra War between the Pandavas and Kauravas, the warrior Arjuna began having doubts about fighting against the unrighteous Kaurava army because among them were his relatives and also military gurus. This was until Krishna reminded Arjuna of his Kshatriya duty in order to arouse his warrior pride and courage. Krishna also told him:

"If slain, you will attain heaven; if victorious, you will enjoy the earth."
Book 6, Section 26

In other words, it is a win-win situation. Prior to battle, the warrior is made to believe he will receive a great reward, whether he lives or dies. With a belief like this, one can go on to fight fearlessly and more viciously than normal and thus likely to cause more casualties and even come out of the battle alive and victorious. In this episode, Arjuna did.

This same divine temptation can be seen in other religions. Convincing a person that some deity is with them and that heaven is reserved for heroes and martyrs, can infuse tremendous courage into them and enable them to perform daring feats which they may otherwise be unable to perform. The evidence of this is that despite believing in distinct deities of different belief systems that contradict one another, people of various faiths, both in ancient and modern times, have been able to fight fearlessly till their last breath, all the while convinced their respective deity was aiding them. Chanakya understood the power and use of faith, which he believed could be very advantageous in military operations.

While Chanakya concludes this section advising a king to avoid fighting soldiers reckless of life, Sun Tzu advises a leader to turn his own troops into reckless fighters in order to squeeze out their full warrior potential:

"Throw your soldiers into positions whence there is no escape, and they will prefer death to flight. If they will face death, there is nothing they may not achieve. Officers and men alike will put forth their uttermost strength."

The Art of War, 11:23

THE BATTLEFIELD

A battlefield (Sanskrit: *Ranbhoomi*) is the location of a battle. The most famous battlefield in Indian history is perhaps Kurukshetra which is located in the modern state of Haryana, northern India. According to the *Mahabharata*, it is the plains upon which the great war between the Pandava and Kaurava armies had taken place. It was also on this battlefield that Krishna imparted spiritual knowledge to the warrior Arjuna (i.e. Bhagavad Gita). Here in this chapter, Chanakya outlines the basics and finer points of the ways of the battlefield.

Men Required for War

The following section is from Book 10, Chapter 4 of the original text.

Men who are trained to fight in the following areas are needed:
- *desert tracts*
- *forests*
- *valleys*
- *plains*
- *ditches*
- *heights*
- *during the day or night*

Also elephants which are bred in countries with rivers, mountains, marshy lands, or lakes, as well as for horses. Such battlefields as they would find suitable (are to be secured).

Quick-lesson:
Have the right men do the right job and train for all conditions.

Good Ground for Chariots
- *splendidly firm*
- *free from mounds and pits*
- *made by wheels and foot-prints of beasts*
- *not offering obstructions to the axle*
- *free from trees, plants, creepers and trunks of trees*
- *not wet*

- *free from pits, ant-hills, sand, and thorns*

Quick-lesson:
Know the ground ahead and establish if vehicles can move along such terrain.

Other Ground Types
For elephants, horses and men, even or uneven grounds are good, either for war or for camp.
That which contains small stones, trees and pits that can be jumped over and which is almost free from thorns is the ground for horses.
That which contains big stones, dry or green trees, and ant-hills is the ground for the infantry.
That which is uneven with assailable hills and valleys, which has trees that can be pulled down and plants that can be torn, and which is full of muddy soil free from thorns is the ground for elephants.
That which is free from thorns, not very uneven, but very expansive, is an excellent ground for the infantry.
That which is doubly expansive, free from mud, water and roots of trees, and which is devoid of piercing gravel is an excellent ground for horses.
That which possesses dust, muddy soil, water, grass and weeds, and which is free from thorns (known as dog's teeth) and obstructions from the branches of big trees is an excellent ground for elephants.
That which contains lakes, which is free from mounds and wet lands, and which affords space for turning is an excellent ground for chariots.

The Use of Horses
- *concentration on occupied positions, in camps and forests*
- *crossing through places and positions favourable to sunny and windy conditions*
- *destruction of the enemy's supplies and reinforcements or protection of one's own*
- *supervising the discipline of the army*
- *extending the length of the army in operations*
- *protecting the sides of the army*
- *launching the initial assault*
- *dispersion (of the enemy's army)*
- *providing rest to one's own army*
- *taking prisoners*
- *freeing one's soldiers from enemy detention*
- *causing the army to take a different direction*

- *carrying the treasury and the princes*
- *falling against the rear of the enemy*
- *chasing the timid*
- *pursuit*
- *gathering one's troops*

These constitute the use of horses.

Quick-lesson:
Fast moving vehicles are needed on the battlefield.

The Use of Elephants
- *marching at the front*
- *preparing the roads, camping grounds and path for bringing water*
- *protecting the sides*
- *firm standing, fording and entering into water while crossing pools of water and ascending from them*
- *forced entrance into impregnable places*
- *setting or quenching the fire*
- *the over-powering of one of the four constituents of the army*
- *gathering the dispersed army*
- *breaking a compact army*
- *protection against dangers*
- *trampling down (the enemy's army)*
- *frightening and driving*
- *adding splendour*
- *seizing*
- *abandoning*
- *destruction of walls, gates and towers*
- *carrying the treasury*

Quick-lesson:
Use heavy and powerful equipment if feasible.

The Work of Chariots
- *protection of the army*
- *repelling an attack made by all the four constituents of the enemy's army*
- *seizing and abandoning (positions) during the time of battle*

- *gathering a dispersed army*
- *breaking the compact array of the enemy's army*
- *frightening it*
- *magnificence*
- *fearful noise*

Quick-lesson:
The 'four constituents' are:
1. infantry
2. cavalry
3. chariots
4. elephants

The Work of the Infantry
Always carrying the weapons to all places and fighting (Fig. 47).

Fig. 47

Quick-lesson:

Think of the following:
- A spearman is a soldier with a bayonet-fixed rifle
- The elephant is a heavy tank
- A chariot is a lightly armoured weapon-mounted jeep (Fig. 48)

Fig. 48

The Work of the Free Labourers
- *the examination of camps, roads, bridges, wells and rivers*
- *carrying the machines, weapons, armours, instruments and provisions*
- *carrying away the men that are knocked down, along with their weapons and armours*

Alterative Vehicles
The king who has a small number of horses may combine bulls with horses; likewise, when he is deficient in elephants, he may fill up the centre of his army with mules, camels and carts.

Roundup
Types of ground and tactics according to each ground down to the work of the labourers are the parts that turn a mass of chaos into a fully functioning army with well-oiled discipline and a functioning command structure. Having secured land, having fortified castles, having governed well and installing correct government will all fall if proper command of troops on the field of battle is not mastered to defend the nation that the leader has built.

THE ARRAY OF TROOPS

Following on from the above, a commander and his army need to understand the formations of troops, their movement and signals. Often military manuals describe in detail the correct formations of armies, and frequently the reality of war is the breakup of these formations to mass combat. Here, Chanakya discusses his ideas and practices on the use of individual elements in war.

Spacing

> The following section is from Book 10, Chapter 5 of the original text.

- *Having fortified a camp at the distance of five hundred bows he should begin to fight. Having detached the flower of the army and kept it on a favourable position not visible (to the enemy), the commander-in-chief and the leader should array the rest of the army.*
- *The infantry should be arrayed such that the space between any two men is a sama (10.5 inches); cavalry with three samas (31.5 inches); chariots with four samas (42 inches); elephants with twice or thrice as much space (as between any two chariots) (84 inches or 7 feet, or 126 inches or 10.5 feet) (Fig. 49). With such an array free to move and having no confusion, one should fight.*
- *A "bow" means five aratnis (90 inches or 7.5 feet), archers should be stationed at the distance of five bows (from one line to another) (450 inches or 37.5 feet); the cavalry at the distance of three bows (270 inches or 22.5 feet); and chariots or elephants at the distance of five bows (450 inches or 37.5 feet)* (Fig. 50)
- *The intervening space between wings, flanks and front of the army should be five bows (450 inches or 37.5 feet)* (Fig. 51)

Fig. 49

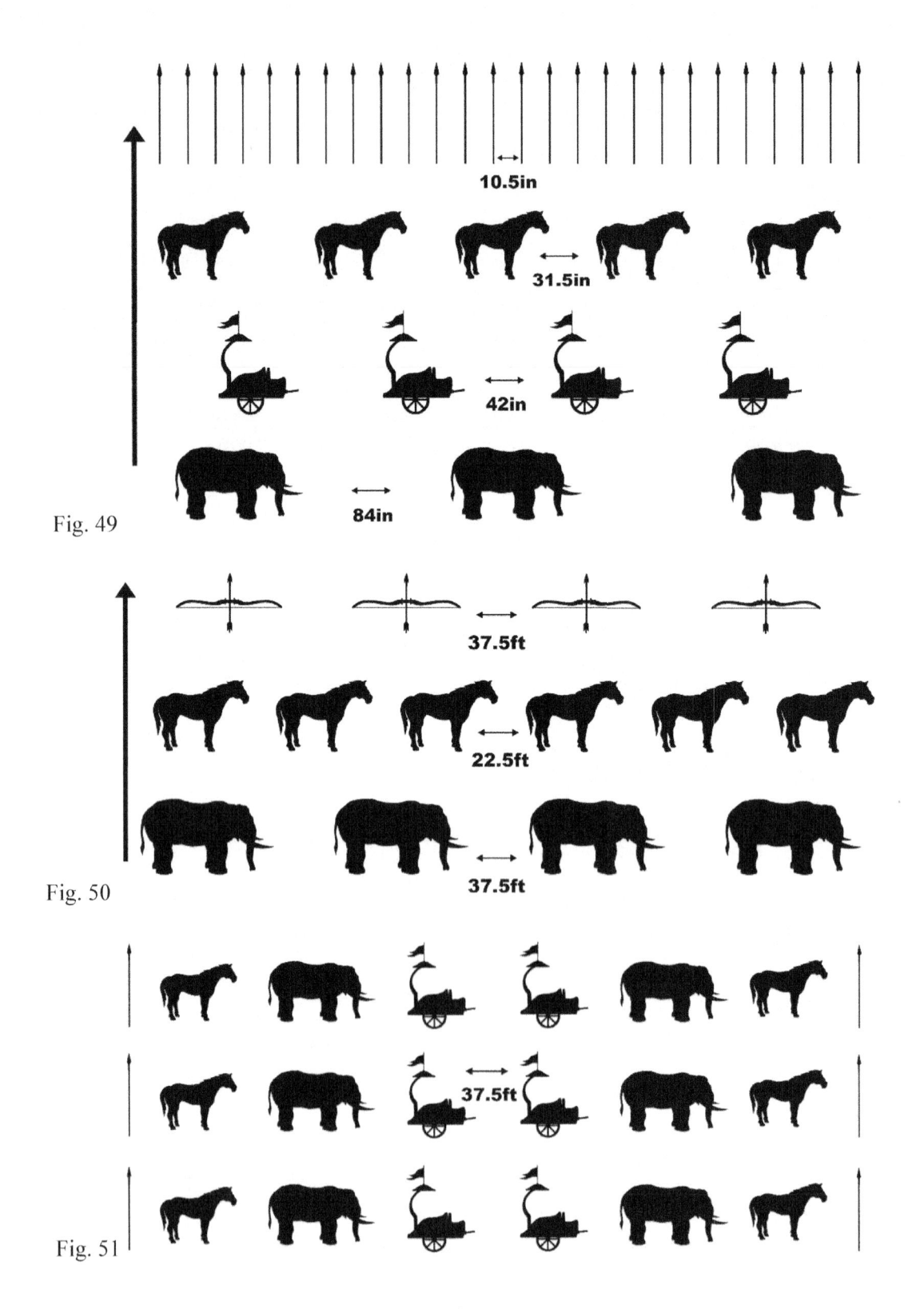

Fig. 50

Fig. 51

Opposing the Enemy
- *three men to oppose a horse*
- *fifteen men or five horses to oppose a chariot or an elephant*

Surplus
- *excess of the army is called surplus*
- *deficiency in infantry is called absence of surplus*
- *excess of any one of the four constituents of the army is akin to surplus*
- *excess of traitors is far from surplus*
- *in accordance with one's own resources, one should increase one's army from four to eight times the excess of the enemy's army or the deficiency in the enemy's infantry*

Quick-lesson:
The enemy should be outnumbered and outgunned.

Strategic Combinations
- *An array of elephants, chariots, and horses mixed together may also be made: at the extremities of the circle (array), elephants; and on the flanks, horses and principal chariots.*
- *The array in which the front is occupied by elephants, the flanks by chariots, and the wings by horses is an array which can break the centre of the enemy's army; the reverse of this can harass the extremities of the enemy's army.*
- *An array of elephants may also be made: the front by such elephants as are trained for war; the flanks by such as are trained for riding; and the wings by rogue elephants.*
- *In an array of horses, the front by horses with mail armour; and the flanks and wings by horses without armour. In an array of infantry, men dressed in mail armour in front, archers in the rear, and men without armour on the wings; or horses on the wings, elephants on the flanks, and chariots in front; other changes may also be made so as to oppose the enemy's army successfully.*

The Best Army
The best army is that which consists of strong infantry and of such elephants and horses as are noted for their breed, birth, strength, youth, vitality and capacity to run even in old age, fury, skill, firmness, magnanimity, obedience, and good habits.

Positioning by Skill
One-third of the best of infantry, cavalry and elephants should be kept in front; two-thirds on both the flanks and wings; the array of the army according to the strength of its constituents is in the direct order; that which is arrayed mixing one-third of strong and weak troops is in the reverse order. Thus, one should know all the varieties of arraying the array.

Proper Positioning
Having stationed the weak troops at the extremities, one would be liable to the force of the enemy's onslaught. Having stationed the flower of the army in front, one should make the wings equally strong. One-third of the best in the rear, and weak troops in the centre – this array is able to resist the enemy; having made an array, he should strike the enemy with one or two of the divisions on the wings, flanks, and front, and capture the enemy by means of the rest of the troops.

Quick-lesson:
A commander should not risk letting inferior troops lead the way. He must have his best men do what they do best.

The Weak Enemy
When the enemy's force is weak, with few horses and elephants, and is contaminated with the intrigue of treacherous ministers, the conqueror should strike it with most of his best troops. He should increase the numerical strength of that constituent of the army which is physically weak. He should array his troops on that side on which the enemy is weak or from which danger is apprehended.

Quick-lesson:
When the enemy is not formed with strength or has internal issues, send the best men.

Waging War with Horses
- *running against*
- *running round*
- *running beyond*
- *running back*
- *disturbing the enemy's halt*
- *gathering the troops*
- *curving*

- *circling*
- *miscellaneous operations*
- *removal of the rear*
- *pursuit of the line from the front*
- *flanks and rear*
- *protection of a broken army*
- *falling upon the broken army*

Quick-lesson:
Have mobile troops understand manoeuvres and precision movement.

Waging War with Elephants
These are same varieties with the exception of (what is called) miscellaneous operations – including;
- *the destruction of the four constituents of the army, either single or combined*
- *the dispersion of the flanks*
- *wings and front trampling down*
- *attacking the army when it is asleep*

Waging War with Infantry
The same varieties [as above] with the exception of disturbing the enemy's halt. Also:
- *running against*
- *running back*
- *fighting from where it stands on its own ground*
- *striking in all places and at all times*
- *striking by surprise* (Fig. 52)

Fig. 52

DIFFERENT FORMATIONS

Indian military texts, scriptures and epics mention and/or describe numerous battle formations (*vyuha*). These formations consisted of the army's four divisions:
1. chariots
2. elephants
3. cavalry
4. infantry

There is a story from the *Mahabharata* epic (found in Book 7: from Section 31 onwards) relating to the *chakravyuha* (circle formation). Arjuna's young, brave warrior son, Abhimanyu, was one of few warriors who knew the secret of penetrating the almost-impenetrable circle formation. However, he had no knowledge of exiting it. In battle, after managing to enter the formation, he killed as many enemies as he could, but once in deep, he found himself trapped and surrounded by several notable enemy warriors of the Kaurava army who then unchivalrously disarmed and wounded him severely, eventually killing him with a mace blow to the crown of his head.

In the *Arthashastra*, Chanakya describes a variety of formations as well as their variations. These formations are named after animals, shapes or battle-winning words.

The following section is from Book 10, Chapter 6 of the original text.

Two great arrays and their variations
- *Wings and front, capable to turn (against an enemy is what is called) a snake-like array.*
- *The two wings, the two flanks, the front and the reserve (form an array) according to the school of Brihaspati.*
- *The principal forms of the array of the army, such as that like a staff, like a snake, like a circle, and in detached order, are varieties of the above two forms of the array consisting of wings, flanks and front.*

Quick-lesson:
Brihaspati – the guru of the gods (Fig. 53). He is the lord of prayer and rituals, and is also identified with the planet Jupiter in Indian astrology. Chanakya refers to his school of thought in his text.

Fig. 53

Formations

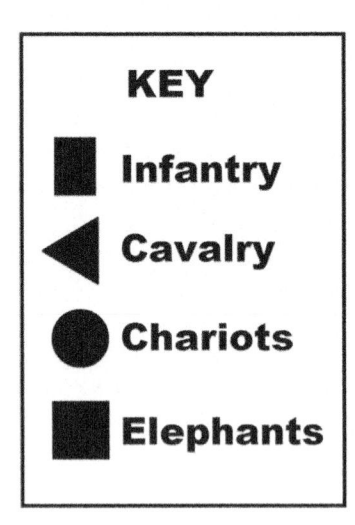

KEY
■ Infantry
◀ Cavalry
● Chariots
■ Elephants

- *Stationing the army so as to stand abreast, is called a 'staff-like array'* (Fig. 54).
- *Stationing the army in a line so that one may follow the other, is called a 'snake-like array'* (Fig. 55).
- *Stationing the army so as to face all the directions, is called a 'circle-like array'.* (Fig. 56).
- *Detached arrangement of the army into small bodies so as to enable each to act for itself, is termed an array in detached order.* (Fig. 57).

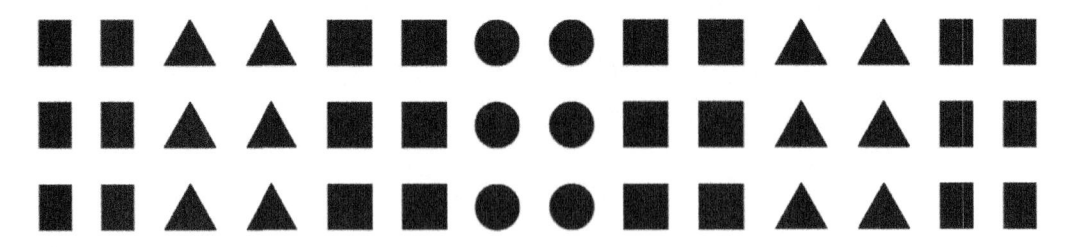

■ ■ ▲ ▲ ■ ■ ● ● ■ ▲ ▲ ■ ■
■ ■ ▲ ▲ ■ ■ ● ● ■ ▲ ▲ ■ ■
■ ■ ▲ ▲ ■ ■ ● ● ■ ▲ ▲ ■ ■

Fig. 54

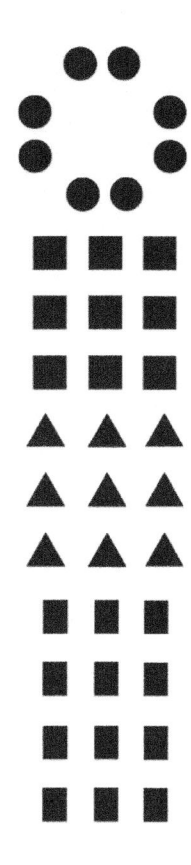

Fig. 55

Fig. 56

108

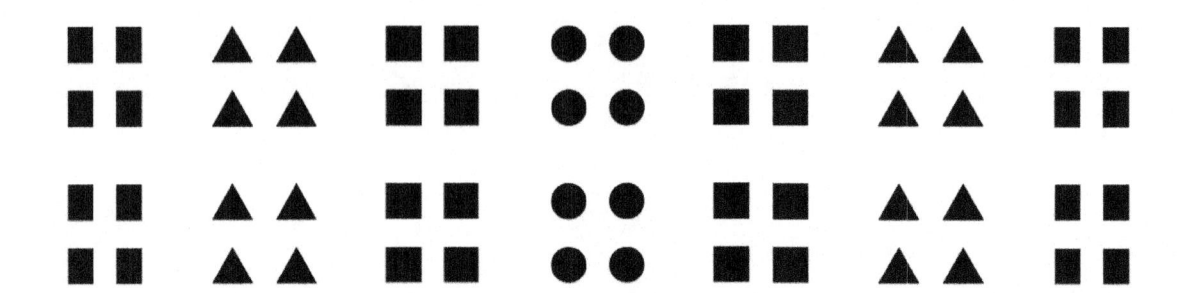

Fig. 57

Staff-like Array
That which is of equal strength on its wings, flanks and front, is a staff-like array.
- *The same array is called 'enemy array-breaker' when its flanks are made to project in front (Fig. 58).*
- *The same is called 'firm' when its wings and flanks are stretched back (Fig. 59).*
- *The same is called 'irresistible' when its wings are lengthened (Fig. 60).*

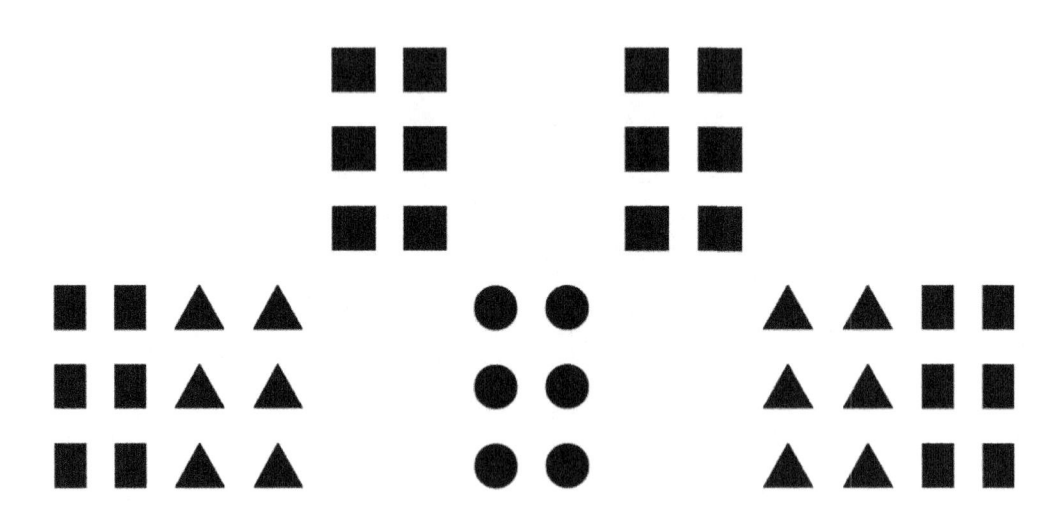

Fig. 58

109

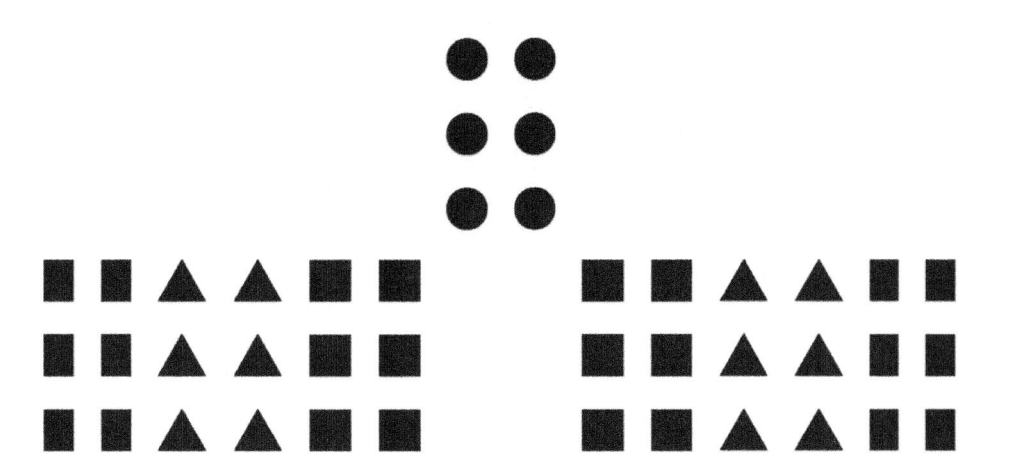

Fig. 59

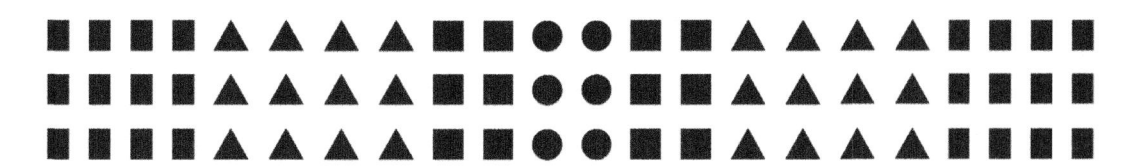

Fig. 60

Eagle Array
When, having formed the wings, the front is made to bulge out, it is called an 'eagle-like array'.

The Victory Array
- *That, of which the wings are arrayed like a bow, is called 'victory' (Fig. 61).*
- *the same with projected front is called 'the conqueror' (Fig. 62).*
- *that which has its flanks and wings formed like a staff is called 'big ear'.*
- *the same with its front made twice as strong as the conqueror, is called 'a vast victory'.*
- *that which has its wings stretched forward is called 'face of the army'.*
- *the same is called 'face of the fish' when it is arrayed in the reverse form.*

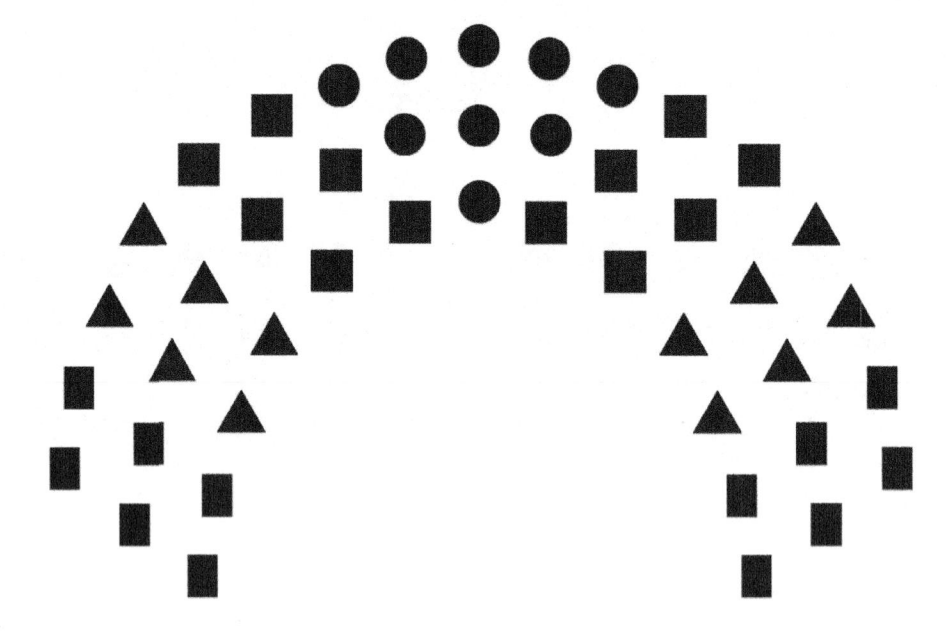

Fig. 61

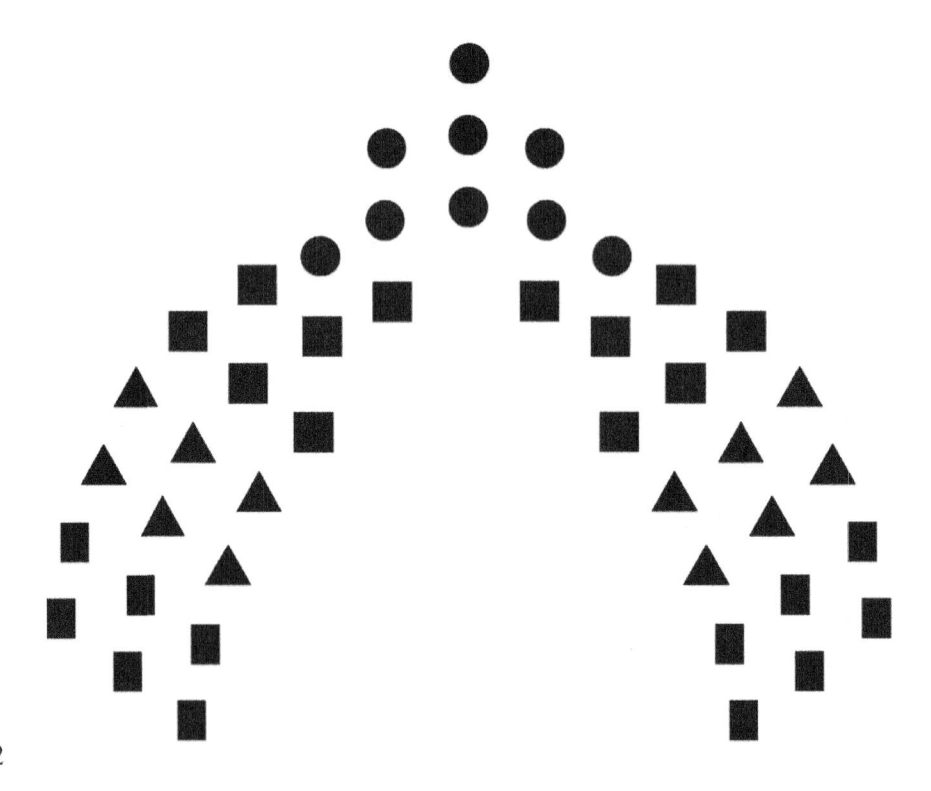

Fig. 62

The staff-like array in which one (constituent of the army) is made to stand behind the other is called a 'pin-like array' (Fig. 63).

Fig. 63

When this array consists of two such lines, it is called an 'aggregate' (Fig. 64); *and when of four lines, it is called an 'invincible array'* (Fig. 65) – *these are the varieties of the staff-like array.*

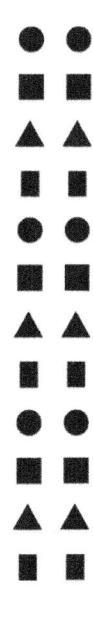

Fig. 64

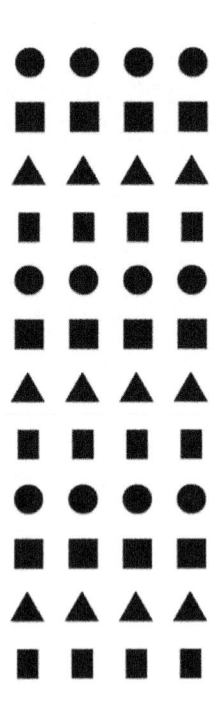

Fig. 65

The snake-like array in which the wings, flanks and front are of unequal depth is called 'serpentine movement', or 'the course of a cow's urine' (Fig. 66).

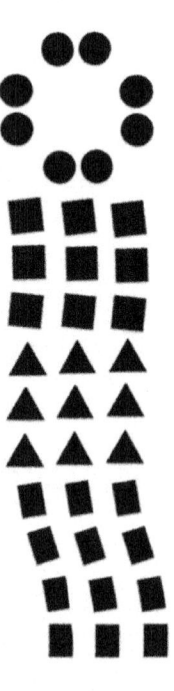

Fig. 66

When it consists of two lines in front and has its wings arranged as in the staff-like array, it is called a 'cart-like array'; the reverse of this is called a 'crocodile-like array'.

The circle-like array in which the distinction of wings, flanks and front is lost is called 'facing all directions', or 'all auspicious, 'one of eight divisions', or 'victory' – these are the varieties of the circle-like array.

That, of which the wings, flanks and front are stationed apart is called an array in detached order; when five divisions of the army are arranged in detached order, it is called 'diamond', or 'alligator'; when four divisions, it is called 'park', or 'crow's foot'; when three divisions, it is called 'half-moon' – these are the varieties of the array in detached-order.

The array in which chariots form the front, elephants the wings, and horses the rear, is called 'auspicious'.

The array in which infantry, cavalry, chariots and elephants stand one behind the other is called 'immovable' (Fig. 67).

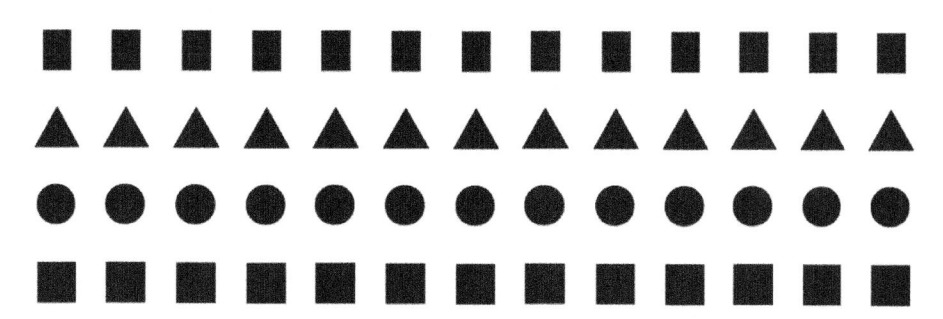

Fig. 67

The array in which elephants, horses, chariots and infantry stand in order one behind the other is called 'invincible'.

Of these, the conqueror should:
- *assail the 'breaking the enemy's array' by means of the 'firm array'*
- *'firm array' by means of the 'irresistible array'*
- *'eagle-like array' by means of 'an array like a bow'*
- *a hold by means of a strong-hold*
- *'victory array' by means of 'conqueror array'*

- *'big ear array' by means of 'vast victory array'*

He may assail all kinds of arrays by means of the 'unconquerable array'.

Of infantry, cavalry, chariots and elephants, he should strike the first-mentioned with that which is subsequently mentioned; and a small constituent of the army with a big one.

For every ten members of each of the constituents of the army, there must be one commander; ten commanders under a commander-in-chief; ten commander-in-chiefs under a leader (Fig. 68).

Fig. 68

The constituents of the array of the army should be called after the names of trumpet sounds, flags and ensigns. Achievement of success in arranging the constituents of the army, in gathering the forces, in camping, in marching, in turning back, in making onslaughts, and in the array of equal strength depends upon the place and time of action.

To Kill in the Womb
By the display of the army, by secret contrivances, by fiery spies employed to strike the enemy engaged otherwise, by witch-craft, by proclaiming the conqueror's association with gods, by carts, by the ornaments of elephants;

By inciting traitors, by herds of cattle, by setting fire to the camp, by destroying the wings and the rear of the enemy's army, by sowing the seeds of dissension through the agency of men under the guise of servants;

Or by telling the enemy that his fort was burnt, stormed, or that some one of his family, or an enemy or a wild chief rose in rebellion – by these and other means the conqueror should cause excitement to the enemy.

The arrow shot by an archer may or may not kill a single man; but skilful intrigue devised by wise men can kill even those who are in the womb.

Quick-lesson:
Cunning is superior to strength.

Roundup
Formations are a complex matter and the question as to the reality of their use in actual warfare always sits in the back of the mind. This topic is a target of debate for many people and the reality of how well or how often formations were used, controlled or changed in ancient warfare is a difficult question to answer. At some point in a battle, a formation may give way to individual combat, thus losing the integrity of the formation itself. Therefore, here we must understand that formations were complex but were recorded for people to study and follow. How long these formations lasted and their success was dependent on many factors.

THE BATTLE OF INTRIGUE

The *Shukraniti* text – which Chanakya was more than familiar with – says:

"...to ensure the destruction of a powerful enemy, there is no fighting equal to unfair fighting."

Spying and intrigue flow throughout this book and while it seems that the original document is full of spy use, it has to be remembered that we have concentrated on the use of spies which may seem to give their position a slightly unbalanced view. In truth, the original text is a massive and eclectic collection and while spies are clearly important to Chanakya, a balanced understanding of their importance must be retained. That being said, they certainly hold a place of importance for the author. In this chapter, Chanakya goes through many aspects of covert operations and the 'games' played behind the walls of power.

A Warning to the Enemy

The following section is from Book 12, Chapter 2 of the original text.

If the enemy does not keep peace, he should be told:
"These kings perished by surrendering themselves to the aggregate of the six enemies; it is not worthy of you to follow the lead of these unwise kings; be mindful of virtue and wealth; those who advise you to brave danger, sin and violation of wealth, are enemies under the guise of friends; it is danger to fight with men who are reckless of their own lives; it is sin to cause the loss of life on both sides; it is violation of wealth to abandon the wealth at hand and the friend of no mean character (meaning the addresser himself); that king has many friends whom he will set against you with the same wealth (that is acquired with your help at my expense), and who will fall upon you from all sides; that king has not lost his influence over the Circle of the middle and neutral States; but you have lost that power over them who are, therefore, waiting for an opportunity to fall upon you; patiently bear the loss of men and money again; break peace with that friend; then we shall be able to remove him from that

stronghold over which he has lost his influence. Hence, it is not worthy of you to lend your ear to those enemies with the face of friends, to expose your real friends to trouble, to help your enemies to attain success, and to involve yourself in dangers costing life and wealth."

Placing Intrigue
If without caring for the advice, the enemy proceeds on his own way, the weak king should create disaffection among the enemy's people by adopting such measures as are explained in "The Conduct of Corporations," and "Enticement of the enemy by secret contrivances" (of the Arthashastra). He should also make use of fiery spies and poison. Against what is described as deserving protection in the chapter, "Safety of his own person," (in the Arthashastra).
Measures to be taken:
- *Fiery spies and poisoners should be employed (in the enemy's court)*
- *Keepers of harlots should excite love in the minds of the leaders of the enemy's army by exhibiting women endowed with youth and beauty*
- *Fiery spies should bring about quarrels among them when one or two of them have fallen in love*

In the affray that ensues they should prevail upon the defeated party to migrate elsewhere or to proceed to help the master (of the spies) in the invasion undertaken by the latter.

Quick-lesson:
A weak leader should use espionage and covert death squads against his powerful enemy to compensate his lack of conventional power.

Deadly Love Potions
Or to those who have fallen in love, spies, under the guise of ascetics, may administer poison under the plea that the medical drugs given to them are capable of securing the object of love (Fig. 69).

Fig. 69

A spy, under the guise of a merchant, may, under the plea of winning the love of an immediate maid-servant of the beautiful queen (of the enemy), shower wealth upon her and then give her up. A spy in the service of the merchant may give to another spy, employed as a servant of the maid-servant, some medical drug, telling the latter that (in order to regain the love of the merchant), the drug may be applied to the person of the merchant (by the maid-servant). On her attaining success (the maid-servant) may inform the queen that the same drug may be applied to the person of the king (to secure his love), and then change the drug for poison.

Quick-lesson:
A love potion should be substituted with poison. In the second situation, a maid servant is placed in the employment of another and when she has gained trust, she administers poison instead of a love potion or medicine.

Face Reading
A spy, under the guise of an astrologer, may gradually delude the enemy's prime minister with the belief that he is possessed of all the physiognomical characteristics of a king; a mendicant woman may tell the minister's wife that she has the characteristics of a queen and that she will bring forth a prince; or a woman, disguised as the minister's wife, may tell him that, "The king is troubling me; and an ascetic woman has brought to me this letter and jewellery."

Quick-lesson:
Face reading is an ancient skill where a person's features would divine their future. The spy should give a false reading to benefit the situation.

Fire, fire, fire!
Spreading the false news of the danger of the enemy, (spies) who may set fire to the harem, the gates of the town and the store-house of grains and other things, and slay the sentinels who are kept to guard them (Fig. 70).

Fig. 70

Quick-lesson:
Spread rumours to force the enemy to do something they would not normally do so as to take advantage of it.

Roundup
Covert operations can come in many formats yet all remain under the banner of 'covert'. Remember that multiple types of operators and agents are required – from the highly-trained and 'danger-loving' to the low-paid lesser agents to the deeply-undercover intelligence operative. The aim of the 'game' is to cause internal strife for the enemy, as much discord as can be brought out of order by a handful of men and women.

SLAYING THE ENEMY COMMANDER

Killing an enemy commander is of strategic importance. It can weaken and demoralise his troops. This is similar to how modern riot police try to spot and remove the major instigator(s) to quell the mayhem, or how striking the gang leader in a street fight can discourage his friends. Here Chanakya explains the ways of killing the enemy leader.

Removing Enemy Chiefs

The following section is from Book 12, Chapter 3 of the original text.

Spies in the service of the (enemy) king or of his courtiers may, under the pretence of friendship, say in the presence of other friends that the king is angry with the chiefs of infantry, cavalry, chariots and elephants. When their men are collected together, fiery spies, having guarded themselves against night watches, may, under the pretence of the (enemy) king's order, invite the chiefs to a certain house and slay the chiefs when returning from the house (Fig. 71). Other spies in the vicinity may say that it has been the king's order to slay them. Spies may also tell those who have been banished from the country: "This is just what we foretold; for personal safety, you may go elsewhere."

Fig. 71

Quick-lesson:
Bring people together under the guise of false orders from the enemy commander or lord. Then have them killed as if the enemy lord had killed them. The enemy should be demonised by making them appear villainous and bloodthirsty.

Interviewed by the Enemy
A spy employed as the personal servant of the (enemy) king may inform him that such and such ministers of his are being interviewed by the enemy's servants. When he comes to believe this, some treacherous persons may be represented as the messengers of the enemy.

Quick-lesson:
Instil paranoia into the enemy king and stir trouble between them and their aides, advisors and troops.

High End Bribes
The chief officers of the army may be induced by offering land and gold to fall against their own men and secede from the enemy (their king). If one of the sons of the commander-in-chief is living near or inside the fort, a spy may tell him:
"You are the most worthy son; still you are neglected; why are you indifferent? Seize your position by force; otherwise the heir-apparent will destroy you."

Or some one of the family (of the commander-in-chief or the king), or one who is imprisoned may be bribed in gold and told:
"Destroy the internal strength of the enemy, or a portion of his force in the border of his country."

Or having seduced wild tribes with rewards of wealth and honour, they may be incited to devastate the enemy's country. Or the enemy's rear-enemy may be told:
"I am, as it were, a bridge to you all; if I am broken like a rafter, this king will drown you all; let us, therefore, combine and thwart the enemy in his march."
Accordingly, a message may be sent to individual or combined states to the effect: "After having done with me, this king will do his work of you: beware of it. I am the best man to be relied upon."

Quick-lesson:
Bribes should be given to the correct people. Choose those who will turn for a price and who have key positions or those who feel resentment towards their lord.

Bribe for Support

In order to escape from the danger from an immediate enemy, a king should frequently send to a madhyama king or a neutral king (whatever would please him); or one may put one's whole property at the enemy's disposal.

Quick-lesson:
When in a difficult situation, use wealth to secure aid and safety.

Roundup
The key point here is the disconnection between a commander or leader of any level from their men. Divide the masses from leadership and force troops to turn on their leaders or even to distrust them. The discord found in such tactics creates gaps for an allied force to use.

> Madhyama means middle, medium and mediatory. A madhyama king is a go-between. He tries to bring rivals to come to an agreement.

FIRE, SPIES, POISON AND DESTRUCTION

Poison and fire both draw out an inherent fear we have of a vile death. In our modern times, the fear of fire has dwindled and the threat of poisoning only exists in ill-prepared food. But in the ancient days, fire and poison were deeply feared. A world without fire-prevention or antidotes meant a gruesome death and for a leader or person of power, being a target of these two malignant forms of death was a fear which stood out among others.

My Enemy's Friend

> The following section is from Book 12, Chapter 4 of the original text.

The conqueror's spies who are residing as traders in the enemy's forts, and those who are living as cultivators in the enemy's villages, as well as those who are living as cowherds or ascetics in the district borders of the enemy's country may send through merchants, information to another neighbouring enemy, or a wild chief, or a scion of the enemy's family, or an imprisoned prince that the enemy's country is to be captured. When their secret envoys come as invited, they are to be pleased with rewards of wealth and honour and shown the enemy's weak points; and with the help of the envoys, the spies should strike the enemy at his weak points.

Quick-lesson:
The enemy of the enemy is a friend. Buy their friendship as well as pass on vital intelligence to them about the common enemy.

Poisoning

Having put a banished prince in the enemy's camp; a spy disguised as a wine-maker in the service of the enemy, may distribute as a toast hundreds of vessels of liquor mixed with the juice of the madana plant; or, for the first day, he may distribute a mild or intoxicating variety of liquor, and on the following days such liquor as is mixed with poison; or having given pure liquor to the officers of the enemy's army, he may give them poisoned liquor when they are in intoxication (Fig. 72).

> The juice produced from the madana plant (Latin name: Randia dumetorum) is said to be intoxicating and poisonous, hence suitable for use by assassins. Spiking enemy drinks and food-stuffs with this were effective methods of administering it.

124

A spy, employed as a chief officer of the enemy's army, may adopt the same measures as those employed by the wine-maker.

Quick-lesson:
Drink and food will be closely monitored. Therefore, gain trust with good wine and food, then at the right time move to poison the enemy.

Bad Fish
Spies, disguised as experts in trading in cooked flesh, cooked rice, liquor, and cakes, may vie with each other in proclaiming in public the sale of a fresh supply of their special articles at cheap price and may sell the articles mixed with poison to the attracted customers of the enemy (Fig. 73).

Fig. 73

Quick-lesson:
Become a trusted supplier to the enemy and poison them.

Poison the Source
Women and children may receive in their poisoned vessels, liquor, milk, curd, ghee, or oil from traders in those articles, and pour those fluids back into the vessels of the traders, saying that at a specified rate the whole may be sold to them. Spies, disguised as merchants, may purchase the above articles, and may so contrive that servants, attending upon the elephants and horses of the enemy, may make use of the same articles in giving

rations and grass to those animals. Spies, under the garb of servants, may sell poisoned grass and water.

Quick-lesson:
Discreetly poison the food-stuffs of innocent traders, after which other spies can purchase those food-stuffs and then sell them on to unaware enemies.

The Extended Use of Spies
Spies, let off as traders in cattle for a long time, may leave herds of cattle, sheep, or goats in tempting places so as to divert the attention of the enemy from the attack which they (the enemy) intend to make.

Quick-lesson:
If you know the enemy will attack, have something to tempt them placed nearby so that their aim is changed.

Scare the horses
Spies as cowherds may let off such animals as are ferocious among horses, mules, camels, buffaloes and others beasts, having smeared the eyes of those animals with the blood of a musk-rat (Fig. 74).

Fig. 74

Spies as hunters may let off cruel beasts from traps (Fig. 75).

Fig. 75

Spies as snake charmers may let off highly poisonous snakes (Fig. 76).

Fig. 76

Those who keep elephants may let off elephants (near the enemy's camp).

127

Those who live by making use of fire may set fire (to the camp, etc.) (Fig. 77).

Fig. 77

Quick-lesson:
Destruction upon the enemy can be given in various forms:
- by fire
- by wild animals
- by venomous animals
- by causing panic in animals

To Slay from the Rear
Secret spies may slay from behind; the chiefs of infantry, cavalry, chariots and elephants (Fig. 78), *or they may set fire to the chief residences of the enemy.*

Fig. 78

Traitors, enemies and wild tribes, employed for the purpose, may destroy the enemy's rear or obstruct his reinforcement; or spies, concealed in forests, may enter into the border of the enemy's country, and devastate it; or they may destroy the enemy's supply, stores, and other things, when those things are being conveyed on a narrow path passable by a single man (Fig. 79).

Fig. 79

Quick-lesson:
Leave troops to destroy enemy:
- supplies
- reserves
- escape

To Kill a King

In accordance with a plan arranged in advance, spies may, on the occasion of a night-battle, go to the enemy's capital, and blowing a large number of trumpets, cry aloud:
"We have entered into the capital, and the country has been conquered."
After entering into the king's (the enemy's) palace, they may kill the king in the tumult;
They may also kill in the following ways:
- *when the king begins to run from one direction to another, Mlechchhas, wild tribes, or chiefs of the army, lying in ambush, or concealed near a pillar or a fence, may slay him* (Fig. 80)
- *spies, under the guise of hunters, may slay the king when he is directing his attack, or in the tumult of attack following the plan of treacherous fights*
- *occupying an advantageous position, they may slay the enemy when he is marching in a narrow path passable by a single man* (Fig. 81)
- *on a mountain*
- *near the trunk of a tree*
- *under the branches of a banyan tree*
- *in water; they may cause him to be carried off by the force of a current of water let off by the destruction of a dam across a river, or of a lake or pond* (Fig. 82)
- *destroy him by means of an explosive fire*
- *with poisonous snakes when he has entrenched himself in a fort* (Fig. 83)
- *in a desert*
- *in a forest*
- *in a valley*

Fig. 80

Fig. 81

Fig. 82

Fig. 83

Advice to the Above Assassins
- *he should be destroyed with fire when he is under a thicket* (Fig. 84)
- *with smoke when he is in a desert* (Fig. 85)
- *with poison when he is in a comfortable place* (Fig. 86)
- *with crocodile and other cruel beasts when he is in water* (Fig. 87)
- *slay him when he is going out of his burning house* (Fig. 88)

Fig. 84

Fig. 85

Fig. 86

Fig. 87

Fig. 88

Roundup

In China, one of India's neighbouring countries, Ying Zheng (259 – 210 BCE), the Qin state king, and later, China's first emperor, took his security seriously but there were flaws in the design. His nearby officials remained unarmed while armed guards were stationed outside the palace. Two individuals named Jing Ke and Qin Wuyang, disguised as envoys, came to the palace, bringing with them a dagger concealed in a map which was to be presented to the king. Once the map was unfolded, Jing Ke took hold of the dagger and tried to stab the king, who evaded the blade strikes until he eventually managed to draw his sword to strike and kill his assassin. His nearby unarmed officials and faraway-stationed armed guards were of no use to him at that time. Chanakya, however, advises different security measures for a king. He wanted the king to never be left by himself nor surrounded by unarmed well-wishers. For example, the entire 21st chapter of the *Arthashastra's* 1st book is devoted to a king's personal safety. However, like the section above, in Chapter 2, Book 13 of the *Arthashastra*, Chanakya provides a list of ideal times and situations to assassinate an enemy king, which includes targeting a king "wherever he is unguarded." China's Jing Ke tried to kill his badly-guarded target and would have succeeded had he not missed his kill-shots.

Chanakya also mentions some uses of fire to target an enemy. Fire as a weapon has been used worldwide throughout history. Chapter 12 of Sun Tzu's *The Art of War* is devoted entirely to incendiary attacks, which opens with the following words:

"Sun Tzu said: There are five ways of attacking with fire. The first is to burn soldiers in their camp; the second is to burn stores; the third is to burn baggage trains; the fourth is to burn arsenals and magazines; the fifth is to hurl dropping fire amongst the enemy."

REMEDIES AND ANTIDOTES

Among Hindus, perhaps the most well-known story related to Indian remedies/antidotes is an incident from Book 6, Canto 102 of the *Valmiki Ramayana*. Lakshman, brother of the warrior prince Rama, falls wounded and ill after being struck by a series of spears and arrows. The monkey warrior Hanuman was ordered to find and bring back a powerful rejuvenating herb known as *sanjivini booti* (life-infusing herb) from the Dunagiri mountain. When Hanuman reached there, he was unable to identify the correct herb. So, using his great strength and ability to fly, he lifted the mountain and flew it back to Lakshman. An expert physician named Sushena then identified the correct herb, administered it and rejuvenated Lakshman.

> The sanjivini booti or sanjeevani is identified as Selaginella bryopteris. This Indian herb is believed by some modern biotechnologists to be beneficial to health but due to lack of credible scientific evidence, it is not currently used medicinally.

In Chanakya's text, methods of harm also come with methods of healing.

Cure Your Own People

> The following section is from Book 14, Chapter 4 of the original text.

With regard to remedies against poisons and poisonous compounds applied by an enemy against one's own army or people: When the things that are meant for the king's use, inclusive of the limbs of women, as well as the things of the army are washed in the tepid water prepared from the decoction of:

- *Sebesten or cordia myxa*
- *Emblica officinalis*
- *Madanti – unknown*
- *ivory*
- *citron tree*
- *Elephantopus scaber*
- *Aconitum ferox*
- *Bignonia suaveolens*

- *Sida cordifolia et rhombifolia*
- *Bignonia indica*
- *Punarnava – unknown*
- *Andropogon aciculatum*
- *Tabernaemontana coronaria*

Mixed with sandal and the blood of jackal, the above removes the bad effects of poison.

The stinking oil extracted from Vangueria spinosa removes madness.

The mixture prepared from panic seed and Galedupa arborea removes, when applied through the nose, leprosy.

The mixture prepared from Costus and Symplocos removes consumption.

A mixture prepared from:
- *Gmelina arborea*
- *Anthericum tuberosum*
- *Vilanga – a kind of seed*

The above removes, when applied through the nose, headaches and other diseases of the head (Fig. 89).

Fig. 89

The application of the mixture prepared from:
- *panic seed*
- *Rubia manjit*
- *tabernmontana coronaria*
- *the juice or essence of lac*
- *madhuka – unknown*
- *turmeric*
- *honey*

Persons who have fallen senseless by being beaten by a rope, by falling into water, or by eating poison, or by being whipped, or by falling, this resuscitates them.

The proportion of a dose is as much as:
- *an aksha (unknown) to men*
- *twice as much to cows and horses*
- *four times as much to elephants and camels*

A round ball prepared from the above mixture and containing gold in its centre, removes the effects of any kind of poison.

A round ball prepared from the wood of:
- *holy fig tree growing wound – with the plants such as jivanti (a medicinal plant)*
- *Andropogon aciculatus*
- *the flower of mushkaka (a species of tree)*
- *Epidendrum tesselloides*

This removes the effects due to any kind of poison.

Magical Trumpets

The sound of trumpets which have been painted with the above mixture destroys poison (Fig. 90); whoever looks at a flag or banner besmeared with the above mixture will get rid of poison (Fig. 91).

Fig. 90

Fig. 91

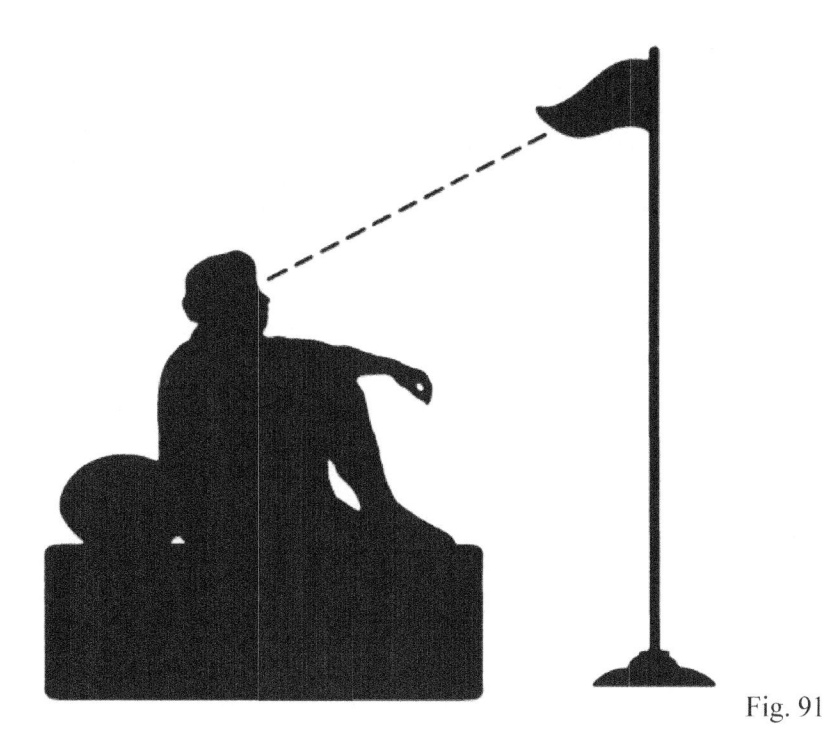

Poisonous Smoke
Having applied these remedies to secure the safety of himself and his army, a king should make use of poisonous smokes and other mixtures to vitiate water against his enemy (Fig. 92).

Fig. 92

Roundup

In this chapter, Chanakya provides counter-measures to various types of poisons and diseases. *The Laws of Manu* advises the following:

"Let him mix all his food with medicines (that are) antidotes against poison, and let him always be careful to wear gems which destroy poison."

Chapter 7, verse 218

The *Atharvaveda* contains several spells and charms to repel the effects of:
- poisoned arrows – Book 4, Hymn 6
- poisonous plants – Book 4, Hymn 7
- venomous snakes – Book 5, Hymn 13

Chanakya makes several references to this *Veda* in his *Arthashastra*. For example, in Book 1, Chapter 9, Chanakya lists the suitable qualities which a priest must possess before a king decides to employ him. Being well-versed in the *Atharvaveda* is one such quality:

"Him whose family and character are highly spoken of, who is well educated in the Vedás and the six Angas, is skilful in reading portents providential or accidental, is well versed in the science of government, and who is obedient and who can prevent calamities providential or human by performing such expiatory rites as are prescribed in the Atharvaveda, the king shall employ as high priest. As a student his teacher, a son his father, and a servant his master, the king shall follow him."

Also:

"When there is fear from snakes, experts in applying remedies against snake poison shall resort to incantations and medicines; or they may destroy snakes in a body; or those who are learned in the Atharvaveda may perform auspicious rites."

Book 4, Chapter 1

STRATAGEMS

From Chanakya's advice, it is quite apparent that might alone is not enough to conquer enemies. Power had to be won through strategy. It should be remembered that it was Chanakya's wisdom that made his protégé, Chandragupta Maurya, one of the most renowned and powerful emperors in history.

In this section, Chanakya lists his four enemy-defeating policies which among all of his teachings are well-known and quoted in present-day India. In Sanskrit, they are:
1. *Saam* – to appease
2. *Dhaam* – to bribe
3. *Dand* – to punish
4. *Bhed* – to divide

These strategies are mentioned in several places throughout the *Arthashastra*. Book 2, Chapter 10 states them briefly:

"Negotiation, bribery, causing dissension, and open attack are forms of stratagem."

Guru Gobind Singh Ji (1666 – 1708 CE), the tenth Sikh guru, makes a reference to Chanakya's strategies in the first chapter of his weaponry-focused composition, the Shastar Naam Mala:

"... Thou (referring to God) *art also Saam, Dhaam, Dand, Bhed and other remedies."*
       Dasam Granth, Shastar Naam Mala, The Praise of the Primal Power, 18

In addition to being the tenth spiritual guide of the Sikhs, Guru Gobind Singh Ji was also a great military leader, having won numerous battles against barbaric Mughals from the tender age of 19, despite his army being outnumbered and 'outgunned'. The questions are: How familiar was the guru with Chanakya's ways, and could these ways have given Sikhs the edge over their foreign enemy?

A comparison can be found between Chanakya's advice and events in the guru's life. One of the numerous battles fought between the Sikhs and Mughals is known as the Battle of Chamkaur, which took place in 1704. Despite being numerically inferior and ill-equipped, the guru and his Sikhs fought bravely. Many Sikhs were martyred, including two of the guru's four sons, Ajit Singh and Jujhar Singh. On the insistence of the remaining Sikhs, the guru was asked to leave the mud fortress they were besieged in, but not before one of his warriors, who resembled him, was dressed up in his attire to fool the

Mughals (the use of a doppelganger is also mentioned by Chanakya in Book 9, Chapter 6 of text). After this, the guru and some Pathan well-wishers again fooled the Mughals when he took on a guise to resemble a mystic who was referred to as "*Uch da Peer*" and was carried upon a sedan chair or litter and passed the Mughals without arousing any suspicion. This event shares some resemblance to the strategic advice given in the *Arthashastra* which says:

"Or having challenged the conqueror at night, he may successfully confront the attack; if he cannot do this, he may run away by a side path; or, disguised as a heretic, he may escape with a small retinue; or he may be carried off by spies as a corpse…"

Book 5, Chapter 12

> The following section is from Book 12, Chapter 1 of the original text.

The Mind is Mightier Than the Sword
Others say:
When a king of poor resources is attacked by a powerful enemy, he should surrender himself together with his sons to the enemy and live like a reed (in the midst of a current of water).

Bháradvája says that he who surrenders himself to the strong, bows down before Indra (the god of rain).

But Visáláksha says that a weak king should rather fight with all his resources, for he bravery destroys all troubles; this (fighting) is the natural duty of a Kshatriya, no matter whether he achieves victory or sustains defeat in battle.

> Throughout his text, Chanakya refers to previous teachings of divine, semi-divine and human scholars, and then states his own opinion which he regards as correct. These scholars include Bháradvája - one of the saptarishi (seven sages who were patriarchs of the Vedic religion) and father of martial Brahmin guru, Drona, who plays a significant role in the *Mahabharata*.

Chanakya disagrees and states:

No, he who bows down to all like a crab on the banks (of a river) lives in despair; whoever goes with his small army to fight perishes like a man attempting to cross the sea without a boat. Hence, a weak king should either seek the protection of a powerful king or maintain himself in an impregnable fort.

Invaders are of three kinds:
1. *a just conqueror*
2. *a greedy conqueror*
3. *a demon-like conqueror*

A Just Conqueror

Of these, the just conqueror is satisfied with mere obeisance. Hence, a weak king should seek his protection.

A Greedy Conqueror

Fearing his own enemies, the greedy conqueror is satisfied with what he can safely gain in land or money. Hence, a weak king should satisfy such a conqueror with wealth.

The Demon Conqueror
The demon-like conqueror satisfies himself not merely by seizing the land, treasure, sons and wives of the conquered, but by taking the life of the latter. Hence, a weak king should keep such a conqueror at a distance by offering him land and wealth.

When any one of these is on the point of rising against a weak king, the latter should avert the invasion by:
- *making a treaty of peace*
- *by taking recourse to the battle of intrigue*
- *by a treacherous fight in the battlefield*
- *he may seduce the enemy's men either by conciliation or by giving gifts* (Fig. 93)
- *he should prevent the treacherous proceedings of his own men either by sowing the seeds of dissension among them or by punishing them*
- *spies, under concealment, may capture the enemy's fort, country, or camp with the aid of weapons, poison, or fire*
- *he may harass the enemy's rear on all sides*
- *he may devastate the enemy's country through the help of wild tribes*
- *he may set up a scion of the enemy's family or an imprisoned prince to seize the enemy's territory.*

When all this mischief has been perpetrated, a messenger may be sent to the enemy, (to sue for peace); or he may make peace with the enemy without offending the latter. If the enemy still continues the march, the weak king may sue for peace by offering more than one-fourth of his wealth and army, the payment being made after the lapse of a day and night.

Fig. 93

Quick-lesson:
Do not give up at the sight of overwhelming forces. There is a way out. Think laterally and use the power of others, deception and geography to your advantage.

Tactics when Brokering a Peace
If the enemy desires to make peace on condition of the weak king surrendering a portion of this army:
- *he may give the enemy such of his elephants and cavalry as are uncontrollable or as are provided with poison*
- *if the enemy desires to make peace on condition of his surrendering his chief men, he may send over to the enemy such portion of his army as is full of traitors, enemies and wild tribes under the command of a trusted officer, so that both his enemy and his own undesirable army may perish*
- *he may provide the enemy with an army composed of fiery spies, taking care to satisfy his own disappointed men (before sending them over to the enemy)*
- *he may transfer to the enemy his own faithful and hereditary army that is capable to hurt the enemy on occasions of trouble*

If the enemy desires to make peace on condition of his paying a certain amount of wealth:
- *he may give the enemy such precious articles as do not find a purchaser or such raw products as are of no use in war*

If the enemy desires to make peace on condition of his ceding a part of his land:
- *he should provide the enemy with that kind of land which he can recover, which is always at the mercy of another enemy, which possesses no protective defences, or which can be colonized at considerable cost of men and money*
- *he may make peace, surrendering his whole state except his capital*

He should so contrive as to make the enemy accept that which another enemy is likely to carry off by force; and he should take care more of his person than of his wealth, for of what interest is perishing wealth?

Chanakya Expands on the Meanings of his Strategies:
By means of conciliation and gifts, he should subdue weak kings; and by means of sowing the seeds of dissension and by threats, strong kings. By adopting a particular, or an alternative, or all of the strategic means, he should subdue his immediate and distant enemies.

He should observe the policy of conciliation by promising the protection of villages, of those who live in forests, of flocks of cattle, and of the roads of traffic as well as the restoration of those who have been banished or who have run away or who have done some harm.

Quick-lesson:
If a powerful enemy is in a position superior to yours, appease them with land and gifts that are either trouble to hold or easy to take back.

Gifts
Gifts of:
- *land*
- *things*
- *girls in marriage*
- *absence of fear*

By declaring these, he should observe the policy of gifts.

Quick-lesson:
The abstract is also a gift. In this case, the absence of fear is the gift of safety.

Roundup
Behind all armies is the strategy. Without a strategy, a force would blow aimlessly with the wind. Good strategy is to consider the beginning, the middle and the end, to have alternative plans and backups in place to counter enemy moves. It is also to predict with good accuracy the enemy reaction to your own movements and to force the enemy into a 'corner'. Internal strategy is the hidden element within a situation, those which are not seen by others, conspiracy, espionage and intelligence, all working together to bring about changes within the enemy.

SOWING THE SEEDS OF DISSENSION

Troop and population morale are an often underestimated factor in warfare from theoretical strategists. If the 'feel' of the people is not positive and their willingness to endure and participate in warfare is lacking, the entire foundation of the army may collapse. Every army in the world is supported by the people that it protects or by the conquering of enemy provinces. Taxation and profit through war is that which keeps soldiers on the front line. If a populace has no faith in its leader, dissention will arise to which a leader can either subjugate with pressure and an 'iron fist', or they can win back the hearts of the people. Therefore, another key factor in warfare is to steal the hearts of the enemy or to 'blacken the hearts' of the enemy against their leaders.

The following section is from Book 13, Chapter 1 of the original text.

Using the Gods
When the conqueror is desirous of seizing an enemy's village, he should infuse enthusiastic spirit among his own men and frighten his enemy's people by giving publicity to his power of omniscience and close association with gods.

Proclamation of his omniscience is as follows:
- *rejection of his chief officers when their secret, domestic and other private affairs are known*
- *revealing the names of traitors after receiving information from spies specially employed to find out such men*
- *pointing out the impolitic aspect of any course of action suggested to him*
- *pretensions to the knowledge of foreign affairs by means of his power to read omens and signs invisible to others when information about foreign affairs is just received through a domestic pigeon which has brought a sealed letter*

Quick-lesson:
A conqueror should convince others their intelligence is gathered via supernatural means. This will demonstrate their power, thereby boosting the morale of his side and demoralising the opposition.

Fake Gods

Proclamation of his association with gods is as follows:
- *holding conversation with, and worshipping, the spies who pretend to be the gods of fire or altar when through a tunnel they come to stand in the midst of fire, altar, or in the interior of a hollow image* (Fig. 94)
- *holding conversation with, and worshipping, the spies who rise up from water and pretend to be the gods and goddesses of snakes* (Fig. 95)
- *placing under water at night a mass of sea-foam mixed with burning oil, and exhibiting it as the spontaneous outbreak of fire, when it is burning in a line*
- *sitting on a raft in water which is secretly fastened by a rope to a rock* (Fig. 96)

Fig. 94

Fig. 95

Fig. 96

Quick-lesson:
Create fake miracles. Examples from the text:
1. using a tunnel, the fake god comes up in the middle of a fire, on to an alter or talks from within a hollow statue
2. using rafts, fake gods can be brought up from water
3. using flammable and floating liquids, fire can be seen to 'magically' spread over water at the command of the fake prophet balanced on a raft

How to Perform the Above Producing of Water Gods
Such magical performance in water as is usually done at night by bands of magicians, using the sack-abdomen or womb of water animals to hide the head and the nose, and applying to the nose the following oil which is prepared from:
- *the entrails of red spotted deer*
- *the serum of the flesh of the crab, crocodile, porpoise and otter*

Holding conversation, as though, with women of Varuna, the god of water, or of the snake-god when they are performing magical tricks in water; and sending out volumes of smoke from the mouth on occasions of anger.

Quick-lesson:
A conqueror should convince others that he is a middleman between deities and humans. This 'prophet-hood' will win him support and power.

Religious Propaganda
Astrologers, sooth-sayers, horologists, story-tellers, as well as those who read the forebodings of every moment, together with spies and their disciples, inclusive of those who have witnessed the wonderful performances of the conqueror should give wide publicity to the power of the king to associate with gods throughout his territory. Likewise, in foreign countries, they should spread the news of gods appearing before the conqueror and of his having received from heaven weapons and treasure. Those who are well versed in horary and astrology and the science of omens should proclaim abroad that the conqueror is a successful expert in explaining the indications of dreams and in understanding the language of beasts and birds. They should not only attribute the contrary to his enemy, but also show to the enemy's people the shower of firebrand with the noise of drums (from the sky) on the day of the birth-star of the enemy.

Quick-lesson:
Religious propaganda is to be used to bring about love for a lord, fear in an enemy and awe in the population. A commander of guile should construct situations which appear to show the gods giving favour to their army.

Winning over the Enemy
The conqueror's chief messengers, pretending to be friendly towards the enemy, should highly speak of the conqueror's respectful treatment of visitors, of the strength of his army, and of the likelihood of impending destruction of his enemy's men. They should also make it known to the enemy that under their master, both ministers and soldiers are equally safe and happy, and that their master treats his servants with parental care in their weal or woe.

Quick-lesson:
Set the enemy mind at ease with promises of fair treatment upon surrender or defeat.

Roundup
Propaganda is a branch of the intelligence service for any army. Alone it may not bring about the goals required but it slowly chips away at the moral foundation of the enemy's reputation and support. If a leader can be made to look incompetent or 'evil' (even when they are not) the general population will believe it to be true. Few people look into the facts themselves to ascertain the truth. Say something enough times and it becomes a truth.

ENTICEMENT OF KINGS

Human rights activists around the globe have accused certain governments of being responsible for extrajudicial killings against alleged members of gangs and terrorist organisations. India's Mumbai "Encounter Squad" is one government body accused of "fake encounters". If true, their actions can be seen as the utilisation of Chanakya's 'punishment' strategy (i.e. the use of *dand*) against the state's enemies.

Moving the Mind of a King

> The following section is from Book 13, Chapter 2 of the original text.

An ascetic, with shaved head or braided hair and living in the cave of a mountain, may pretend to be four hundred years old, and, followed by a number of disciples with braided hair, halt in the vicinity of the capital city of the enemy. The disciples of the ascetic may make presentations of roots and fruits to the king and his ministers and invite them to pay a visit to the venerable ascetic. On the arrival of the king on the spot, the ascetic may acquaint him with the history of ancient kings and their states, and tell him:

"Every time when I complete the course of a hundred years, I enter into the fire and come out of it as a fresh youth. Now, here in your presence, I am going to enter into the fire for the fourth time. It is highly necessary that you may be pleased to honour me with your presence at the time. Please request three boons."

When the king agrees to do so, he may be requested to come and remain at the spot with his wives and children for seven nights to witness the sacrificial performance. When he does so, he may be caught hold of.

Quick-lesson:
Know what actions or situations will sway the mind of a king. Provide for him an opportunity that even a king would not decline. In this manner and the ones below, the movements and placement of the king can be directed – at which point he can be snatched.

Magic Gold

An ascetic, with shaved head or braided hair, and followed by a number of disciples with shaved heads or braided hair, and pretending to be aware of whatever is contained in the interior of the earth, may put in the interior of an ant-hill either a bamboo stick wound round with a piece of cloth drenched in blood and painted with gold dust, or a hollow golden tube into which a snake can enter and remain. One of the disciples may tell the king:

"This ascetic can discover flourishing treasure trove."

When he asks the ascetic (as to the veracity of the statement), the latter should acknowledge it, and produce confirmatory evidence (by pulling out the bamboo stick); or having kept some more gold in the interior of the ant-hill, the ascetic may tell the king:

"This treasure trove is guarded by a snake and can possibly be taken out by performing necessary sacrifice. When the king agrees to do so, he may be requested to come and remain with his wives as stated before so that he can get hold of him.

Quick-lesson:
This is an alternative version of the above, with the aim of getting close to the king.

The Burning Body

When an ascetic, pretending to be able to find out hidden treasure trove, is seated with his body burning with magical fire at night in a lonely place, his disciples may bring the king to see him and inform the king that the ascetic can find out treasure troves. While engaged in performing some work at the request of the king, the latter may be requested to come and remain at the spot for seven nights . . . (as before).

Quick-lesson:
This is an alternative version of the above, with the aim of getting close to the king.

Fool the King

An accomplished ascetic may beguile a king by his knowledge of the science of magic known as jambhaka, and request him to come and remain.

An accomplished ascetic, pretending to have secured the favour of the powerful guardian deity of the country, may often beguile the king's chief ministers with his wonderful performance and gradually impose upon the king.

Imitating the Gods
Any person, disguised as an ascetic and living under water or in the interior of an idol entered into through a tunnel or an underground chamber, may be said by his disciples to be Varuna, the god of water, or the king of snakes, and shown to the king. While going to accomplish whatever the king may desire, the latter may be requested to come and remain.

Quick-Lesson:
Like in the above examples, create a situation where a leader would venture out of his normal security circle so as to kill or take him.

Divine Punishment
Getting into an altar at night in the vicinity of the capital city of the enemy and blowing through tubes or hollow reeds the fire contained in a few pots, some fiery spies may shout aloud:
"We are going to eat the flesh of the king or of his ministers; let the worship of the gods go on."
Spies, under the guise of sooth-sayers and horologists may spread the news abroad (Fig. 97).

Fig. 97

Quick-lesson:
Spies must cause people to believe divine punishment is coming to their leaders.

Snake-gods in the Fire
Spies, disguised as Nagas (snake-gods) and with their body besmeared with burning oil, may stand in the centre of a sacred pool of water or of a lake at night, and sharpening their iron swords or spikes, may shout aloud as before (Fig. 98).

Fig. 98

Dance of the Demons:
Spies, wearing coats formed of the skins of bears and sending out volumes of smoke from their mouth, may pretend to be demons, and after circumambulating the city thrice from right to left, may shout aloud as before at a place full of the horrid noise of antelopes and jackals (Fig. 99).

Fig. 99

Quick-lesson:
Create the illusion and appearance of that which people fear on the edge of their fortification to cause panic to spread.

Burning Altars
Spies may set fire to an altar or an image of a god covered with a layer of mica besmeared with burning oil at night, and shout aloud as before. Others may spread this news abroad

Bleeding Gods to Kill a King
They may cause (by some contrivance or other) blood to flow out in floods from revered images of gods. Others may spread this news abroad and challenge any bold or brave man to come out to witness this flow of divine blood. Whoever accepts the challenge may be beaten to death by others with rods, making the people believe that he was killed by demons. Spies and other witnesses may inform the king of this wonder. Then spies, disguised as sooth-sayers and astrologers may prescribe auspicious and expiatory rites to avert the evil consequences which would otherwise overtake the king and his country. When the king agrees to the proposal he may be asked to perform in person special

sacrifices and offerings with special mantras every night for seven days. Then (while doing this, he may be slain) as before (Fig. 100).

Fig. 100

Quick-lesson:
Create an area where hidden assassins can move freely. Entice a leader to enter this area and kill him.

Various Ways to Kill a King
An accomplished ascetic, halting in the vicinity of the capital city, may invite the king to witness the person (of his enemy) when he comes to witness the invocation of his enemy's life in the image to be destroyed, he may be murdered in an unguarded place.

Spies, under the, guise of merchants come to sell horses, may invite the king to examine and purchase any of the animals. While attentively examining the horses, he may be murdered in the tumult or trampled down by horses (Fig. 101).

Fig. 101

When the enemy is fond of elephants, spies may delude him with the sight of a beautiful elephant reared by the officer in charge of elephant forests. When he desires to capture the elephant, he may be taken to a remote desolate part of the forest, and killed or carried off as a prisoner. This explains the fate of kings addicted to hunting.

When the enemy is fond of wealth or women, he may be beguiled at the sight of rich and beautiful widows brought before him with a plaint for the recovery of a deposit kept by them in the custody of one of their kinsmen; and when he comes to meet with a woman at night as arranged, hidden spies may kill him with weapons or poison (Fig. 102).

Fig. 102

When the enemy is in the habit of paying frequent visits to ascetics, altars, sacred pillars, and images of gods, spies hidden in underground chambers or in subterranean passages, or inside the walls, may strike him down (Fig. 103).

Fig. 103

Whatever may be the sights or spectacles which the king goes in person to witness; wherever he may engage himself in sports or in swimming in water.

Wherever he may be careless in uttering such words of rebuke as "Tut" or on the occasions of sacrificial performance or during the accouchement of women or at the time of death or disease (of some person in the palace), or at the time of love, sorrow, or fear.

Whatever may be the festivities of his own men, which the king goes to attend, wherever he is unguarded or during a cloudy day, or in the tumultuous concourse of people.

Or in an assembly of Bráhmins, or whenever he may go in person to see the outbreak of fire, or when, he is in a lonely place, or when he is putting on dress or ornaments, or garlands of flower, or when he is lying in his bed or sitting on a seat.

When he is eating or drinking, on these and other occasions, spies, together with other persons previously hidden at those places, may strike him down at the sound of trumpets.

And they may get out as secretly as they came there with the pretence of witnessing the sights; thus it is that kings and other persons are enticed to come out and be captured.

Quick-lesson:
A spy, knowing the positioning or the whereabouts of a leader, waits in hiding. Then upon killing the enemy uses the ensuing panic to make an escape.

Roundup
Here, psychological warfare is also present. Chanakya advises taking advantage of the fearful and superstitious nature of the religious targets in order to eliminate them.

One of the assassination tactics Chanakya describes is informally known today as the 'honey-trap' whereby one or more females lure an unsuspecting male to a location where attackers/thieves, known to the female(s), await. Baiting victims with a 'damsel in distress' was also utilised by Thuggees, India's assassin/serial killer cult. An 1837 book entitled, *Illustrations of the history and practices of the Thugs*, contains the secrets of Thuggee tactics from accounts obtained from the ruthless stealth killers themselves. According to page 19:

"They have another cunning trick, also, to catch travellers with. They send out a handsome woman upon the road, who, with her hair dishevelled, seems to be all in tears. Sighing and complaining of some misfortunes which she pretends has befallen her. Now, as she takes the same way that the traveller goes, he easily falls into conversation with her, and, finding her beautiful, offers her his assistance, which she accepts: but he hath no sooner taken her up behind him on horseback, but she throws the snare about his neck and strangles him; or at least stuns him, until the robbers, who lie hid, come running to her assistance, and complete what she hath begun."

If propaganda is to smear a leader's name, then this chapter is about confusing and fooling that leader directly. A target of such skills, if they fall for such a trap, will become ensnared within it, bringing their leadership to an end, or causing issues with their command.

FORTIFICATIONS

Even to this day, India is peppered with ancient and medieval forts, some preserved and others in ruins. Elaborately designed and standing sturdily (Fig. 104).

Fig. 104

There are numerous descriptions of forts in various Indian texts. The *Ramayana* contains a description of Ravan's massive fortified palace, as witnessed by Hanuman whose mission it was to penetrate it:

"He saw the grisly legions wait, in strictest watch at Ravan's gate, whose palace on the mountain crest rose proudly towering over the rest, fenced with high ramparts from the foe, and lotus-covered moats below."

Book 5, Canto 4

The *Arthashastra's* chapters concerning fortifications detail their construction and stockpile requirements. These chapters detail the construction materials required, along with measurements of walls, ramparts, etc. They call for the stockpiling of tools, weapons, foodstuffs, and the need for shops, hospitals, water supplies, enemy obstructions, using doors/gates of different types for various purposes, living quarters for animals and people of various duties, etc. The fortress had to be siege-proof and its occupants had to be well-provided in order for it to be an efficient fortification.

> Several cities in India have the suffix 'garh' (fort) to their name, such as Chandigarh (fort of Chandi – the fearsome warrior goddess), Lohgarh (Iron fort – iron is metal sacred to warriors), etc.

> The following section is from Book 2, Chapter 3 of the original text.

Construction of Forts

On all the four quarters of the boundaries of the kingdom, defensive fortifications against an enemy in war shall be constructed on grounds best fitted for the purpose these include:
- *a water-fortification such as an island in the midst of a river*
- *a plain surrounded by low ground*
- *a mountainous fortification such as a rocky tract or a cave*
- *a desert such as a wild tract devoid of water and overgrown with thicket growing in barren soil*
- *or a forest fortification full of wagtail*
- *in water and thickets*

Water and mountain fortifications (Fig. 105) *are best suited to defend populous centres; whereas desert and forest fortifications are habitations in wilderness.*

Fig. 105

The Retreat
With ready preparations for flight the king may have his fortified capital as the seat of his sovereignty in the centre of his kingdom: in a locality naturally best fitted for the purpose, such as the bank of the confluence of rivers, a deep pool of perennial water, or of a lake or tank, a fort, circular, rectangular, or square in form, surrounded with an artificial canal of water, and connected with both land and water paths (may be constructed).

Around this fort, three ditches with an intermediate space of one danda (6ft) from each other, fourteen, twelve and ten dandas respectively in width, with depth less by one quarter or by one-half of their width, square at their bottom and one-third as wide as at their top, with sides built of stones or bricks, filled with perennial flowing water or with water drawn from some other source, and possessing crocodiles and lotus plants shall be constructed.

Quick-lesson:
A fortress with numerous security measures will make it formidable and ensure a king's safety.

A view of the fort
Of the first floor, five parts (are to be taken) for the formation of a hall, a well, and a boundary-house; two-tenths of it for the formation of two platforms opposite to each other; an upper storey twice as high as its width; carvings of images; an upper-most

storey, half or three-fourths as broad as the first floor; side walls built of bricks; on the left side, a staircase circumambulating from left to right; on the right, a secret staircase hidden in the wall; a top-support of ornamental arches projecting as far as two hastas; two door-panels, (each) occupying three-fourths of the space; two and two cross-bars (parigha, to fasten the door); an iron-bolt as long as an aratni; a boundary gate five hastas in width; four beams to shut the door against elephants; and turrets (outside the rampart) raised up to the height of the face of a man, removable or irremovable, or made of earth in places devoid of water.

A turret above the gate and starting from the top of the parapet shall be constructed, its front resembling an alligator up to three-fourths of its height.

In the centre of the parapets, there shall be constructed a deep lotus pool; a rectangular building of four compartments, one within the other; an abode of the Goddess Kumari, having its external area one-and-a-half times as broad as that of its innermost room; a circular building with an arch way; and in accordance with available space and materials, there shall also be constructed hallways to hold weapons and three times as long as broad.

In those hallways, there shall be collected:
- *stones*
- *spades*
- *axes*
- *varieties of staffs*
- *cudgels*
- *hammers*
- *clubs*
- *flat bladed rings*
- *machines*
- *such weapons as can destroy a hundred persons at once*
- *spears*
- *tridents*
- *bamboo-sticks with pointed edges made of iron*
- *hot oil vessels*
- *explosives*

And whatever else can be devised and formed from available materials (Fig 106).

Fig. 106

Trident in Sanskrit is trishul. The word 'trident' comes from Latin. Both words are similar because Sanskrit and Latin are branches of Indo-European languages.

Quick-lesson:
One must prepare their base to the fullest so there is no chance of penetration by enemy forces. Weapons and tools to repel the enemy must be made ready.

Gods within the Fort

> The following section is from Book 2, Chapter 4 of the original text.

In the centre of the city, the shrines [should be erected] of gods such as
- *Aparájita*
- *Apratihata*
- *Jayanta*
- *Vaijayanta*
- *Shiva*
- *Vaisravana*
- *Ashvina*
- *Sri*
- *Madira*

Quick-lesson:
Hindu deities have numerous names. The god Vishnu, for instance, has one thousand names. Each name has a meaning which describes the deity. Several deities share the same name, such as "Unconquerable". Therefore, sometimes knowing which god or goddess is being referred to in texts can become confusing. Many of the names Chanakya uses in his text for Hindu deities are not those commonly used by most Hindus today:

- Aparájita – another name of the Durga, the tiger- or lion-riding war goddess (Fig. 107). She has numerous arms and each hand grasps a different weapon which was gifted to her by various gods to vanquish almost-invincible demon warriors, such as Mahishasura
- Apratihata – another name for the god Vishnu, preserver of the universe. He is one of the three chief gods of Hinduism, along with Brahma and Shiva. He comes to the rescue whenever evil humans or demons cause chaos, defeating them using weapons, miraculous powers or wisdom (Fig. 108)
- Jayanta – a son of the rain and thunder god, Indra

> Apratihata is another name for Vishnu, the Hindu preserver of the universe. Hindus believe he has come to Earth several times to fight injustice in various avatars (incarnations) including Narsimha, Parushurama, Ramachandra, Krishna, Buddha and others. It is believed he will appear in his final form, Kalki, towards the end of the present age, Kali Yuga, the age of darkness.

- Vaijayanta – another name for Indra, god of rain and thunder and king of gods.
- Shiva – the destroyer/transformer of the universe. He is one of the three chief gods of Hinduism, along with Brahma and Vishnu (Fig. 109)
- Vaisravana – another name for Kubera, god of wealth
- Ashvina – the twin deities of medicine and the physicians of the gods
- Sri – another name for Lakshmi, goddess of wealth and consort of Vishnu
- Madira – the goddess of wine

Fig. 107

Fig. 108

Fig 109

In the corners, the guardian deities of the ground shall be appropriately set up.

Likewise, the principal gates such as Bráhma, Indra, Yáma, and Senápati shall be constructed; and at a distance of 100 bows (dhanus = 108 angulas) from the ditch (on the counterscarp side), places of worship and pilgrimage, groves and buildings shall be constructed.

Quick-lesson:
- Bráhma – the god of creation. He is one of the three chief gods of Hinduism, along with Vishnu and Shiva (Fig. 110)
- Indra – the god of rain and thunder. His primary weapon is the *Vajra* (thunderbolt) (Fig. 111)
- Yáma – the god of death
- Senápati – a name referring to Kartikeya, a son of Shiva and commander-in-chief of the army of the gods. He is also known as Skanda, Subramanya and Murugan

Fig. 110

Fig. 111

Guardian deities of all quarters shall also be set up in quarters appropriate to them.

Either to the north or the east, burial or cremation grounds shall be situated; but that of the people of the highest caste shall be to the south (of the city).

Heretics and outcasts shall live beyond the burial grounds.

Families of workmen may in any other way be provided with sites befitting with their occupation and field work. Besides working in flower-gardens, fruit-gardens, vegetable-gardens, and paddy-fields allotted to them, they (families) shall collect grains and merchandise in abundance as authorised.

There shall be a water-well for every ten houses.

Oils, grains, sugar, salt, medicinal articles, dry or fresh vegetables, meadow grass, dried flesh, hay stock, firewood, metals, skins, charcoal, tendons, poison, horns, bamboo, fibrous garments, strong timber, weapons, armour, and stones shall also be stored (in the fort) in such quantities as can be enjoyed for years together without feeling any want. Of such collection, old things shall be replaced by new ones when received.

Elephants, cavalry, chariots, and infantry shall each be officered with many chiefs inasmuch as chiefs, when many, are under the fear of betrayal from each other and scarcely liable to the insinuations and intrigues of an enemy.

The same rule shall hold good with the appointment of boundary, guards, and repairers of fortifications.

Never shall outsiders who are dangerous to the wellbeing of cities and countries be kept in forts. They may either be thrown in country parts or compelled to pay taxes.

Roundup
The fortress may seem bland in description; however, in reality the Indian fortress or castle is equally as impressive as both its western or eastern counterpart. Often the European castle is imagined with its knights, townsfolk, entertainers and court life. It is set against a bleak grey windy day with rain lashing down, or against the blazing sun and green fields. To the East, the Japanese castle is whitewashed, perched upon massive stones and the Chinese fortress is vast and complex with bright colours (all of which are only stereotypes). There should be no reason why the Indian fortress cannot hold as much of a fascination with its exotic imagery and grand structures.

SPIES IN A SIEGE

When either attacking in a siege or defending against one, there are ways that the enemy can cross the threshold of sides. Often the attacking force and the defenders know that the result will be siege warfare and because of this, good leaders will try to place agents among the enemy and the defender will surely defend against them. Having someone on the inside of a siege is like having a well in a sand castle; the foundations of the fortress are at serious risk. Furthermore, there are ways to entice an enemy out or even use their stationary position against them.

The 'Trojan Horse'

> The following section is from Book 13, Chapter 3 of the original text.

The conqueror may dismiss a confidential chief of a corporation. The chief may go over to the enemy as a friend and offer to supply him with recruits and other help collected from the conqueror's territory or followed by a band of spies, the chief may please the enemy by destroying a disloyal village or a regiment or an ally of the conqueror and by sending as a present the elephants, horses, and disaffected persons of the conqueror's army or of the latter's ally; or a confidential chief officer of the conqueror may solicit help from a portion of the territory (of the enemy), or from a corporation of people or from wild tribes; and when he has gained their confidence, he may send them down to the conqueror to be routed down on the occasion of a farcical attempt to capture elephants or wild tribes.

This explains the work of ministers and wild chiefs under the mission of the conqueror.

Quick-lesson:
The easiest way to get past enemy lines is to fake defection to the enemy side. Once in, lure the enemy into a trap.

The Devious Minister
After making peace with the enemy, the conqueror may dismiss his own confidential ministers. They may request the enemy to reconcile them to their master. When the enemy

sends a messenger for this purpose, the conqueror may rebuke him and say: "Your master attempts to sow the seeds of dissension between myself and my ministers; so you should not come here again."

Then one of the dismissed ministers may go over to the enemy, taking with him a band of spies, disaffected people, traitors, brave thieves, and wild tribes who make no distinction between a friend and a foe. Having secured the good graces of the enemy, the minister may propose to him the destruction of his officers, such as the boundary-guard, wild chief, and commander of his army, telling him:

"These and other persons are in concert with your enemy."

Then these persons may be put to death under the unequivocal orders of the enemy.

Quick-lesson:
Spreading suspicion and disunity among an enemy is advantageous, especially when the enemy starts killing their own.

Unification with an Enemy to Slay Him
The conqueror may tell his enemy:
"A chief with a powerful army means to offend us, so let us combine and put him down; you may take possession of his treasury or territory."
When the enemy agrees to the proposal and comes out honoured by the conqueror, he may be slain in a tumult or in an open battle with the chief (in concert with the conqueror).
Alternatively:
Having invited the enemy to be present as a good friend on the occasion of a pretended gift of territory, or the installation of the heir-apparent, or the performance of some expiatory rites, the conqueror may capture the enemy. Whoever withstands such inducements may be slain by secret means.
Alternatively:
If the enemy refuses to meet any man in person, then also attempts may be made to kill him by employing his enemy.
Alternatively:
If the enemy likes to march alone with his army, but not in company with the conqueror, then he may be hemmed in between two forces and destroyed. If, trusting to none, he wants to march alone in order to capture a portion of the territory of an assailable enemy, then he may be slain by employing one of his enemies or any other person provided with all necessary help.
Alternatively:

When he goes to his subdued enemy for the purpose of collecting an army, his capital may be captured.

Alternatively:
He may be asked to take possession of the territory of another enemy or a friend of the conqueror; and when he goes to seize the territory, the conqueror may ask his (the conqueror's) friend to offend him (the conqueror), and then enable the friend to catch hold of the enemy.
These and other contrivances lead to the same end.

Quick-lesson:
A leader can kill or capture an enemy by luring them through a variety of ways, including unity, gifts, alliances and agreements. Bring an enemy into the allied force and then destroy them.

The Enemy of My Enemy is Actually My Friend and it was All a Plan
When the enemy is desirous of taking possession of the territory of the conqueror's friend, then the conqueror may, under the pretence of compliance, supply the enemy with an army. Then having entered into a secret concert with the friend, the conqueror may pretend to be under troubles and allow himself to be attacked by the enemy combined with the neglected friend. Then, hemmed from two sides, the enemy may be killed or captured alive to distribute his territory among the conqueror and his friend (Fig. 112).

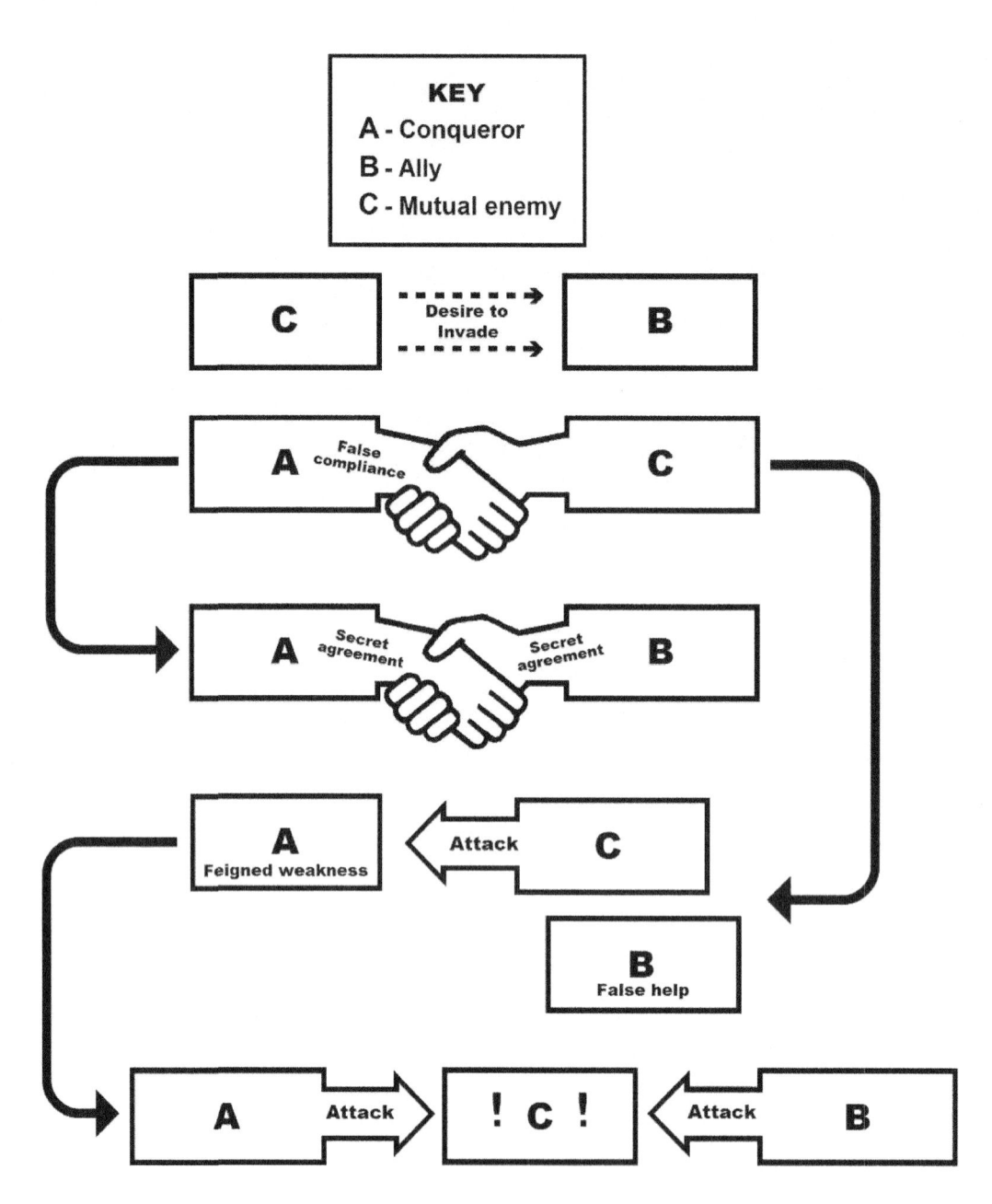

Fig. 112

Quick-lesson:
A leader can help their friend by deceiving the enemy of their ally. They make an agreement with the enemy of their ally, but during the agreement, switch sides.

Divide the United
If the enemy, helped by his friend, shuts himself in an impregnable fort, then his neighbouring enemies may be employed to lay waste his territory. If he attempts to defend his territory by his army, that army may be annihilated. If the enemy and his ally cannot be separated, then each of these may be openly asked to come to an agreement with the conqueror to seize the territory of the other. Then they will, of course, send such of their messengers as are termed friends and recipients of salaries from two states to each other with information:
"This king (the conqueror), allied with my army, desires to seize your territory."
Then one of them may, with enragement and suspicion, act as before (i.e., fall upon the conqueror or the friend).

Quick-lesson:
A leader should separate two inseparable allies by stirring rivalry among them. He should have them believe that one of them will turn on the other.

The Classic 'Doomed Spy' Trick
The conqueror may dismiss his chief officers in charge of his forests, country parts, and army, under the pretence of their intrigue with the enemy. Then going over to the enemy, they may catch hold of him on occasions of war, siege, or any other troubles; or they may sow the seeds of dissension between the enemy and his party, corroborating the causes of dissension by producing witnesses specially tutored.

Quick-lesson:
A leader should use their men to infiltrate the opposition and cause chaos from within. This skill directly resembles Sun Tzu's *The Art of War* and the Doomed Spy. The Japanese shinobi-trained Chikamatsu Shigenori and the shinobi, Fujibayashi Yasutake, give examples of using your own men by making it appear that they have been driven from the land and relieved of their position, at which point the enemy takes them in, to gain information. However, as they are still loyal, they spread disinformation.

Open the Gates!
Spies, disguised as hunters, may take a stand near the gate of the enemy's fort to sell flesh, and make friendship with the sentinels at the gate. Having informed the enemy of

the arrival of thieves on two or three occasions, they may prove themselves to be of reliable character and cause him to split his army into two divisions and to station them in two different parts of his territory. When his villages are being plundered or besieged, they may tell him that thieves have come very near, that the tumult is very great, and that a large army is required. They may take the army supplied, and surrendering it to the commander laying waste the villages, return at night with a part of the commander's army, and cry aloud at the gate of the fort that the thieves are slain, that the army has returned victorious, and that the gate may be opened. When the gate is opened by the watchmen under the enemy's order or by others in confidence, they may strike the enemy with the help of the army (Fig. 113).

Fig. 113

Quick-lesson:
Having sent an agent to make friends with the enemy forces, the agent allows the enemy to catch out spies or thieves – which again is a classic doomed spy tactic – and after having gained the trust of the enemy, inform them of a large raid. Then during the night, an allied force pretends to be the army returning from the fray. When they are admitted to the fortress, they kill the people within.

Sneak the Soldiers In
Painters, carpenters, heretics, actors, merchants, and other disguised spies belonging to the conqueror's army may also reside inside the fort of the enemy. Spies, disguised as agriculturists, may supply them with weapons taken in carts loaded with firewood, grass, grains, and other commodities of commerce (Fig. 114)*, or disguised as images and flags*

of gods. Then spies, disguised as priests, may announce to the enemy, blowing their conch shells and beating their drums, that a besieging army, eager to destroy all, and armed with weapons, is coming closely behind them (Fig. 115). *Then in the ensuing tumult, they may surrender the fort-gate and the towers of the fort to the army of the conqueror or disperse the enemy's army and bring about his fall.*

Fig. 114

Fig. 115

Quick-lesson:
Once the enemy's stronghold has been infiltrated, the spirit of defeatism should be spread among the enemy forces to the point that it causes the enemy's downfall. Here, forces take up residence inside the enemy's castle long before the allied force attacks. These hidden agents smuggle weapons and tools. Then when the call of attack is given, they will take the fort gates in the surprise.

Smuggle the Weapons
Or taking advantage of peace and friendship with the enemy, army and weapons may be collected inside the enemy's fort by spies disguised as merchants, caravans, processions leading a bride, merchants selling horses, peddlers trading in miscellaneous articles, purchasers or sellers of grains, and as ascetics. These and others are the spies aiming on the life of a king.

Quick-lesson:
Before any hint of war is given, have men and supplies take up residence and position within an enemy fort. This will allow allied forces to remain on the inside.

Drug the Shepherds
The same spies, together with those described in "Removal of thorns" section (of the Arthashastra) may, by employing thieves, destroy the flock of the enemy's cattle or merchandise in the vicinity of wild tracts. They may poison with the juice of the madana plant, the food-stuffs and beverage kept, as previously arranged, in a definite place for the enemy's cowherds, and go out unknown. When the cowherds show signs of intoxication in consequence of their eating the above food-stuffs, spies, disguised as cowherds, merchants, and thieves, may fall upon the enemy's cowherds, and carry off the cattle.

> Sankarshana is another name of Balarama, elder brother of Krishna. He is noted for his great combat skills with mace and plough.

Spies disguised as ascetics with shaved head or braided hair and pretending to be the worshippers of god, Sankarshana, may mix their sacrificial beverage with the juice of the madana plant (and give it to the cowherds), and carry off the cattle.

A spy, under the guise of a wine maker, may, on the occasion of procession of gods, funeral rites, festivals, and other congregations of people, go to sell liquor and present the cowherds with some liquor mixed with the juice of the madana plant. Then others may fall upon the intoxicated cowherds (and carry off the cattle).

Quick-lesson:
Drugging an enemy makes it easy work to kill and loot.

Spies under the Garb of Thieves
Those spies, who enter into the wild territories of the enemy with the intention of plundering his villages, and who, leaving that work, set themselves to destroy the enemy, are termed spies under the garb of thieves.

Roundup
A leader should always consider a third party. Often warfare is viewed simplistically with the idea of two sides, two commanders and a war over land. However, often third parties are on the outskirts of the conflict, either as reserve forces for one side or to join the victor to gain a massive victory. The politics in either keeping the third party out or having them come over to the allied side is a long and drawn out process that is ongoing. Nations, states, tribes and villages will be in a constant flux of treaties and agreements, pre-empting that moment when war tests the strength of such agreements.

THE OPERATION OF A SIEGE

Here Chanakya introduces the tactics to be used in an actual siege and the principles of siege warfare. Often the terms castle, fortress, citadel, etc. are used in an interchangeable way, and 'Indian fortress' has become more prevalent than 'Indian castle'. When investigating Indian fortification, grand examples such as the Mehrangarh Fort quickly come to the forefront; however, this type of castle was built well over a millennium after the time period we are considering. Remember, when considering the tactics below, contextualise and place the combatants in their correct period and with the correct fortifications.

Reduction of the Enemy

The following section is from Book 13, Chapter 4 of the original text.

Reduction (of the enemy) must precede a siege. The territory that has been conquered should be kept so peacefully that it might sleep without any fear. When it is in rebellion, it is to be pacified by bestowing rewards and remitting taxes, unless the conqueror means to quit it. Or he may select his battle fields in a remote part of the enemy's territory, far from the populous centres; for, in my opinion (Chanakya's), *no territory deserves the name of a kingdom or country unless it is full of people. When a people resist the attempt of the conqueror, then he may destroy their stores, crops, and granaries, and trade.*

Quick-lesson:
- Reduce the power of an enemy that is to be sieged
- Keep the peace in a territory conquered
- End rebellion by lifting tax and giving gifts
- Tax a conquered enemy heavily before abandoning the land
- Destroy stores and crops if needs be

Prep the Enemy for a Fall
By the destruction of trade, agricultural produce, and standing crops, by causing the people to run away, and by slaying their leaders in secret, the country will be denuded of its people.

Quick-lesson:
A leader should crush an enemy who is suffering hardships because they will be at their weakest. Victory will be swift.

The State before a Siege
When the conqueror thinks:
"My army is provided with abundance of staple corn, raw materials, machines, weapons, dress, labourers, ropes and the like, and has a favourable season to act, whereas my enemy has an unfavourable season and is suffering from disease, famine and loss of stores and defensive force, while his hired troops as well as the army of his friend are in a miserable condition," then he may begin the siege.

Quick-lesson:
The conqueror must be in a state of substantial and of preparation. The enemy must be in a state of insubstantial and unpreparedness

Harassing the Enemy Camp
Having well-guarded his camp [take the following into account]:
- *transport*
- *supplies*
- *roads of communication*
- *having dug up a ditch and raised a rampart round his camp, he may vitiate the water in the ditches round the enemy's fort, or empty the ditches of their water or fill them with water if empty*
- *he may assail the rampart and the parapets by making use of underground tunnels and iron rods*
- *if the ditch is very deep, he may fill it up with soil*
- *if it is defended by a number of men, he may destroy it by means of machines.*
- *horse soldiers may force their passage through the gate into the fort and smite the enemy.*

Quick-lesson:
One whose own fortification is up-to-date, should tamper with the enemy's fortification in order to disturb its security and overpower the enemy.

Setting Fire to Thatch
Having captured the birds such as the vulture, crow, naptri, bhása, parrot, máina, and pigeon which have their nests in the fort-walls, and having tied to their tails inflammable powders, he may let them fly to the forts. If the camp is situated at a distance from the fort and is provided with an elevated post for archers and their flags, then the enemy's fort may be set on fire. Spies, living as watchmen of the fort, may tie inflammable powder to the tails of mongooses, monkeys (Fig. 116), cats and dogs and let them go over the thatched roofs of the houses. A splinter of fire kept in the body of a dried fish may be caused to be carried off by a monkey, or a crow, or any other bird (to the thatched roofs of the houses).

Fig. 116

Quick-lesson:

The use of animals to set fire to buildings is also found extensively in Chinese warfare, as well as in Japanese military manuals and within shinobi literature. It is without doubt that Japan imported this skill from China. *Could and did China have in turn imported this skill from neighbouring India?* is a question that needs to be asked and asked.

Fire Balls

Small balls prepared from the mixture of:
- *Pinus roxburghii* (changed from the obsolete name, Pinus longifolia)
- *Deodar*
- *stinking grass*
- *Bdellium*
- *turpentine*
- *the juice of Vatica robusta*
- *lac*

Combined with the dung of an ass, camel, sheep, and goat, these balls are flammable (Fig. 117).

Fig. 117

Quick-lesson:

The use of fire is an effective means to cause havoc among an enemy. Various means to apply fire should be prepared and utilised. Shinobi literature states that these types of small balls can be held in the hand as lights, thrown into dark corridors to illuminate places or thrown into a thatch.

Incineration of the Enemy

The mixture of the powder of;
- *Chironjia Sapida*
- *the charcoal of Oanyza, serratula and Anthelmintica*
- *wax*

Combined with the dung of a horse, ass, camel, and cow is an inflammable powder to be hurled against the enemy (Fig. 118).

Fig. 118

Quick-lesson:
This is most likely a pot which contains the above which is set on fire, thrown and broken over the enemy or poured over them in some way.

An Alternative Recipe
The powder of all the metals:
- *iron*
- *the mixture of the powder of Gmelina arborea*
- *lead*
- *zinc*

Mixed with the charcoal powder of the flowers:
- *Deodar*
- *Butea Frondosa*

Then include:
- *hair*
- *oil*
- *wax*
- *turpentine*

The fire arrow
A stick of visvásagháti painted with the above mixture and wound round with a bark made of hemp, zinc, and lead, is a fire-arrow (to be hurled against the enemy) (Fig. 119).

Fig. 119

To Take Without Fire
When a fort can be captured by other means, no attempt should be made to set fire to it; for fire cannot be trusted; it not only offends gods, but also destroys the people, grains, cattle, gold, raw materials and the like. Also the acquisition of a fort with its property all destroyed is a source of further loss. Such is the aspect of a siege.

Quick-lesson:
Do not destroy those things that can be kept whole.

Time to Take a Fort
When the conqueror thinks:
"I am well provided with all necessary means and with workmen whereas my enemy is diseased with officers proved to be impure under temptations, with unfinished forts and deficient stores, allied with no friends, or with friends inimical at heart."
Then he should consider it as an opportune moment to take up arms and storm the fort.

The Time to Make an Assault
- *when fire, accidental or intentionally kindled, breaks out*
- *when the enemy's people are engaged in a sacrificial performance*
- *in witnessing spectacles or the troops*
- *in a quarrel due to the drinking of liquor*
- *when the enemy's army is too tired by daily engagements in battles and is reduced in strength in consequence of the slaughter of a number of its men in a number of battles*
- *when the enemy's people wearied from sleeplessness have fallen asleep*
- *on the occasion of a cloudy day*
- *during floods*
- *a day of thick fog or snow*

Quick-lesson:
Fire can be extinguished if it is not set at an opportune time.

Lying in Wait
Having concealed himself in a forest after abandoning the camp, the conqueror may strike the enemy when the latter comes out.

Tricking the Enemy Commander
A king pretending to be the enemy's chief friend or ally, may make the friendship closer with the besieged, and send a messenger to say:
"This is your weak point; these are your internal enemies; that is the weak point of the besieger; and this person (who, deserting the conqueror is now coming to you) is your partisan."
When this partisan is returning with another messenger from the enemy, the conqueror should catch hold of him and, having published the partisan's guilt, should banish him, and retire from the siege operations. Then the pretending friend may tell the besieged: "Come out to help me, or let us combine and strike the besieger."
Accordingly, when the enemy comes out, he may be hemmed between the two forces (the conqueror's force and the pretending friend's force) and killed or captured alive to distribute his territory (between the conqueror and the friend). His capital city may be razed to the ground; and the flower of his army made to come out and destroyed.

Quick-lesson:
A king should feign friendship with an enemy in order to lower the enemy's guard so that killing or stealing from them will be no difficult task.

All is Safe
Either a conquered enemy or the chief of a wild tribe (in conspiracy with the conqueror) may inform the besieged:
"With the intention of escaping from a disease, or from the attack in his weak point by his enemy in the rear, or from a rebellion in his army, the conqueror seems to be thinking of going elsewhere, abandoning the siege."
When the enemy is made to believe this, the conqueror may set fire to his camp and retire. Then the enemy coming out may be hemmed . . . as before.

Quick-lesson:
An enemy can be lured out and trapped if they can be convinced that the dangers posed against them have ceased.

The Poisoned Gift
Having collected merchandise mixed with poison, the conqueror may deceive the enemy by sending that merchandise to the latter.

Quick-lesson:
Fill the enemy's stores with poison by deceptive means.

To Strike from the Inside
Spies, disguised as friends or relatives and with passports and orders in their hands, may enter the enemy's fort and help to its capture (Fig. 120).

Fig. 120

Quick-lesson:
Spies should aid external destruction by causing internal damage.

False Attacks as a Lure
Pretending ally of the enemy may send information to the besieged:
"I am going to strike the besieging camp at such a time and place; then you should also fight along with me."
When the enemy does so, or when he comes out of his fort after witnessing the tumult and uproar of the besieging army in danger, he may be slain as before.

Quick-lesson:
Arrange an agreement between yourself and an intended enemy. Construct a plan to kill a mutual enemy of you both but use this as a ruse so that when your 'ally' comes out of their defences, they can be killed.

Surrender
Having captured the fort or having returned to the camp after its capture, he should give quarter to those of the enemy's army who, whether as lying prostrate in the field, or as standing with their back turned to the conqueror, or with their hair dishevelled, with their weapons thrown down or with their body disfigured and shivering under fear, surrender themselves. After the captured fort is cleared of the enemy's partisans and is well guarded by the conqueror's men both within and without, he should make his victorious entry into it.

Quick-lesson:
Once victory has been secured with surety, be benevolent to the defeated and enjoy victory.

Seizing the World
Having thus seized the territory of the enemy close to his country, the conqueror should direct his attention to that of the mediatory king; this being taken, he should catch hold of that of the neutral king. This is the first way to conquer the world. In the absence of the mediatory and neutral kings, he should, in virtue of his own excellent qualities, win the hearts of his enemy's subjects, and then direct his attention to other remote enemies. This is the second way. In the absence of a Circle of States (to be conquered), he should conquer his friend or his enemy by hemming each between his own force and that of his enemy or that of his friend respectively. This is the third way.

Quick-lesson:
A leader can conquer the world in three ways:
1. neutralising a middle king
2. gain support from the enemy's people
3. neutralising friends and enemy's alike with strategy and might

On a roll
He may first put down an almost invincible immediate enemy. Having doubled his power by this victory, he may go against a second enemy; having trebled his power by this victory, he may attack a third. This is the fourth way to conquer the world.

Govern Well
Having conquered the earth with its people of distinct castes and divisions of religious life, he should enjoy it by governing it in accordance with the duties prescribed to kings.

Quick-lesson:
To keep captured land, govern with grace and correctness.

The Five Means to Capture a Fort
1. *intrigue*
2. *spies*
3. *winning over the enemy's people*
4. *siege*
5. *assault*

Roundup
In this section, Chankaya mentions tying inflammable powders to the tails of a variety of animals, including the monkey. This tactic of war may have been inspired by a major event in the ancient epic, the *Ramayana,* which involved Hanuman, the ultra-strong monkey army general devoted to Rama, having his tail set on fire. He then set alight Lanka, the island kingdom of the demon king Ravan, the epic's antagonist. According to Book 5, Canto 54:

"Reflecting thus, his tale ablaze as through the cloud red lightning plays, he scaled the palaces and spread the conflagration where he sped. From house to house he hurried on, and the wild flames behind him shone. Each mansion of the foe he scaled, and furious fire its roof assailed till all the common ruin shared..."

In some places in his text, Chanakya lays down some rules that are in the interest of animal welfare, but in certain circumstances he makes some exceptions, as can be seen in this chapter's section entitled "Setting Fire to Thatch." A 1584 German manual on munitions and explosive devices authored by Franz Helm, entitled *Feuer Buech* (literally, fire book), suggests a similar idea to Chanakya's use of animals on fire. One illustration depicts a cat and bird each with a small rocket pack strapped to their back, heading towards a castle to cause a blazing destruction (Fig. 121). These are also images passed down in Chinese military manuals.

Fig. 121

According to Helm:

"Create a small sack like a fire-arrow… if you would like to get at a town or castle, seek to obtain a cat from that place. And bind the sack to the back of the cat, ignite it, let it glow well and thereafter let the cat go, so it runs to the nearest castle or town, and out of fear it thinks to hide itself where it ends up in barn hay or straw it will be ignited."

It is evident from Chanakya's words, that good knowledge of flammable powders existed in ancient India as he lists in his text (authored nearly 2,400 years ago) the ingredients necessary to produce them.

Defeating the Fort

The following section is from Book 12, Chapter 5 of the original text.

- *Grass and firewood should be set on fire as far as a yojana*
- *water should be vitiated and caused to flow away*
- *mounds, wells, pits and thorns (outside the fort wall) should be destroyed*
- *having widened the mouth of the underground tunnel of the enemy's fort, his stores and leaders may be removed*
- *the enemy may also be likewise carried off*
- *when the underground tunnel has been made by the enemy for his own use, the water in the ditch outside the fort may be made to flow into it*
- *in suspicious places along the parapet (of the enemy's fort) and in the house containing a well outside the fort, empty pots or bronze vessels may be placed in order to find out the direction of the wind (blowing from the underground tunnel)*
- *when the direction of the tunnel is found out, a counter-tunnel may be formed*
- *having opened the tunnel, it may be filled with smoke or water*

Having arranged for the defence of the fort by a scion of his family, the enemy may run in an opposite direction where it is possible for him to meet with friends, relatives, or wild tribes, or with his enemy's treacherous friends of vast resources, or where he may separate his enemy from the latter's friends, or where he may capture the enemy's rear, or country, or where he may prevent the transport of supplies to his enemy, or whence he may strike his enemy by throwing down trees at hand, or where he can find means to defend his own country or to gather reinforcements for his hereditary army; or he may go to any other country whence he can obtain peace on his own terms.

His enemy's (the conqueror's) allies may send a mission to him, saying: "This man, your enemy, has fallen into our hands; under the plea of merchandise or some presentation, send gold and a strong force; we shall either hand over to you your enemy bound in chains, or banish him." If he approves of it, the gold and the army he may send may be received (by the conqueror).

Having access to the enemy's castle, the officer in charge of the boundaries (of the enemy's country) may lead a part of his force and slay the enemy in good faith under the plea of destroying a people in some place, he may take the enemy to an inimical army; and having led the enemy to the surrounded place, he may slay the enemy in good faith.

A pretending friend may send information to an outsider: "Grains, oil and jaggery and salt stored in the fort (of the enemy) have been exhausted; a fresh supply of them is expected to reach the fort at such and such a place and time; seize it by force." Then traitors, enemies, or wild tribes, or some other persons, specially appointed for the purpose, may send a supply of poisoned grains, oil, jaggery, and salt to the fort. This explains the seizure of all kinds of supply.

Having made peace with the conqueror, he may give the conqueror part of the gold promised and the rest gradually. Thus he may cause the conqueror's defensive force to be slackened and then strike them down with fire, poison or sword; or he may win the confidence of the conqueror's courtiers deputed to take the tribute.

Or if his resources are exhausted, he may run away abandoning his fort; he may escape through a tunnel or through a hole newly made or by breaking the parapet.

AWARDS AND PUNISHMENTS

Awarding merit and riches is equally as important as dispensing justice and punishment. Multiple war manuals from the East describe that punishment should be fairly distributed, showing no one favour or prejudice and that it should be done after careful deliberation. Reward should be given equally, fairly, without prejudice and should be given quickly to capture the moment of a person's success. Here Chanakya gives an overview of tactics which can dismantle a person's reputation or bring them to an end by using punishment and reward as part of an intelligence plan.

The Seeds of Doubt

The following section is from Book 5, Chapter 1 of the original text.

With regard to those chiefs who, though living by service under the king, are inimically disposed towards him, or have taken the side of his enemy, a spy with secret mission or one in the guise of an ascetic and devoted to the king's cause shall set to work as described before; or a spy trained in the art of sowing the seeds of dissension may set to work, as will be described in connection with the 'Invasion of an enemy's villages.'

Quick-lesson:
One overlooked aim of the spy is to sow discontent among the enemy. This can be done in two main ways:
1. the spy may infiltrate themselves among the high ranking officers of the enemy, causing arguments between them
2. multiple spies moving around the lower echelons of the population of a target area, spreading stories and false rumours about certain people so that the news of their treachery spreads throughout, effecting the trust given to them by the lord

Secret Punishments
The king in the interests of righteousness may inflict punishment in secret on those courtiers or confederacy of chiefs who are dangerous to the safety of the kingdom and who cannot be put down in open daylight.

Quick-lesson:
Remove anyone who is not loyal or obedient.

Examples of the 'Frame'
A spy may instigate the brother of a seditious minister and with necessary inducements, take him to the king for an interview. The king, having conferred upon him the title to possess and enjoy the property of his seditious brother, may cause him to attack his brother; and when he murders his brother with a weapon or with poison, he shall be put to death in the same spot under the plea that he is a parricide.

> A parricide is someone who kills their parents or other near relative.

Quick-lesson:
A spy can kill a rebellious minister by getting a jealous member of the minister's own family, such as a brother, to carry out the task. Once the brother is successful, they should be demonised so that they are also removed.

The same measure will explain the proceedings to be taken against a seditious person who is begotten by a Bráhmin on Shûdra wife, and a seditious son of a woman-servant.

Quick-lesson:
Spies can eliminate targets by causing family strife.

Instigated by a spy, the brother of a seditious minister may put forward his claim for inheritance. While the claimant is lying at night at the door of the house of the seditious minister or elsewhere, a fiery spy may murder him and declare:
"Oh no! The claimant for inheritance is thus murdered (by his brother)."
Then taking the side of the injured party, the king may punish the other (the seditious minister).

Spies in the presence of a seditious minister may threaten to beat his brother claiming inheritance. Then "while the claimant is lying at the door of, etc." ... as before.

Quick-lesson:
By causing internal strife, a spy can cause deaths without suspicion. To 'frame' an unwanted minister, a leader may murder the minister's next of kin so that it appears that

the minister has killed the next of kin to secure his own position, upon which a leader can lawfully execute the minister.

To Inherit or Not
A spy may flatter to the vanity of a seditious minister's son, of gentle manners and dignified conduct by telling him:
"Though you are the king's son, you are kept here in fear of enemies."
The king may secretly honour this deluded person and tell him that:
"Apprehending danger from the minister, I have put off your installation, though you have attained the age of heir apparent."
Then the spy may instigate him to murder the minister. The task being accomplished, he, too, may be put to death in the same spot under the plea that he is a parricide.

Quick-lesson:
A spy should turn son against father by misinforming them and tempting them with a position of power that they have a 'right' to. However, the son will not achieve what he desires as he too will be demonised and then eliminated.

Poisoned Love
A mendicant woman, having captivated the wife of a seditious minister by administering such medicines as excite the feelings of love, may through that wife contrive to poison the minister.

Quick-lesson:
Poison an enemy through making a connection with their family.

A Kill on the Road
Failing these measures, the king may send a seditious minister with an army of inefficient soldiers and fiery spies to put down a rebellious wild tribe or a village, or to set up a new superintendent of countries or of boundaries in a locality bordering upon a wilderness, or to bring under control a highly-rebellious city, or to fetch a caravan bringing in the tribute due to the king from a neighbouring country. In an affray (that ensues in consequence of the above mission) either by day or at night, the fiery spies, or spies under the guise of robbers may murder the minister and declare that he was killed in the battle.

Quick-lesson:
A leader wishing to eradicate an unwanted minister may send them on a fake mission and then have spies kill them upon the road.

To Kill a Spy
While marching against an enemy or being engaged in sports, the king may send for his seditious ministers for an interview. While leading the ministers to the king, fiery spies with concealed weapons shall, in the middle enclosure of the king's pavilion, offer themselves to be searched for admittance into the interior, and, when caught, with their weapons by the door-keepers, declare themselves to be the accomplices of the seditious ministers. Having made this affair known to the public, the door-keepers shall put the ministers to death, and in the place of the fiery spies, some others are to be hanged.

Quick-lesson:
A leader may need to keep excellent spies. Therefore, after use, give them the death sentence but replace them with common folk at the execution – allowing them to live on and continue their espionage.

The Sex Set-up
While engaged in sports outside the city, the king may honour his seditious ministers with accommodation close to his own. A woman of bad character under the guise of the queen may be caught in the apartment of these ministers and steps may be taken against them as before.

Quick-lesson:
Bring the target close, embroil them in a sex scandal and have rid of them.

The Fake Poisoning
A sauce-maker or a sweetmeat-maker may request of a seditious minister some sauce and sweetmeat by flattering him:
"Only you alone are worthy of such things."
Having mixed those two things and half a cup of water with poison, he may substitute those things in the luncheon (of the king) outside the city. Having made this event known to the public, the king may put them (the minister and the cook) to death under the plea that they are poisoners.

Quick-lesson:
Create a situation where it appears that a leader's target has tried to kill the leader. Then have them executed as a punishment.

Death by Witchcraft
If a seditious minister is addicted to witchcraft, a spy under the guise of an accomplished wizard may make him believe that by manifesting (in witchcraft) any one of the beautiful things; a pot containing an alligator, or a tortoise or crab, he can attain his desired end. While, with this belief, he is engaged in the act of witchcraft, a spy may murder him either by poisoning him or by striking him with an iron bar, and declare that he brought his own death by his proclivity to witchcraft (Fig. 122).

Fig. 122

Quick-lesson:
Make the death of a target look like it resulted due to a misadventure during something they have a passion for.

The Healing Poison
A spy under the guise of a physician may make a seditious minister believe that he is suffering from a fatal or incurable disease and contrive to poison him while prescribing medicine and diet to him (Fig. 123).

Fig. 123

Quick-lesson:
Convince the target of an illness by adopting the guise of a trusted person (such as a doctor) then poison them with the cure.

The King cannot be Blamed
When a seditious person is to be got rid of, another seditious person with an army of inefficient soldiers and fiery spies may be sent with the following missions:
- *raise an army or some revenue*
- *deprive a courtier of his gold*
- *bring by force the daughter of a courtier*
- *build a fort*
- *open a garden*
- *construct a road for traffic*
- *set up a new village*
- *exploit a mine*
- *form forest-preserves for timber or elephants*
- *set up a district or a boundary*

Also inform them that they should "arrest and capture those who prevent your work or do not give you help".

Similarly, another party may be instructed to curb the spirit of the above person. When a quarrel arises between the two parties at work, fiery spies under cover may throw their weapons and murder the seditious person; and others are to be arrested and punished for the crime.

Quick-lesson:
A leader may send out someone they wish dead to undertake a fake task. Next, send out a second group to enter into conflict with the first. Spies will take the opportunity to kill the target during the upcoming fight, making people believe that the target was killed due to a confrontation which has no connection to the leader.

The Fire Attack
When there arises a quarrel among seditious persons, fiery spies may set fire to their fields, harvest-grounds, and houses, hurl weapons on their relatives, friends and beasts of burden, and say that they did so at the instigation of the seditious; and for this offence others may be punished.

Quick-lesson:
Order a raid on a property, then push the blame and punishment for this on another person.

A Dinner Date with Death
Spies may induce seditious persons in forts or in country parts to be each other's guests at a dinner in which poisoners may administer poison; and for this offence others may be punished.

Quick-lesson:
Poison a dinner party and force blame onto others.

The Love Triangle
A mendicant woman may delude a seditious chief of a district into the belief that the wife, daughter, or daughter-in-law of another seditious chief of another district loves the former. She may take the jewellery which the deluded chief gives her (for delivery to the wife, daughter, etc.), and, presenting it before the other chief, narrate that this chief in the pride of his youth makes love to the other's wife, daughter, or daughter-in-law. When at night a duel arises between the two chiefs, etc., as before.

Quick-lesson:
Anger and cause two people to fight over the same woman and a leader may not have to get his hands dirty to have one of them killed.

Leave a Loyal Son Alive
Whoever among the sons of the seditious persons thus put down shows no mental uneasiness shall receive his father's property. It is only thus that the whole of the country will loyally follow the sons and grandsons of the king, and will be free from all troubles caused by men.

Quick-lesson:
If a rebellious minister is put down but their son is loyal to the leader, leave them in authority.

Roundup
The above skill sets are examples of 'plans within plans', each of which works on the element of presenting a situation that will seem beneficial to sections of those involved, so that they support the idea. However, attached to those benefits are secondary consequences that are not first detected or the fact that they will bring about a situation that can be manipulated to achieve benefit to a leader who sets such plans in motion.

ASSASSINATION

In the following chapter, Chanakya lists a huge variety of assassination methods. Chanakya's words unveil the treacherous lengths Indian warriors went in order to attain victory. The methods described are cunning, and range from simple to advanced. In his text (Book 1, Chapter 20), Chanakya even presents some colorful case studies:

"When in the interior of the harem, the king shall see the queen only when her personal purity is vouchsafed by an old maid-servant. He shall not touch any woman (unless he is apprised of her personal purity); for hidden in the queen's chamber, his own brother slew king Bhadrasena; hiding himself under the bed of his mother, the son killed king Kárusa; mixing fried rice with poison, as though with honey, his own queen poisoned Kásirája; with an anklet painted with poison, his own queen killed Vairantya; with a gem of her zone bedaubed with poison, his own queen killed Sauvíra; with a looking glass painted with poison, his own queen killed Jálútha; and with a weapon hidden under her tuft of hair, his own queen slew Vidúratha."

Assassination even found its way into the family of Chanakya's protégé, Chandragupta Maurya, as told in the *Ashokavadana*, a 2nd century CE Buddhist narrative of history and legends concerning Ashoka, Chandragupta's grandson. According to the text, Chandragupta's son, Bindusara, the second Mauryan emperor who ruled for nearly thirty years, was to be succeeded by his son Sushima, the legitimate heir to the throne. However, Sushima's younger brother, Ashoka, who felt he himself was more worthy of the throne, utilised a plan devised by a minister named Radhagupta and removed his elder brother permanently by causing him to fall into a ditch of burning coals.

> After all the tactical bloodshed, Chandragupta would step down as emperor and embrace the ultra-pacifist religion of Jainism in his later years. His grandson, Ashoka, who become a more powerful and destructive emperor, later embraced Buddhism out of remorse and helped propagate it in and outside India.

Shivaji (1627 – 1680 CE), the founder and first emperor of the Maratha Empire, was noted for being a Hindu nationalist and skilful warrior who emphasised the use of guerrilla warfare against the Mughals and other enemies. One event he is perhaps most well-known for is his counter-measure to an assassination attempt. A friendly meeting between him and a commander of the Adil Shahi dynasty named Afzal Khan was arranged. When Khan arrived at the tent, they both embraced each other, but then Khan suddenly struck Shivaji in the back with a concealed blade. Suspecting such treachery, Shivaji had fortunately decided to put on armour beneath his clothing and concealed small weapons prior to the meeting. After Khan struck, Shivaji responded by stabbing and slashing Khan's abdomen with a *bagh-nakh*, a metal tiger-claw weapon (Fig. 124). The assassin became the assassinated.

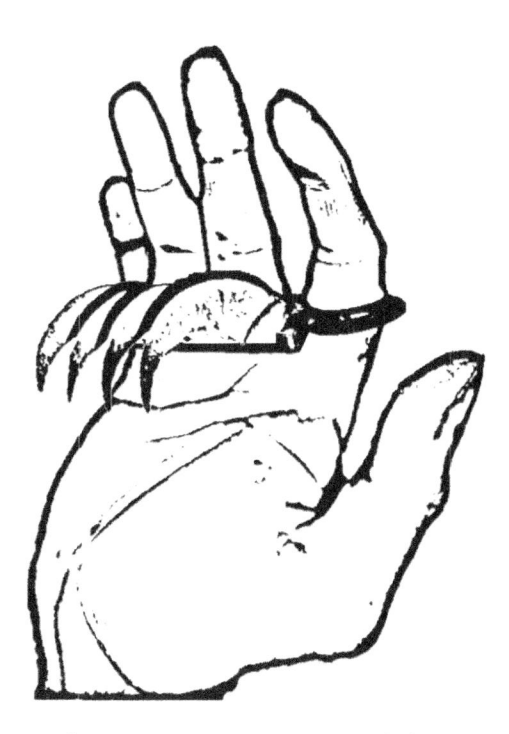

Fig. 124. The *bagh-nakh*, one of India's traditional concealed weapons, similar to the Japanese *shuko*, a metal hand claw believed to have been used by the shinobi.

The British colonialists in India found themselves trying to supress an organised cult of Indian serial killers/assassins, known as the Thuggees (Fig. 125). A Thuggee was a killer who worshipped the Hindu deity, Goddess Kali, and whose primary tool of murder was the *rumal* (scarf) which he used to strangle his victims, killing them without spilling blood. Usually operating in small groups, Thuggees would cunningly prey upon those who were vulnerable, distracted and benevolent. Several old books, paintings, sketches and even photographs exist revealing the Thuggee *modus operandi*. One 19th century watercolour depicts four Thuggees distracting a traveller by conversing with him and pointing up, whilst the fifth sneaks up behind ready to wrap his scarf around the unsuspecting traveller's exposed neck. Another watercolour (from the British Library) depicts a band of three Thuggees targeting a European traveller: one holds down his hands, another his ankles, while the third kneels on his back and garrottes him with a scarf.

Fig. 125. Thuggees at work. Image derived from a 19th century watercolour.

"Thuggee" is derived from the Hindi word "thag" meaning "thief/deceiver". From it, we get the English word "thug".

According to Hinduism, the Goddess Kali is a demon-slayer who, after decapitating demons, caught the demon blood in a bowl and drank it in order to prevent it from falling to the ground and giving birth to more demons.

It may be interesting to mention the story of a 16th century Indian serial killer-thug named Sajjan Thag. He set up an inn at which exhausted travellers could stay the night.

He would overwhelm them with his hospitality, tending to their every need. However, at the dead of night, Sajjan Thag would mercilessly kill his customers in their sleep and steal their possessions. One day, – as the story goes – Guru Nanak Dev Ji (1469 – 1539 CE), the founder of the Sikh faith, visited the inn. He was with his friend and musician, Mardana, who was accompanying the guru on his missionary journeys. However, before Guru Nanak Dev Ji and his friend could fall victim to Sajjan Thag's *modus operandi*, the guru read the killer's cruel mind and sang a hymn encouraging repentance whilst his friend played the Rabab, a stringed instrument. On hearing the guru's words, the heartless thug confessed to his wrong-doings and vowed to make a positive transformation.

Assassination skills from the original manual:

Temples of Death

> The following section is from Book 12, Chapter 5 of the original text.

Contrivances to kill the enemy may be formed in those places of worship and visit, which the enemy, under the influence of faith, frequents on occasions of worshipping gods, and of pilgrimage (Fig. 126).

Fig. 126

Methods include:
- *a wall or a stone, kept by mechanical contrivance, may, by loosening the fastenings, be let to fall on the head of the enemy when he has entered into a temple*

- *stones and weapons may be showered over his head from the topmost storey* (Fig. 127)
- *a door-panel may be let to fall* (Fig. 128)
- *a huge rod kept over a wall or partly attached to a wall may be made to fall over him* (Fig. 129)
- *weapons kept inside the body of an idol may be thrown over his head* (Fig. 130)
- *the floor of those places where he usually stands, sits, or walks may be sprinkled with poison mixed with cow-dung or with pure water* (Fig. 131)
- *under the plea of giving him flowers* (Fig. 132), *scented powders causing scented smoke, he may be poisoned*
- *by removing the fastenings made under a cot or a seat, he may be made to fall into a pit containing pointed spears* (Fig. 133)
- *when he is eager to escape from impending imprisonment in his own country, he may be led away to fall into the hands of a wild tribe or an enemy waiting for him not far from his country* (Fig. 134)

Fig. 127

Fig. 128

Fig. 129

Fig. 130

Fig. 131

Fig. 132

Fig. 133

Fig. 134

Making Good an Escape
If there is a need to flee use the following:
- *run away by a side path*
- *disguised as a heretic*
- *escape with a small retinue*
- *be carried off by spies as a corpse* (Fig. 135)
- *be disguised as a woman*
- *follow a corpse (as it were, of her husband to the cremation ground)*

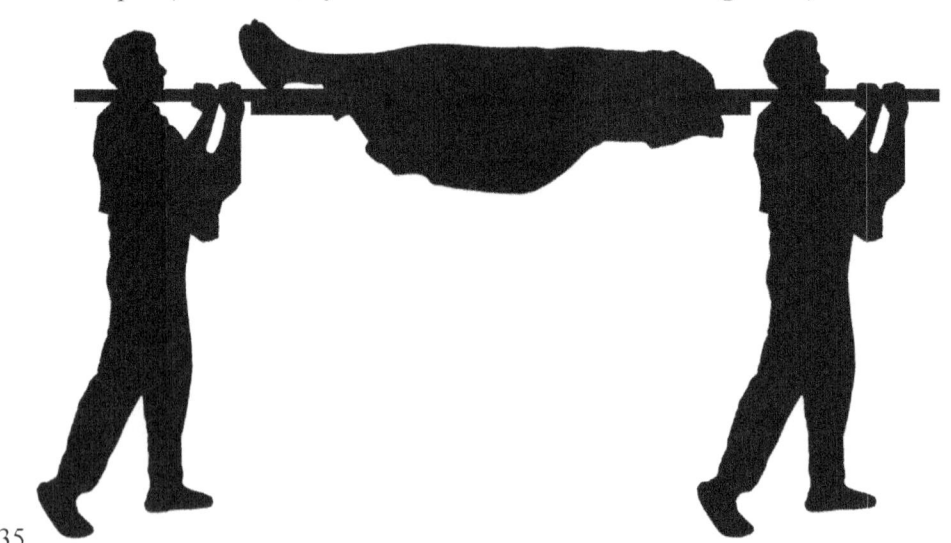

Fig. 135

Hidden Assassination Strikes

- *on the occasion of feeding the people in honour of gods or of ancestors or in some festival, he may make use of poisoned rice and water, and having conspired with his enemy's traitors, he may strike the enemy with his concealed army* (Fig. 136)
- *when he is surrounded in his fort, he may lie concealed in a hole bored into the body of an idol after eating sacramental food and setting up an altar* (Fig 137)
- *he may lie in a secret hole in a wall*
- *lie in a hole made in the body of an idol in an underground chamber and when he is forgotten, he may get out of his concealment through a tunnel, and, entering into the palace, slay his enemy while sleeping*
- *by loosening the fastenings of a machine he may let it fall on his enemy* (Fig. 138)
- *when his enemy is lying in a chamber which is besmeared with poisonous and explosive substances or which is made of lac, he may set fire to it.* (Fig. 139)
- *Fiery spies, hidden in an underground chamber, or in a tunnel, or inside a secret wall, may slay the enemy when the latter is carelessly amusing himself in a pleasure park or any other place of recreation* (Fig. 140)
- *spies under concealment may poison him*
- *women under concealment may throw a snake* (Fig. 141), *or poison, or fire or poisonous smoke over his person when he is asleep in confined place*
- *spies, having access to the enemy's harem, may, when opportunities occur, do to the enemy whatever is found possible on the occasion, and then get out unknown. On such occasions, they should make use of the signs indicative of the purpose of their society* (Fig. 142)

Fig. 136

Fig. 137

Fig. 138

Fig. 139

Fig. 140

Fig. 141

Fig. 142

Quick-lesson:
A spy or assassin should use hidden compartments to conceal themselves. They should also disguise themselves as people that are expected to be there and to use a person's lust against them.

Roundup
Despite listing a number of chivalrous laws of combat, Manu seems to include some advice on asymmetric warfare. According to *The Laws of Manu*, Chapter 7, 195-198:

"When he has shut up his foe (in a town), let him sit encamped, harass his kingdom, and continually spoil his grass, food, fuel, and water. Likewise let him destroy the tanks, ramparts, and ditches, and let him assail the (foe unawares) and alarm him at night. Let him instigate to rebellion those who are open to such instigations, let him be informed of his (foe's) doings, and, when fate is propitious, let him fight without fear, trying to conquer. He should (however) try to conquer his foes by conciliation, by (well-applied) gifts, and by creating dissension, used either separately or conjointly, never by fighting, (if it can be avoided.)"

Prithviraj Chauhan (1149 – 1192 CE) is one of India's best known warrior kings and was noted for his fairness and mercy. However, his chivalrous nature can be said to have led to his downfall, leaving India vulnerable to further foreign invaders. He had defeated the forces of a powerful invader named Shahabuddin Muhammad Ghori, whom Chauhan, out of benevolence, permitted to retreat and live rather than annihilate. Victory, however, was eventually attained by Ghori in battle and his valiant rival, Chauhan, was captured, imprisoned, taunted and blinded.

One of the methods detailed in this chapter is assassinating a target whilst they are asleep. Guru Gobind Singh Ji, the tenth Sikh guru, survived such a method. As the guru slept, a blade was plunged into his chest by one of two Pathans, Wasil Beg and Jamshed Khan, believed to have been sent by a tyrannical governor named Wazir Khan. The guru survived the assassination attempt because the blade missed his heart. The assassin was soon cut down by the guru's sword while his accomplice too fell by the sword as he tried to escape. The attack, however, caused a severe wound which would eventually lead to the guru's passing.

BIOLOGICAL AND CHEMICAL AGENTS

Chanakya's biological and chemical warfare may seem ridiculous to many, but according to reporter Shaikh Azizur Rahman's 2002 BBC news story, the Indian military took a very enthusiastic interest in the martial aspects of the *Arthashastra*. George Fernandez, the then Defence Minister of India approved nearly one million rupees to fund the project. Space scientist, Professor SV Bhavasar said regarding the project:

"All of us are excited about the possibilities and do not for a moment think that the idea is crazy."

The Indo-Asian News Service also reported on this unusual project. Professor Vikram Ghole, the project's principal investigator and coordinator told the IANS that they were testing formulations from the *Arthashastra* on mice and that any progress would be passed onto the DRDO (Defence Research and Development Organisation) who will then continue the research carrying out more advanced experiments.

One will note that the names of several ingredients in Chanakya's biological and chemical weapon recipes appear to be untranslatable. He may have deliberately used obscure words in case his manual fell into the wrong hands.

Disguise

The following section is from Book 14, Chapter 1 of the original text.

In order to protect the institution of the four castes, such measures as are treated of in secret science shall be applied against the wicked. Through the instrumentality of such men or women of Mlechchha class as can put on disguises, appropriate to different countries, arts, or professions, or as can put on the appearance of:
- *a hump-backed person*
- *a dwarfish, or short-sized person*
- *a dumb, deaf or idiot*
- *a blind person*

Deadly poison named kálakúta and other manifold poisons should be administered in the diet and other physical enjoyments of the wicked. Spies lying in wait or living as inmates (in the same house) may make use of weapons on occasions of royal sports or musical and other entertainments. Spies, under the disguise of night-walkers or of fire-keepers may set fire (to the houses of the wicked).

Quick-lesson:
Spies must be able to disguise themselves, to act out a role and to adopt a persona. The shinobi of Japan centred their arts of disguise and the adoption of persona, taking on the mantle of other identities and becoming that person.

Death Gas
The powder (prepared from the carcass) of animals such as:
- *frog*
- *Perdix sylvatika – a kind of partridge*
- *centipede*
- *crab*
- *lizard, with the powder of the bark of Physalis flexuosa* (spelling corrected from phyalis flexuosa)
- *a small house-lizard*
- *andháhika – a blind snake*
- *krakanthaka – a kind of partridge*
- *pútikíta – a stinking insect*

The smoke caused by burning the above powders causes instantaneous death.
Any of the (above) insects may be heated with a black snake and panic seed and reduced to powder. This mixture, when burnt, causes instantaneous death.

Slow Death
The powder prepared from the roots of:
- *Lufta foetida (possibly Lutea foetida)*
- *yátudhána – unknown*

Mixed with the powder of the flower of Semecarpus anacardium when administered this causes death in the course of half a month.

Powder:
- *The root of Cassia fistula* (spelling corrected from Casia fistula)
- *the flower of Semecarpus anacardium*

Mixed with the essence of an insect, when administered causes death in the course of a month.

Death on the Wind
The smoke caused by burning the powder of:
- *satakardama – unknown*
- *crab*
- *Nerium odorum*
- *katutumbi – a kind of bitter gourd*
- *fish together with the chaff of the grains of madana*
- *Paspalum scrobiculatum* (spelling corrected from Paspalam scrobiculatum) *or with the chaff of the seeds of castor oil tree*
- *Butea frondosa*

The above destroys animal life as far as it is carried off by the wind.

The smoke caused by burning the powder made of the mixture of:
- *the dung and urine of pigeons, frogs, flesh-eating animals, elephants, men, and boars*
- *the chaff and powder of barley mixed with green sulphate of iron*
- *rice*
- *the seeds of cotton*
- *Nerium antidysentericum*
- *Lufta pentandra*
- *cow's urine*
- *the root of Hydroeotyle asiatica*
- *the powder of Nimba meria*
- *Hyperanthera moringa*
- *phanirjaka – a kind of tulasi (also tulsi) plant*
- *ripe Careya arborea*
- *hemp*
- *the skin of a snake and fish*
- *and the powder of the nails and tusk of an elephant,*

Mix the above with the chaff of madana and Paspalum scrobiculatum, or with the chaff of the seeds of castor oil tree and Butea frondosa causes instantaneous death wherever the smoke is carried off by the wind.

Blinding Powders
The smoke caused by burning:

- *the powder of pútikita – a stinking insect*
- *fish*
- *katutumbi – a kind of bitter gourd*
- *the bark of satakardama – unknown*
- *the cochineal insect*

The powder of:
- *pútikita – a stinking insect*
- *the resin of the plant, Shorea robusta, and hemavidári – unknown*

Mixed with the powder of the hoof and horn of a goat causes blindness.

The smoke caused by burning of:
- *the leaves of Guilandina bonducella*
- *yellow arsenic*
- *Realgar*
- *the seeds of Abrus precatorius*
- *the chaff of the seeds of red cotton*
- *Careya arborea*
- *khácha – salt?*
- *the dung and urine of a cow* (Fig. 143)

Fig. 143

The smoke caused by burning:
- *the skin of a snake*
- *the dung of a cow and a horse*
- *the head of a blind snake*

When a man who has kept his eyes secure with the application of ointment and medicinal water burns; on the occasion of the commencement of a battle and the assailing of forts:
- *the roots of tragia involucrata*
- *Costus*
- *nada – a kind of reed*
- *Asparagus racemosus*
- *or the powder of (the skin of) a snake*
- *the tail of a peacock*
- *krikana – a kind of partridge*
- *panchakushtha – unknown*

Mix with the chaff as previously described or with wet or dry chaff, the smoke caused thereby destroys the eyes of all animals.

The ointment prepared by mixing:
- *the excretion of maina*
- *pigeon*
- *crane*
- *baláka – a kind of small crane*

Mix with the milk of Hyperanthera moringa
- *píluka – a species of Careya arborea*
- *Euphorbia*

This causes blindness and poisons water.

The mixture of:
- *yavaka – a kind of barley*
- *the root of Achyrantes triandria*
- *the fruit of madana*
- *the leaves of nutmeg?*
- *the urine of a man mixed with the powder of the root of fig tree*
- *liquorice*

- *the essence of the decoction of musta – a kind of poison*
- *Glomerulus fig tree*
- *Paspalum scrobiculatum*
- *with the decoction of castor oil tree*
- *Butea frondosa*

is termed the juice of madana.

The mixture of the powders of:
- *Atis betula, gaumevriksha (?)*
- *Solanum xanthocarpum*
- *mayúrapadi (?)*
- *the powder of Abrus precatorius seeds*
- *Jussiena repens*
- *vishamúlika (?)*
- *heart-pea, and the powder of Oleander*
- *Careya arborea*
- *Arka plant*
- *mrigamáríni (?)*
- *combined with the decoction of madana*
- *Paspalum scrobiculatum*
- *or with that of castor oil tree*
- *Butea frondosa*

is termed madana mixture.

The combination of (the above two) mixtures poisons grass and water when applied to them.

The smoke caused by burning the mixture of the powders:
- *krikana – a kind of partridge*
- *lizard*
- *a small house-lizard*
- *a blind snake*

This destroys the eyes and causes madness.

Fever
The mixture of:
- *panchakushtha – unknown*
- *kaundinyaka – unknown*
- *Cassia fistula*
- *Bassia latifolia*
- *madhu – honey?*

This causes fever.

Deaf and Dumb
The mixture prepared from the powder of:
- *the knot of the tongue of bhája – unknown*
- *mongoose*

Reduced to a paste with the milk of a she-donkey this causes both dumbness and deafness.

Preparation
Mixtures become very powerful when, in the case of drugs, they are prepared by the process of decoction; and in the case of animals, by the process of making powders; or in all cases by the process of decoction.

Zombie outbreaks
Whoever is pierced by the arrow prepared from;

- *the grains of Bombax heptaphyllum*
- *liquorice*

When reduced to powder and mixed with the powder of múlavatsanábha (a kind of poison) and smeared over with the blood of musk-rat, he who bites some ten other persons in their turn bite others (Fig. 144).

Fig. 144

Poison the well

The mixture prepared from:
- *the flowers of Semecarpus anacardium*
- *yátudhána – unknown*
- *Achyranthes aspera*
- *sal tree mixed with the powder of large cardamom*
- *red aluminous earth*
- *Bdellium*
- *háláhala – a kind of poison*

Together with the blood of a goat and a man causes biting madness.

When half a dharana of this mixture together with flour and oil-cakes is thrown into water of a reservoir measuring a hundred bows in length, it vitiates the whole mass of water; all the fish swallowing or touching this mixture become poisonous; and whoever drinks or touches this water will be poisoned.

Unquenchable fires

When, on the days of the stars of krittiká or bharaní and following the method of performing fearful rites, an offering with a black cobra emitting froth at the shock of lightning or caught hold of by means of the sticks of a tree struck by lightning and perfumed is made into the fire, that fire continues to burn unquenchably.

An oblation of honey shall be made into the fire fetched from the house of a blacksmith; of spirituous liquor into the fire brought from the house of a vintner; of clarified butter into the fire of a sacrificer.

Of a garland into the fire kept by a sacrificer with one wife; of mustard seeds into the fire kept by an adulterous woman; of curds into the fire kept during the birth of a child; of rice-grain into the fire of a sacrificer;

> Krittiká and Bharani are stars in Hindu astronomy. The former is located in the constellation of Taurus and its ruling deity is by Agni, the god of fire. The latter is ruled by the planet Venus.

Of flesh into the fire kept by an outcast of human flesh into the fire burning in cremation grounds; an oblation of the serum of the flesh of a goat and a man shall be made by means of a sacrificial ladle into the fire which is made of all the above fires;

Repeating the mantras addressed to the fire, an oblation of the wooden pieces of cassia fistula into the same fire.

The above fires will unquenchably burn deluding the eyes of the enemies.

The prayer

Salutation to Aditi, salutation to Anumati, salutation to Sarasvati and salutation to the Sun; oblation to Agni, oblation to Soma, oblation to the earth, and oblation to the atmosphere.

Quick-lesson:
- Aditi – the mother of gods
- Anumati – a lunar goddess
- Sarasvati – goddess of knowledge, music and arts
- Sun – known as Surya in Sanskrit. He is the solar deity and chief of the planets
- Agni – the god of fire (Fig. 145)
- Soma – the god of a certain plant and its intoxicating elixir

Fig. 145

Roundup

Even in today's modern India, many fear the power of Tantrik gurus. Revenge-seekers approach them for help on casting spells and curses upon their rivals. In exchange for money, the gurus promise their clients the desired results.

In several Hindu scriptures and epics, one can find numerous references to poisons, such as *kálakúta* and *háláhala* (two names of the same ultra-lethal poison). Interestingly, Chanakya names both here. According to Hindu legends, large amounts of this poison was consumed by the Hindu god Shiva, thus saving the world from its dire effects. The poison turned his throat blue-coloured, earning him the name, Neelkanth – *blue throat*.

Elsewhere in the *Arthashastra*, Chanakya tells how to examine a corpse to determine if the deceased was killed by poisoning:

"Any dead person with dark coloured hands, legs, teeth, and nails, with loose skin, hairs fallen, flesh reduced, and with face bedaubed with foam and saliva, may be regarded as having been poisoned."

And:

"Any dead person, with body spread and dress thrown out after excessive vomiting and purging may be considered as having been killed by the administration of the juice of the madana plant."

Book 4, Chapter 7

Chanakya also warns of the penalty which poisoners face:

"Any man who poisons another... shall be drowned."

Book 4, Chapter 11

WONDERFUL AND DELUSIVE CONTRIVANCES

Following on from biological and chemical warfare, Chanakya moves on to other agents and recipes which have a wide range of applications. Often the problem attached to these lists are the lack of dosage or instructions. Nonetheless, that does not stop them from being highly interesting as they truly give a glimpse of the exotic and esoteric. However, testing their practicality is essential, otherwise they hold no real value.

In the first section, Chanakya shares a recipe for meals that would enable soldiers to fast for half a month and another recipe for a whole month. This particular section intrigued the modern Indian scientists, led by Dr. Vikram Ghole, who were researching the *Arthashastra* to give their nation's soldiers an advantage in battle. Soumya Ghosh, a research fellow of Dr. Ghole's government-backed *Arthashastra* experiments told *The Times of India* that the *Arthashastra* does not mention exact dose compositions and discovering them was difficult and in order to unlock these secrets, the article says tests were being done on mice.

Hunger Pills

The following section is from Book 14, Chapter 2 of the original text.

A dose of the powder of:
- *Mimosa siríssa* (spelling corrected from Mimosa sirísa)
- *Glomerulus fig tree*
- *Acacia suma*

Mixed with clarified butter, renders fasting possible for half a month.

The scum prepared from the mixture of:
- *the root of kaseruka – a kind of water-creeper*
- *Costus*
- *sugar cane mixed with water-lily*
- *grass*

Mixed with clarified butter enables a man to fast for a month.

The powder of:
- *Phaseolus radiatus* (spelling corrected from Phraseolus radiatus)

- *barley*
- *horse-gram*
- *root of darbha – a sacred Vedic sacrificial grass*

Mixed with milk and clarified butter.

Quick-lesson:
Give the men high-energy foods to help them keep hunger at bay.

Bleaching Agent
The oil prepared from mustard seeds previously kept for seven nights in the urine of a white goat will, when used (externally) after keeping the oil inside a large bitter gourd for a month and a half, alter the colour of both biped and quadruped animals.

The oil extracted from white mustard seeds mixed with the barley-corns contained in the dung of a white donkey, which has been living for more than seven nights on a diet of butter, milk and barley, causes alteration in colour.

The oil prepared from mustard seeds which have been previously kept in the urine and fluid dung of any of the two animals, a white goat and a white donkey, causes (when applied) such white colour as that of the fibre of arka plant or the down of a (white) bird.

The mixture of the dung of a white cock and Boa constrictor causes white colour.

The Boa constrictor is a large, heavy-bodied snake that flourishes in countries of high temperatures, such as India and the Americas.

The pastry made from white mustard seeds kept for seven nights in the urine of a white goat mixed with butter-milk, the milk of arka plant, salt, and grains, causes, when applied for a fortnight, white colour.

The paste, prepared from white mustard seeds which have been previously kept within a large bitter gourd and with clarified butter prepared from the milk of a creeper for half a month, makes the hair white.

A bitter gourd, a stinking insect, and a white house-lizard; when a paste prepared from these is applied to the hair, the latter becomes as white as a conch-shell.

Black or White

Whoever eats the mixture of the powders of the roots of Marsilia dentata, Duffa pentandra, Asparagus racemosus for a month will become white.

Whoever bathes in the decoction of banyan tree and rubs his body with the paste prepared from yellow barleria becomes black.

Sulphuret of arsenic and red arsenic mixed with the oil extracted from sakuna (a kind of bird) and a vulture causes blackness.

Leprosy Paste

When any part of the body of a man is rubbed over with:
- *the pastry prepared from glutinosa*
- *soap-berry*
- *the dung of a cow*

The part of the body being also smeared over with the juice of Semecarpus anacardium, he will catch leprosy in the course of a month.

The application of the paste prepared from) Abrus precatorius seeds kept previously for seven nights in the mouth of a white cobra or in the mouth of a house-lizard brings on leprosy.

External application of the liquid essence of the egg of a parrot and a cuckoo brings on leprosy.

Quick-lesson:
Use chemical warfare to make the enemy sick.

Light emitting Powders

The powder of khadyota – fire-fly mixed with the oil of mustard seeds emits light at night.

Quick-lesson:
Luminescence at night can be used for various activities.

Ignition Powder
The powder of:

- *fire-fly and earthworm or the powder of ocean animals mixed with the powder of malabathrum*
- *kapála – a pot-herb*
- *mimosa catechu*
- *Pentapetes acerifolia*
- *combined with the oil of sakuna – a bird and vulture*

This is ignition powder.

Quick-lesson:
The *Bansenshukai* ninja manual states that ignition powder is a wondrous invention and can be a great assist in arson.

Fireproof Paste
When the body of a man is rubbed over with the powder of the charcoal of the bark of Erythrina indica, mixed with the serum of the flesh of a frog, it can be burnt with fire (without causing hurt) (Fig. 146).

Fig. 146

The body which is painted with the pastry (prepared from the bark of Erythrina indica) and Sesamum seeds burns with fire (without causing hurt).

When the body of a man is smeared over with the serum of the flesh of a frog, it burns with fire (with no hurt).

When the body of a man is smeared over with the above serum as well:
- *the oil extracted from the fruits of Ficus religiosa*
- *mango tree*

Also:
The powder prepared from:
- *an ocean frog*
- *sea-foam*
- *the juice of Vatica robusta*

When this is sprinkled over the body, it burns with fire (without being hurt).

When the body of a man is smeared over with Sesamum oil mixed with equal quantities of the serum of the flesh of a frog, crab, and other animals, it can burn with fire (without hurt).

The body which is smeared over with the serum of the flesh of a frog burns with fire.

The body of a man, which is rubbed over with the powder of:
- *the root of bamboo*
- *saiväla (an aquatic plant)*
- *the serum of the flesh of a frog*

This burns with fire.

Whoever has anointed his legs with the oil extracted from the paste prepared from:
- *roots of Erythrina indica*
- *pratibala – unknown*
- *vanjula (a kind of ratan or tree)*
- *Andropogon muricatum or euphorbia*
- *banana*

Mixed with the serum of the flesh of a frog, can walk over fire (without hurt).

Oil should be extracted from the paste prepared from the roots of pratibala (unknown), vanjula and Erythrina indica, all growing near water, the paste being mixed with the serum of the flesh of a frog. Having anointed one's legs with this oil, one can walk over a white-hot mass of fire as though on a bed of roses (Fig. 147).

Fig. 147

Quick-lesson:
Use fireproof pastes so that men can move through burning places and awe spectators.

Fire Balls
The ball prepared from the powder of the charcoal of the bark of Careya arborea can be held in hand and burnt with fire.

Quick-lesson:
Japanese warriors would use such fire balls to throw into dark corridors or to hold in the hand and use as a torch. They could extinguish it by simply closing their hands.

Fire from Heaven
When birds such as a goose, heron, peacock and other large swimming birds are let to fly at night with a burning reed attached to their tail it presents the appearance of a firebrand falling from the sky.

Fire extinguisher
Ashes caused by lightning quench the fire.

Fire Breathing
By keeping in the mouth a ball-like piece of Careya arberea or a knot of the root of linseed tree with fire inserted within the mass of the ball and wound round with threads and cotton, volumes of smoke and fire can be breathed out (Fig. 148).

Fig. 148

Windproof Fire
When the oil extracted from the fruits of Ficus religiosa and mango is poured over the fire, it burns even in a storm.

Floating Fire
Sea-foam wetted with oil and ignited keeps burning when floating on water.

Monkey Bones
The fire generated by churning the bone of a monkey by means of a bamboo stick of white and black colour burns in water instead of being quenched.

Oil for the Legs
The paste prepared from the powder of:
- *the rib-bone of náraka – unknown*
- *donkey*
- *kanka – a kind of vulture*
- *bhása – a bird*

Mixed with the juice of water-lily, is applied to the legs of bipeds and quadrupeds (while making a journey).

Footsore
When a man makes a journey, wearing the shoes made of the skin of a camel, smeared over with the serum of the flesh of an owl and a vulture and covered over with the leaves of the banyan tree, he can walk fifty yojanas without any fatigue.
Also:
(When the shoes are smeared over with) the pith, marrow or sperm of the birds, eagle, kanka (a kind of vulture), kaka (a kind of bird), gridhra (a kind of vulture), goose, heron, and vichiralla (a kind of vulture) (the traveller wearing them) can walk a hundred yojanas (without any fatigue).
Also:
The fat or serum derived from roasting a pregnant camel together with Lechites scholaris or from roasting dead children in cremation grounds, is applied to render a journey of a hundred yojanas easy.

The Application of Terror
Terror should be caused to the enemy by exhibiting these and other wonderful and delusive performances; while anger causing terror is common to all, terrification by such wonders is held as a means to consolidate peace.

Roundup
Throughout this chapter, Chanakya lists numerous methods of causing insanity, loss of sight, leprosy, death and even gonorrhoea using a variety of poisonous mixtures and smoke weapons. This is ancient Indian biological and chemical warfare.

It is interesting to note that Chanakya suggests shooting an enemy with an arrow contaminated with a mixture of several ingredients which would cause an enemy to become somewhat similar to a flesh-eating zombie who creates more like him after gnawing on their flesh.

While Chanakya permits the use of deceptive and excessive violence in war, the laws laid down by him in his *Arthashastra*, however, prohibit such fighting outside of war. Non-war combat would incur various punishments. For example:

"For catching hold of a man by his legs, clothes, hands or hair, fines ranging above 6 panas shall be imposed. Squeezing, rounding with arms, thrusting, dragging, or sitting over the body of another person shall be punished with the first amercement."

"…Causing a bloodless wound with a stick, mud, a stone, an iron bar, or a rope shall be punished with a fine of 24 panas."

"Beating a person almost to death, though without causing blood, breaking the hands, legs, or teeth, tearing off the ear or the nose, or breaking open the flesh of a person except in ulcers or boils shall be punished with the first amercement. Causing hurt in the thigh or the neck, wounding the eye, or hurting so as to impede eating, speaking, or any other bodily movements shall not only be punished with the middlemost amercement, but also be made liable to the payment (to the sufferer) of such compensation as is necessary to cure him."

Book 3, Chapter 19

THE APPLICATION OF MANTRAS AND MEDICINES

Adherents of the Dharmic religions (i.e. Hinduism, Buddhism, Jainism and Sikhism) firmly believe in the powers of mantras. Without doubt, deep inhaling and exhaling whilst focusing on positive thoughts/images can help quell stress and achieve a relaxed state of mind, but the religious believe that mantras are more than just about stress relief.

To them, the words of mantras contain supernatural powers which can help in various ways such as summon deities, ward off evil spirits, repel the curses of enemies, etc.

Many mantras begin with the word 'Om' (also Aum), considered the primordial sound of creation.

There are special, secretive mantras for launching divine missiles. India's ancient texts tell of warriors often using a variety of magical weapons in battle. A story in the *Mahabharata* (Book 3: Section 60) tells of how the warrior Arjuna, who after performing penance, received an extraordinarily powerful divine missile called the *Pashupat-astra* as a boon from the deity, Shiva. One of Lord Shiva's forms is called Pashupati, meaning "Lord/Protector of the animals", hence the name of the missile (i.e. Pashupata missile). Lord Shiva says to Arjuna: *"I will give to you that favourite weapon of mine called the Pasupata"*, but also warns: *"...this weapon should not be hurled without adequate cause; for if hurled at any foe of little might, it may destroy the whole universe. In the three worlds with all their mobile and immobile creatures, there is none who is incapable of being slain by this weapon. And it may be hurled by the mind, by the eye, by words, and by the bow."* However, the secret mantra for summoning and discharging this missile is not revealed in the epic, but fortunately it is revealed in the *Dhanurveda Samhita*:

"For operating the Pashupat-astra, a warrior should utter 'praṇava' (Om) then recite 'ślīṁ paśuṁ huṁ phaṭ' 'amuk śatrūn hana huṁ phaṭ' twice, keeping in view the enemy in

mind. For withdrawing the Pashupat-astra, one has to recite the mentioned phrase in reverse order."

Such mantras are not widely known of. Indian epics mention numerous names of many divine missiles but not their usage. However, those who read the rare Indian martial manual, *Dhanurveda Samhita,* will be pleasantly surprised to find several mantras for notable divine missiles mentioned in the epics, such as the one mentioned above. Such divine weapons were summoned by mantras and then launched in various ways i.e. by the mind, hand, bow or other instruments (Fig. 149).

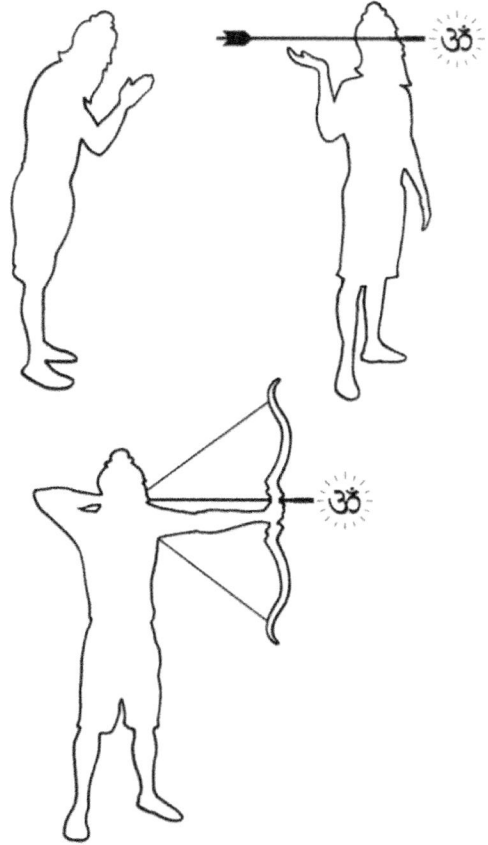

Fig. 149

Chanakya includes several mantras in his text that invoke various Hindu gods and even demons for aiding the chanter in achieving various objectives, such as chanting a mantra that causes enemy guards and animals to fall into a deep sleep, allowing the mantra-chanting spy/assassin to gain access to the guarded area, etc. Being a Brahmin (member of the Vedic priest class), Chanakya would have been well-versed in various mantras, especially those from the four *Vedas*, Hinduism's holiest scriptures. He mentions these scriptures in his text and emphasises the *Atharvaveda*, the fourth *Veda*. Chanakya says in his text:

"Persons acquainted with the rituals of the Atharvaveda, and experts in sacred magic and mysticism shall perform such ceremonials as ward off the danger from demons."

Book 4, Chapter 1

This particular *Veda* is full of herbal remedies, charms and prayers for curing physical and mental ailments, repelling demons, supressing evil dreams, succeeding at playing dice, blessing a house being built, attaining prosperity for cattle, securing the love of a woman, cursing hostile charm users, winning victory in war, and numerous other remedies. For example, a battle-charm of a king on the eve of battle is given as follows:

"I call-upon thee, O Indra, from afar, upon thee for protection against tribulation. I call the strong avenger that has many names, and is of unequalled birth. Where the hostile weapon now rises against us, threatening to slay, there do we place the two arms of Indra round about. The two arms of Indra, the protector, do we place round about us: let him protect us! O god Savitar, and king Soma, render me of confident mind, that I may prosper!"

Atharvaveda, Book 6, Hymn 99

Magical Night Vision

The following section is from Book 14, Chapter 3 of the original text.

Having pulled out both the right and the left eye-balls of [one or more of the following]:

- *cat*
- *camel*
- *wolf*
- *boar*
- *porcupine*
- *váguli – unknown*
- *naptri – unknown*
- *crow*
- *owl*

Or of any one, two, or three, or many of such animals that roam at night, one should reduce them to two kinds of powder. Whoever anoints

239

his own right eye with the powder of the left eye and his left eye with the powder of the right eye-ball can clearly see things even in pitch dark at night.

One is the eye of a boar; another is that of a fire-fly, or a crow, or a mina bird. Having anointed one's own eyes with the above, one can clearly see things at night (Fig. 150).

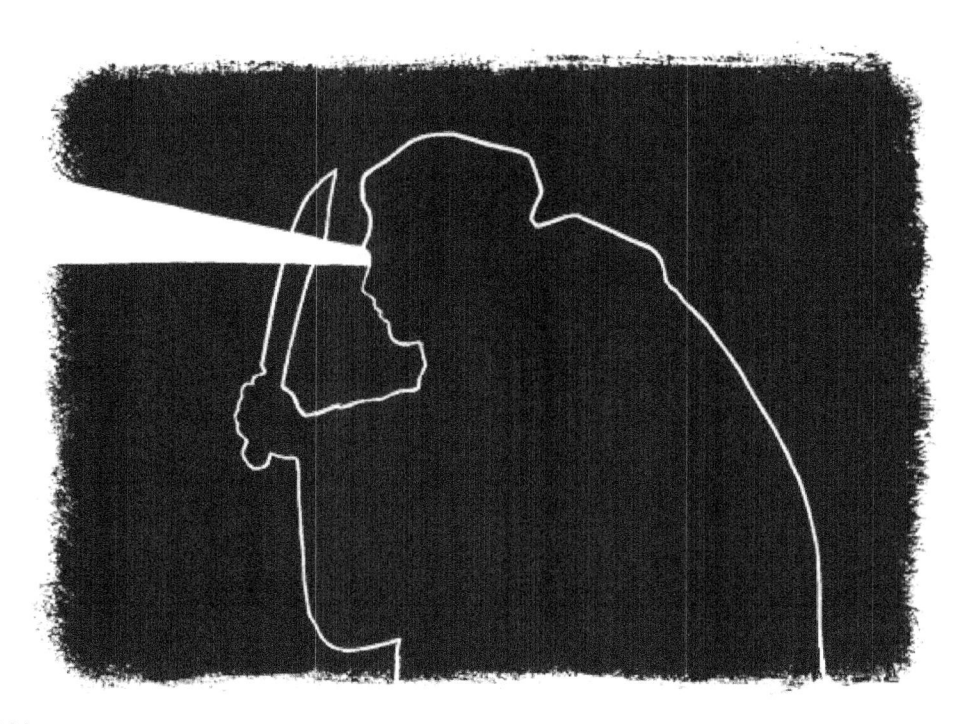

Fig. 150

Quick-lesson:
This is echoed in several Japanese shinobi schools, in particular, Fukushima-Ryu, where the eyes of a dog are placed on a string of hair and kept upon the ninja. In this way, he has "vision" at night. A version of this also appears in the shinobi lessons of Chikamatsu Shigenori.

Invisibility
Having fasted for three nights, one should, on the day of the star, Pushya, catch hold of the skull of a man who has been killed with a weapon or put to the gallows. Having filled the skull with soil and barley seeds, one should irrigate them with the milk of goats and sheep (Fig. 151). *Putting on the garland formed of the sprouts of the above barley crop, one can walk invisible to others.*

Fig. 151

Having fasted for three nights and having afterwards pulled out on the day of the star of Pushya both the right and the left eyes of a dog, a cat, an owl one should reduce them to two kinds of powder. Then having anointed one's own eyes with this ointment as usual, one can walk invisible to others.

Quick-lesson:
Similar magic is found in shinobi scrolls of Japan. According to the skills of the Iga and Koka shinobi, if one wished to infiltrate an enemy castle or mansion without being seen by the enemy, they are advised to trace certain Sanskrit words on a black dog's liver, dry it, grind it, wrap in gold brocade, carry it and when needed, crumble the powder above one's head.

The Female Power of Invisibility
Having fasted for three nights, one should, on the day of the star of Pushya, prepare a round-headed pin from the branch of punnága

Pushya is a star in Indian Hindu astronomy. Being born on the day of Pushya or undertaking new tasks on that day is considered auspicious.

241

(Rottleria tinctoria) tree. Then having filled with ointment the skull of any of the animals which roam at nights, and having inserted that skull in the organ of procreation of a dead woman, one should burn it (Fig. 152). Having taken it out on the day of the star of Pushya and having anointed one's own eyes with that ointment, one can walk invisible to others.

Fig. 152

The Bag of Invisibility

Wherever one may happen to see the corpse burnt or just being burnt of a Bráhmin who kept sacrificial fire (while alive), there one should fast for three nights; and having on the day of the star of Pushya formed a sack from the garment of the corpse of a man who has died from natural causes, and having filled the sack with the ashes of the Bráhmin's corpse, one may put on the sack on one's back, and walk invisible to others (Fig. 153).

Fig. 153

Snake Invisibility
The shed skin of a snake filled with the powder of the bones and marrow or fat of the cow sacrificed during the funeral rites of a Bráhmin, can, when put on the back of cattle, render them invisible.

The shed skin of a snake filled with the powder of the bone of the knee-joint mixed with that of the tail and dung of an owl and a váguli (unknown) can render birds invisible.

Quick-lesson:
It is difficult not to make connections between these above spells and some of the historical ninja scrolls of Japan. The question is: just what was transmitted alongside Buddhism when it reached Asia?

Sleep Magic
The incantation:
I bow to Bali, son of Virochana; to Sambara acquainted with a hundred kinds of magic; to Bhandírapáka, Naraka, Nikumbha, and Kumbha.
I bow to Devala and Nárada; I bow to Sávarnigálava; with the permission of these I cause deep slumber to thee.
Just as the snakes, known as boa constrictor fall into deep slumber, so may the rogues of the army who are very anxious to keep watch over the village;
With their thousands of dogs and hundreds of ruddy geese and donkeys, fall into deep slumber; I shall enter this house, and may the dogs be quiet.
Having bowed to Manu, and having tethered the roguish dogs, and having also bowed to those gods who are in heaven, and to Bráhmins among mankind;
To those who are well versed in their Vedic studies, those who have attained to Kailash (a mountain of god Shiva) by observing penance, and to all prophets, I do cause deep slumber to thee.
The fan comes out; may all combinations retire. Oblation to Manu, O Aliti and Paliti.

The application of the above mantra is as follows:
Having fasted for three nights, one should, on the fourteenth day of the dark half of the month, the day being assigned to the star of Pushya, purchase from a low-caste woman vilikhávalekhana (finger nails?). Having kept them in a basket, one should bury them apart in cremation grounds. Having unearthed them on the next fourteenth day, one should reduce them to a paste with aloe, and prepare small pills out of the paste.

> Is it possible that some ancient Indian magic travelled to the shinobi of Japan through the Asian mainland? The use of Sanskrit words and/or writing and mudras could suggest that it did.

Wherever one of the pills is thrown, chanting the above mantra, there the whole animal life falls into deep slumber.

Following the same procedure, one should separately bury in cremation grounds three white and three black dart-like hairs of a porcupine. When, having on the next fourteenth day taken them out, one throws them together with the ashes of a burnt corpse, chanting the above mantra, the whole animal life in that place falls into deep slumber.

The incantation:
I bow to Bali, the son of Virochana, to S'atamáya, Sambara, Nikumbha, Naraka, Kumbha, Tantukachchha, the great demon;
To Armálava, Pramíla, Mandolúka, Ghatodbala, to Krishna with his followers, and to the famous woman, Paulomi.
Chanting the sacred mantras, I do take the pith or the bone of the corpse productive of my desired ends – may S'alaka demons be victorious; salutation to them; oblation! – May the dogs which are anxiously keeping watch over the village fall into deep and happy slumber.
May all prophets fall into happy sleep about the object which we are seeking from sunset to sunrise and till the attainment of my desired end. Oblation!

The application of the above mantra is as follows:
Having fasted for four nights and having on the fourteenth day of the dark half of the month performed animal sacrifice in cremation grounds, one should, repeating the above mantra, collect the pith of a corpse and keep it in a basket made of leaves. When this basket, being pierced in the centre by a dart-like hair of a porcupine, is buried, chanting the above mantra, the whole animal life therein falls into deep slumber.

Dream Magic for Dogs
The incantation:
I bow to the goddess Suvarnapushpi and to Brahmáni, to the god Bráhma, and to Kusadhvaja; I bow to all serpents and goddesses; I bow to all ascetics.
May all Bráhmins and Kshatriyas come under my power; may all Vaishyas and, Shúdras be at my beck and call,
Oblation to thee, O, Amile, Kimile, Vayujáre, Prayoge, Phake, Kavayusve, Vihále, and Dantakatake, oblation to thee.
May the dogs which are anxiously keeping watch over the village fall into deep and happy slumber; these three white dart-like hairs of the porcupine are the creation of Bráhma.

All prophets have fallen into deep slumber. I do cause sleep to the whole village as far as its boundary till the sun rises. Oblation!

Quick-lesson:
The above mantras invoke several gods and demons which, according to Hindu scriptures and epics, possess great strength and magical powers. It is believed that they also grant blessings and boons to those who worship them. The following is a list of those who are more identifiable than the others:
- Bráhma – the god of creation. He is one of the three chief gods of Hinduism, along with Vishnu and Shiva.
- Brahmáni – the Divine Mother associated with the god Brahma
- Narada – son of Brahma. He has many supernatural powers such as travelling vast distances throughout the universe
- Devala – a great sage who was a disciple of the renowned sage, Vyasa, author of the *Mahabharata*. Like other sages, he possessed supernatural powers attained through spiritual practices. He is noted for cursing a Gandarva (celestial musician) to become a crocodile for annoying him during worship
- Krishna – the eighth incarnation of Vishnu, the preserver of the universe. He fought and defeated numerous evil men, such as Kamsa, and demons, such as Keshi, using hand-to-hand combat as well as divine powers
- Manu – the Hindu progenitor of humanity
- Paulomi – also known as Shachi, goddess of wrath and wife of thunder god, Indra. Her father was a demon
- Bali – a benevolent demon king and son of Vairochana, grandson of Prahlad (also compassionate demon kings) and great-grandson of the evil demon king, Hiranyakashipu (Fig. 154)
- Ghatodbala – possibly another name for Ghatotkacha, the half-demon son of Pandava warrior, Bhima. He helped the Pandava army fight the unrighteous Kaurava army using his supernatural abilities (Fig. 155)
- Naraka – also known as Narakasura, a malevolent being, son of Mother Earth who acquired magical powers and became full of pride and evil (Fig. 156)
- Sambara – also known as Shambarasura, a demon greatly skilled in the use of magic and illusions. He is also noted for kidnapping Krishna's son, Pradyumna, as well as engaging Krishna in combat using his powers (Fig. 157)
- Nikumbha and Kumbha – demonic warrior sons of Kumbhakarna, the gigantic younger brother of the demon king, Ravan (Fig. 158)

Fig. 154

Fig. 155

Fig. 156

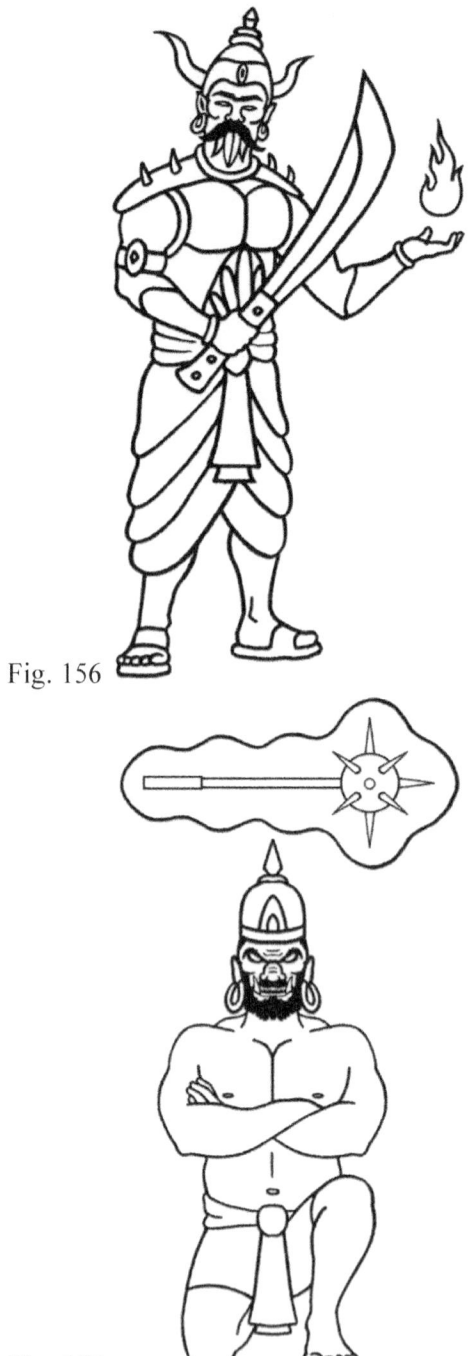

Fig. 157

247

Fig. 158

The application of the above mantra is as follows:
When a man, having fasted for seven nights and secured three white dart-like hairs of a porcupine, makes on the fourteenth day of the dark half of the month oblations into the fire with 108 pieces of the sacrificial fire-wood of mimosa catechu and other trees together with honey and clarified butter chanting the above mantra, and when, chanting the same mantra, he buries one of the hairs at the entrance of either a village or a house within it, he causes the whole animal life therein to fall into deep slumber.

Quick-lesson:
The above spells are to force any guard dog or the guards themselves to fall asleep so that the person can infiltrate.

Open Doors
The incantation:
I take refuge with the god of fire and with all the goddesses in the ten quarters; may all obstructions vanish and may all things come under my power. Oblation.

The application of the above mantra is as follows:
Having fasted for three nights and having on the day of the star of Pushya prepared twenty-one pieces of sugar-candy, one should make oblation into the fire with honey and clarified butter; and having worshipped the pieces of sugar-candy with scents and garlands of flowers, one should bury them. When, having on the next day of the star of

Pushya unearthed the pieces of sugar-candy, and chanting the above mantra, one strikes the door-panel of a house with one piece and throws four pieces in the interior, the door will open itself.

Travel to the Stars
Having fasted for four nights, one should on the fourteenth day of the dark half of the month get a figure of a bull prepared from the bone of a man, and worship it, repeating the above mantra. Then a cart drawn by two bulls will be brought before the worshipper who can (mount it and) drive in the sky and tell all that is connected with the sun and other planets of the sky (Fig. 159).

Fig. 159

> Ancient Indian texts mention various forms of air transport, known as Vimana, used by gods and demons for the purposes of travel and battle. For example, Book 3, Canto 35 and Book 5, Canto 7-8 of the *Ramayana* gloriously describes the Pushpaka, the aircraft of the demon king Ravan. Canto 10, Chapter 76-77 of the *Srimad Bhagavatam* includes a story about Krishna battling against a malicious king named Shalva who launches strikes from an aircraft named Saubha.

Even more Dream Magic

O, Chandáli Kumbhi, Tumba Katuka, and Sárigha, you are possessed of the power of a woman, oblation to you. When this mantra is repeated, the door will open and the inmates fall into sleep (Fig. 160).

Fig. 160

To Cut a String
Having fasted for three nights, one should on the day of the star of Pushya fill with soil the skull of a man killed with weapons or put to the gallows, and, planting in it vallari plants, should irrigate them with water. Having taken up the grown-up plants on the next day of the star of Pushya (i.e., after 27 days), one should manufacture a rope from them. When this rope is cut into two pieces before a drawn bow or any other shooting machine, the string of those machines will be suddenly cut into two pieces.

Organ Inflation
When the shed skin of a water-snake is filled with the breathed-out dirt of a man or woman (and is held before the face and nose of any person), it causes those organs to swell.

Increasing Your Size
When the sack-like skin of the abdomen of a dog or a boar is filled with the breathed-out dirt of a man or woman and is bound (to the body of a man) with the ligaments of a monkey, it causes the man's body to grow in width and length (Fig. 161).

Fig. 161

Blindness via Voodoo Dolls
When the figure of an enemy carved out of Cassia fistula is besmeared with the bile of a brown cow killed with a weapon on the fourteenth day of the dark half of the month, it causes blindness (to the enemy).

Unlucky Charms
Having fasted for four nights and offered animal sacrifice on the fourteenth day of the dark half of the month, one should get a few bolt-like pieces prepared from the bone of a man put to the gallows. When one of these pieces is put in the faeces or urine (of an enemy), it causes (his) body to grow in size; and when the same piece is buried under the feet or seat (of an enemy), it causes death by consumption; and when it is buried in the shop, fields, or the house (of an enemy), it causes him loss of livelihood.

The same process of smearing and burying holds good with the bolt-like pieces prepared from vidyuddanda tree.

- *When the nail of the little finger (punarnavam aváchínam?), Nimba melia, Bdellium, Celtis orientalis, the hair of a monkey, and the bone of a man, all wound round with the garment of a dead man is buried in the house of, or is trodden down by, a man, that man with his wife, children and wealth will not survive three fortnights.*
- *When the nail of the little finger, Nimba melia, Bdellium, Celtis orientalis, and the bone of a man dead from natural causes are buried under the feet of or near the house of, a man or in the vicinity of the camp of an army, of a village, or of a city, that man (or the body of men) with wife, children, and wealth will not survive three fortnights.*
- *When the hair of a sheep and a monkey, of a cat and mongoose, of Bráhmins, of low-caste men, and of a crow and an owl is collected, and is made into a paste with faeces, its application brings on instantaneous death.*
- *When a flower garland of a dead body, the ferment derived from burning corpse, the hair of a mongoose, and the skin of scorpion, a bee, and a snake are buried under the feet of a man, that man will lose all human appearance so long as they are not removed.*

The 'Horn of Plenty'
Having fasted for three nights and having on the day of the star of Pushya planted Abrus precatorius seeds in the skull, filled with soil, of a man killed with weapons or put to the

gallows, one should irrigate it with water. On the new or full moon day with the star of Pushya, one should take out the plants when grown, and prepare out of them circular pedestals. When vessels containing food and water are placed on these pedestals, the food stuffs will never decrease in quantity.

Magic Butter Dish
When a grand procession is being celebrated at night, one should cut off the nipples of the udder of a dead cow and burn them in a torch-light flame. A fresh vessel should be plastered in the interior with the paste prepared from these burnt nipples, mixed with the urine of a bull. When this vessel, taken round the village in circumambulation from right to left, is placed below, the whole quantity of the butter produced by all the cows (of the village) will collect itself in the vessel.

The Magic Fruit Bowl
On the fourteenth day of the dark half of the month combined with the star of Pushya, one should thrust into the organ of procreation of a dog or heat an iron seal and take it up when it falls down of itself. When, with this seal in hand, a collection of fruits is called out, it will come of itself (before the magician).

By the power of mantras, drugs, and other magical performances, one should protect one's own people and hurt those of the enemy.

Roundup
Modern soldiers use the 'five S's' to conceal their presence from their enemy, i.e.:
1. shape
2. shadow
3. spacing
4. shine
5. silhouette

Texts from Japan and India, such as the *Arthashastra*, show that the ancient warriors used smoke bombs, shields, powders, and spells to conceal themselves and their escape.

While Chanakya appears to be superstitious and an advocator of pseudo-sciences such as astrology, he points out some clearly logical advice:

"*Wealth will pass away from that childish man who inquires most after the stars; for wealth is the star for wealth; what will the stars do?*"

Book 11, Chapter 4

ASSORTED SECTIONS

Up until this point we have attempted to keep the text in the same position as it is in the original, having to move the position of only a few sections. Here on we have taken from the remaining chapters those points of interest and therefore they are eclectic. While there are still vast amounts of sections left out of this book – sections which are by no means uninteresting – the following selection should be considered as the parts that are easily assessable or which take less effort to interpret allowing the focus of introducing the *Arthashastra* to remain.

Encampment
A military camp is a temporarily facility for an army which is set up when an army is engaged in training or operations. Chanakya's plan for a camp appears organised and secure. He details the measures necessary to keep the king safe and indicates where every person and animal should dwell.

Layout
On a site declared to be the best according to the science of buildings, the leader, the carpenter, and the astrologer should measure a circular, rectangular, or square spot for the camp which should, in accordance with the available space, consist of four gates, six roads, and nine divisions (Fig. 162).

The following section is from Book 10, Chapter 1 of the original text.

Fig. 162

The Kings Quarters

Provided with ditches, parapets, walls, doors, and watch towers for defence against fear, the quarters of the king, 1,000 bows long and half as broad, should be situated in one of the nine divisions to the north from the centre, while to the west of it his harem, and at its extremity the army of the harem are to be situated. In his front, the place for worshipping gods; to his right the departments of finance and accounts; and to his left the quarters of elephants and horses mounted by the king himself. Outside this and at a distance of 100 bows from each other, there should be fixed four cart-poles pillars and walls. In the first (of these four divisions), the prime minister and the priest (should have their quarters); to its right the store-house and the kitchen: to its left the store of raw products and weapons; in the second division the quarters of the hereditary army and of horses and chariots: outside this, hunters and keepers of dogs with their trumpets and with fire; also spies and sentinels; also, to prevent the attack of enemies, wells, mounds and thorns should be arranged. The eighteen divisions of sentinels employed for the purpose of securing the safety of the king should be changing their watches in turn. In order to ascertain the movements of spies, a time-table of business should also be prepared during the day. Disputes, drinking, social gatherings, and gambling should also be prohibited. The system of passports should also be observed. The officer in charge of the boundary (of the camp) should supervise the conduct of the commander-in-chief and the observance of the instructions given to the army.

The instructor with his retinue and with carpenters and free labourers should carefully march in front on the road, and should dig wells of water.

The following section is from Book 5, Chapter 3 of the original text.

Wages

The chiefs of military corporations, the chiefs of elephants, of horses, of chariots and of infantry and commissioners, 8,000 (panas). With this amount they can have a good following in their own communities.

The Superintendents of infantry, of cavalry, of chariots and of elephants, the guards of timber and elephant forests, 4,000.

The chariot-driver, the physician of the army, the trainer of horses, the carpenter, and those who rear animals, 2,000.

Spies such as the fraudulent, the indifferent, the house-holder, the merchant, and the ascetic 1,000.
The village-servant, fiery spies, poisoners and mendicant women, 500.
Servants leading the spies, 250 or in proportion to the work done by them.

Quick-lesson:
Have a set pay for set positions so that the men have clarity.

The Use of Spies

> The following section is from Book 1, Chapter 13 of the original text.

Spies shall also know the rumours prevalent in the state. Spies with shaved heads or braided hair shall ascertain whether there prevails content or discontent among those who live upon the grains, cattle, and gold of the king, among those who supply the same (to the king) in weal or woe, those who keep under restraint a disaffected relative of the king or a rebellious district, as well as those who drive away an invading enemy or a wild tribe. The greater the contentment of such persons, the more shall be the honour shown to them; while those who are disaffected shall be ingratiated by rewards or conciliation; or dissension may be sown among them so that they may alienate themselves from each other, from a neighbouring enemy, from a wild tribe, or from a banished or imprisoned prince. Failing this measure, they may be so employed in collecting fines and taxes as to incur the displeasure of the people. Those who are inebriated with feelings of enmity may be put down by punishment in secret or by making them incur the displeasure of the whole country. Or having taken the sons and wives of such treacherous persons under State protection, they may be made to live in mines, lest they may afford shelter to enemies.

Quick-lesson:
Spies must be utilised to the full and information must find its way back to a central hub.

Discover Hidden Relationships

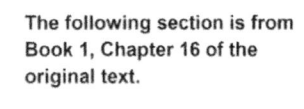

The following section is from Book 1, Chapter 16 of the original text.

Those that are angry, those that are greedy, those that are alarmed, as well as those that despise the king are the instruments of enemies. Spies under the guise of astrologers and tellers of omens and augury shall ascertain the relationship of such persons with each other and with foreign kings.

Quick-lesson:
Discover who is in league with whom. Do not be unaware of any hidden relationships.

Duties of the envoy-spy
- *transmission of missions*
- *maintenance of treaties*
- *issue of ultimatum*
- *gaining of friends*
- *intrigue*
- *sowing dissension among friends*
- *fetching secret force*
- *carrying away by stealth relatives and gems*
- *gathering information about the movements of spies*
- *bravery*
- *breaking of treaties of peace*
- *winning over the favour of the envoy and government officers of the enemy*

The envoy shall make friendship with the enemy's officers such as those in charge of wild tracts, of boundaries, of cities, and of country parts. He shall also contrast the military stations, sinews of war, and strong-holds of the enemy with those of his own master. He shall ascertain the size and area of forts and of the state, as well as strongholds of precious things and assailable and unassailable points.

The king shall employ his own envoys to carry on works of the above description, and guard himself against (the mischief of) foreign envoys by employing counter envoys, spies, and visible and invisible watchmen.

Quick-lesson:
While on a mission as an envoy, discover important facts about the enemy, to defend against others and to be the eyes and ears of the king.

Tricks with a Prince

(The following section is from Book 1, Chapter 17 of the original text.)

Allure the prince towards hunting, gambling, liquor, and women, and instigate him to attack his own father and snatch the reins of government in his own hands. Another spy shall prevent him from such acts.

Tricks with the king

(The following section is from Book 1, Chapter 18 of the original text.)

Or having disguised himself as a painter, a carpenter, court-bard, a physician, a buffoon, or a heretic, and assisted by spies under similar disguise, he may, when opportunity affords itself, present himself armed with weapons and poison before the king, and address him:

"I am the heir-apparent; it does not become thee to enjoy the state alone when it is enjoyable by both of us, or when others justly desire such enjoyment; I ought not to be kept away by awarding an allowance of double the subsistence and salary."

Spies or his mother, natural or adoptive, may reconcile an heir-apparent under restraint and bring him to the court.

Or secret emissaries armed with weapons and poison may kill an abandoned prince. If he is not abandoned, he may be caught hold of at night by employing women equal to the occasion, or by making use of liquor, or on the occasion of hunting, and brought back (to the court).

Generational Retainers

The following section is from Book 1, Chapter 21 of the original text.

The king shall employ as his personal attendants those whose fathers and grandfathers had been royal servants, those who bear close relationship to the king, those who are well trained and loyal, and those who have rendered good service.

Neither foreigners, nor those who have earned neither rewards nor honour by rendering good service, nor even natives found engaged in inimical works shall form the bodyguard of the king or the troops of the officers in charge of the harem.

Quick-lesson:
Keep those who are proved loyal about the leader.

Poison in the Food

In a well-guarded locality, the head-cook shall supervise the preparation of varieties of relishing dishes. The king shall partake of such fresh dishes after making an oblation out of them first to the fire and then to birds.

The reason for this is thus:
- *when the flame and the smoke turn blue and crackle, and when birds (that eat the oblation) die, presence of poison (in the dish) shall be inferred*
- *when the vapour arising from cooked rice possesses the colour of the neck of a peacock, and appears chill as if suddenly cooled, when vegetables possess an unnatural colour, and are watery and hardened, and appear to have suddenly turned dry, being possessed of broken layers of blackish foam, and being devoid of smell, touch and taste natural to them*
- *when utensils reflect light either more or less than usual, and are covered with a layer of foam at their edges*
- *when any liquid preparation possesses streaks on its surface*
- *when milk bears a bluish streak in the centre of its surface*
- *when liquor and water possess reddish streaks*

- *when curd is marked with black and dark streaks, and honey with white streaks*
- *when watery things appear parched as if overcooked and look blue and swollen*
- *when dry things have shrunk and changed in their colour*
- *when hard things appear soft, and soft things hard*
- *when microscopic animals die in the vicinity of the dishes*
- *when carpets and curtains possess blackish circular spots, with their threads and hair fallen off*
- *when metallic vessels set with gems appear tarnished as though by roasting, and have lost their polish, colour, shine, and softness of touch*

In all the above presence of poison shall be inferred.

Quick-lesson:
When food or eating utensils appear different to how they should, consider that poison has been administered.

The Culprit
As to the person who has administered poison, the marks that display them are:
- *parched and dry mouth*
- *hesitation in speaking*
- *heavy perspiration*
- *yawning*
- *too much bodily tremor*
- *frequent tumbling*
- *evasion of speech*
- *carelessness in work*
- *unwillingness to keep to the place assigned to him*

Quick-lesson:
If a person who is committing an act of treason does not have the correct amount of 'nerve', a change in their behaviour can give them away.

Target Practice
With a view of acquiring efficiency in the skill of shooting arrows at moving objects, he shall engage himself in sports in such forests as are cleared by hunters and hound-keepers from the fear of high-way-robbers, snakes, and enemies.

Quick-lesson:
Shooting areas should be designated and cleared of dangers. Shooting practice may be done here.

More Spy Disguises

The following section is from Book 4, Chapter 4 of the original text.

The Collector-general shall employ spies disguised as persons endowed with:
- *supernatural power*
- *persons engaged in penance*
- *ascetics*
- *world trotters*
- *bards*
- *buffoons*
- *mystics*
- *astrologers*
- *prophets foretelling the future*
- *persons capable of reading good or bad time*
- *physicians*
- *lunatics*
- *the dumb*
- *the deaf*
- *idiots*
- *the blind*
- *traders*
- *painters*
- *carpenters*
- *musicians*
- *dancers*
- *wine makers*
- *manufacturers of cakes, flesh and cooked rice*

Send the above abroad into the country for espionage.

> The following section is from Book 7, Chapter 3 of the original text.

The Six-fold Policy

A king desirous of expanding his own power shall make use of the six-fold policy:

Agreements of peace shall be made with equal and superior kings; and an inferior king shall be attacked.

Whoever goes to wage war with a superior king will be reduced to the same condition as that of a foot-soldier opposing an elephant.

Just as the collision of an unbaked mud-vessel with a similar vessel is destructive to both, so war with an equal king brings ruin to both.

Like a stone striking an earthen pot, a superior king attains decisive victory over an inferior king.

If a superior king discards the proposal of an inferior king for peace, the latter should take the attitude of a conquered king, or play the part of an inferior king towards a superior.

When a king of equal power does not like peace, then the same amount of vexation as his opponent has received at his hands should be given to him in return; for it is power that brings about peace between any two kings: no piece of iron that is not made red-hot will combine with another piece of iron.

When an inferior king is all submissive, peace should be made with him; for when provoked by causing him troubles and anger, an inferior king, like a wild fire, will attack his enemy and will also be favoured by (his) Circle of States.

When a king in peace with another finds that greedy, impoverished, and oppressed as are the subjects of his ally, they do not yet immigrate into his own territory lest they might be called back by their master, then he should, though of inferior power, proclaim war against his ally.

When a king at war with another finds that greedy, impoverished, and oppressed as are the subjects of his enemy, still they do not come to his side in consequence of the troubles of war, then he should, though of superior power, make peace with his enemy or remove the troubles of war as far as possible.

When one of the two kings at war with each other and equally involved in trouble finds his own troubles to be greater than his enemy's, and thinks that by getting rid of his (enemy's) trouble his enemy can successful wage war with him, then he should, though possessing greater resources, sue for peace.

When, either in peace or war, a king finds neither loss to his enemy nor gain to himself, he should, though superior, observe neutrality.

When a king finds the troubles of his enemy irremediable, he should, though of inferior power, march against the enemy.

When a king finds himself threatened by imminent dangers or troubles, he should, though superior, seek the protection of another.

When a king is sure to achieve his desired ends by making peace with one and waging war with another, he should, though superior, adopt the double policy.

Thus it is that the six forms of policy are applied together.

> The following section is from Book 1, Chapter 13 of the original text.

Spy on the Leaders
Having set up spies over his prime ministers, the king shall proceed to espy both citizens and country people.

Quick-lesson:
Spy on your own leaders.

Target Those Angered
Those that are angry, those that are greedy, those that are alarmed, as well as those that despise the king are the instruments of enemies. Spies under the guise of astrologers and tellers of omens and

augury shall ascertain the relationship of such persons with each other and with foreign kings.

Quick-lesson:
Build relationships with those who have been outcast by a leader and gain information from them. Hattori Hanzo in his ninja scroll *Shinobi Hiden* gives the same advice.

Mark the Weapons

> The following section is from Book 5, Chapter 3 of the original text.

Weapons and armour shall be entered into the armoury only after they are marked with the king's seal.

Quick-lesson:
Mark the equipment kept in the arsenal so that it can be identified.

Stop the Movement of Armed Persons
Persons with weapons shall not be allowed to move anywhere unless they are permitted by a passport. Boundary-guards shall take away the weapons and armour possessed by caravans unless the latter are provided with a passport to travel with weapons.

Quick-lesson:
Prevent the general populace from bearing arms to ensure superiority.

Spy on the Ways of the Allied Forces
Spies, prostitutes, artisans, singers, and aged military officers shall vigilantly examine the pure or impure conduct of military men.

> The following section is from Book 7, Chapter 2 of the original text.

Quick-lesson:
Send out people among your own men to get a true feeling for their qualities.

Make Peace Not War
When the advantages derivable from peace and war are of equal character, one should prefer peace; for disadvantages, such as the loss of power and

wealth, sojourning, and sin, are ever-attending upon war.
The same holds good in the case of neutrality and war. Of the two (forms of policy), double policy and alliance, double policy (i.e., making peace with one and waging war with another) is preferable; for whoever adopts the double policy enriches himself, being ever attentive to his own works, whereas an allied king has to help his ally at his own expense.

Quick-lesson:
If war does not give enough prospects for profit, then remain at peace, for war is costly.
The two forms of policy:
- Double policy – being at peace with one but going to war with another; the only costs are the costs you yourself amass
- Alliance – to be allied with another means that costs may be dictated by their plans.

Sometimes it is best to be at war without allies instead of being allied with someone who may cost you more.

Pick Your Friends
One shall make an alliance with a king who is stronger than one's neighbouring enemy; in the absence of such a king, one should ingratiate oneself with one's neighbouring enemy, either by supplying money or army or by ceding a part of one's territory and by keeping oneself aloof; for there can be no greater evil to kings than alliance with a king of considerable power, unless one is actually attacked by one's enemy.

Quick-lesson:
If there is an enemy close by, chose a more powerful ally or sue for peace.

When the Enemy Falls
A powerless king should behave as a conquered king (towards his immediate enemy); but when he finds that the time of his own ascendancy is at hand due to a fatal disease, internal troubles, increase of enemies, or a friend's calamities that are vexing his enemy, then under the pretence of performing some expiatory rites to avert the danger of his enemy, he may get out (of the enemy's court); or if he is in his own territory, he should not go to see his suffering enemy; or if he is near to his enemy, he may murder the enemy when opportunity affords itself.

Quick-lesson:
If a leader is lacking in power but the enemy suddenly falls from theirs, use this opportunity to ascend.

Strike the Fallen

> The following section is from Book 7, Chapter 4 of the original text.

When a king finds that his enemy has fallen into troubles; that the troubles of his enemy's subjects can by no means be remedied; that as his enemy's subjects are oppressed, ill-treated, disaffected, impoverished, become effeminate and disunited among themselves, they can be prevailed upon to desert their master; that his enemy's country has fallen a victim to the inroads of such calamities, as fire, floods, pestilence epidemics, and famine and is therefore losing the flower of its youth and its defensive power, then he should march after proclaiming war.

Quick-lesson:
When an enemy's lands are in turmoil, attack after a declaration of war has been given.

Enemies to the Front and Rear
When a king is so fortunate as to have a powerful friend in front and a powerful ally in the rear, both with brave and loyal subjects, while the reverse is the case with enemies both in front and in the rear, and when he finds it possible for his friend to hold his frontal enemy in check, and for his rear-ally to keep his rear-enemy at bay, then he may march after proclaiming war against his frontal enemy.

When a king finds it possible to achieve the results of victory single-handed in a very short time, then he may march (against his frontal enemy) after proclaiming war against his rear-enemies; otherwise he should march after making peace (with his rear-enemies).

When a king finds himself unable to confront his enemy single-handed and when it is necessary that he should march, then he should make the expedition in combination with kings of inferior, equal, or superior powers.

Quick-lesson:
When commencing a campaign of war, make sure to correctly predict and account for the actions of other states around you.

Spoils of War
When the object aimed at is of a definite nature, then the share of spoils should be fixed; but when it is of a manifold or complex nature, then with no fixity in the share of the spoils. When no such combination is possible, he may request a king either to supply him with the army for a fixed share, or to accompany him for an equal share of the spoils.

When profit is certain, then they should march with fixed shares of profit; but when it is uncertain, with no fixity of shares.

Share of profit proportional to the strength of the army is of the first kind; that which is equal to the effort made is the best; shares may be allotted in proportion to the profit earned or to the capital invested.

> The following section is from Book 7, Chapter 5 of the original text.

Quick-lesson:
Have a definite contract about the splitting of war booty. If the amount is known then a fixed split can be decided upon, if it is not known then the split should be in relation to amount of forces each leader gives.

Who to Kill?
When two enemies, one an assailable enemy and another a strong enemy, are equally involved in troubles, which of them is to be marched against first?

The strong enemy is to be marched against first; after vanquishing him, the assailable enemy is to be attacked, for, when a strong enemy has been vanquished, an assailable enemy will volunteer of his own accord to help the conqueror; but not so, a strong enemy.

Which is to be marched against; an assailable enemy involved in troubles to a greater degree or a strong enemy troubled to a lesser degree?

Others say:
My teacher says that as a matter of easy conquest, the assailable enemy under worse troubles should be marched against first.

Chanakya disagrees and states:
Not so: The conqueror should march against the strong enemy under less troubles, for the troubles of the strong enemy, though less, will be augmented when attacked. True, that the worse troubles of the assailable enemy will be still worse when attacked. But when left to himself, the strong enemy under less troubles will endeavour to get rid of his troubles and unite with the assailable enemy or with another enemy in the rear of the conqueror.

When there are two assailable enemies, one of virtuous character and under worse troubles, and another of vicious character, under less troubles, and with disloyal subjects, which of them is to be marched against first?

When the enemy of virtuous character and under worse troubles is attacked, his subjects will help him; whereas, the subjects of the other of vicious character and under less troubles will be indifferent. Disloyal or indifferent subjects will endeavour to destroy even a strong king. Hence the conqueror should march against that enemy whose subjects are disloyal.

Which is to be marched against; an enemy whose subjects are impoverished and greedy or an enemy whose subjects are being oppressed?

Others say:
My teacher says that the conqueror should march against that enemy whose subjects are impoverished and greedy, for impoverished and greedy subjects suffer themselves to be won over to the other side by intrigue, and are easily excited. But not so the oppressed subjects whose wrath can be pacified by punishing the chief men (of the State).

Chanakya disagrees and states:
Not so, for though impoverished and greedy, they are loyal to their master and are ready to stand for his cause and to defeat any intrigue against him; for it is in loyalty that all other good qualities have their strength. Hence the conqueror should march against the enemy whose subjects are oppressed.

Which enemy is to be marched against; a powerful enemy of wicked character or a powerless enemy of righteous character?

The strong enemy of wicked character should be marched against, for when he is attacked, his subjects will not help him, but rather put him down or go to the side of the conqueror. But when the enemy of virtuous character is attacked, his subjects will help him or die with him.

Quick-lesson:
While an opportunity for war may seem positive, you may be vastly wrong about the reaction of the people on the 'knock on effects' that a war may have. Make sure to correctly predict the reaction of the people that you are to conquer.

Improper conduct as a ruler
- *by insulting the good and commending the wicked*
- *by causing unnatural and unrighteous slaughter of life*
- *by neglecting the observance of proper and righteous customs*
- *by doing unrighteous acts and neglecting righteous ones*
- *by doing what ought not to be done and not doing what ought to be done*
- *by not paying what ought to be paid and exacting what ought not to be taken*
- *by not punishing the guilty and severely punishing the less guilty*
- *by arresting those who are not to be caught hold of and leaving those who are to be arrested*
- *by undertaking risky works and destroying profitable ones*
- *by not protecting the people against thieves and by robbing them of their wealth*
- *by giving up manly enterprise and condemning good works*
- *by hurting the leaders of the people and despising the worthy*
- *by provoking the aged, by crooked conduct, and by untruthfulness*
- *by not applying remedies against evils and neglecting works in hand*
- *by carelessness and negligence of himself in maintaining the security of person and property of his subjects*

With the above, the king causes impoverishment, greed, and disaffection to appear among his subjects and when a people are impoverished, they become greedy; when they are greedy, they become disaffected; when disaffected, they voluntarily go to the side of the enemy or destroy their own master. Hence, no king should give room to such causes as would bring about impoverishment, greed or disaffection among his people. If, however, they appear, he should at once take remedial measures against them.

Quick-lesson:
If a leader has constant improper conduct, the far-reaching consequences will be that the people will support the enemy in a time of war so that such an improper ruler is overthrown.

The Three Types of People
Which (of the three) is the worst?
 1. *impoverished people*
 2. *greedy people*
 3. *disaffected people*

Impoverished people are ever apprehensive of oppression and destruction (by overtaxation, etc.), and are therefore desirous of getting rid of their impoverishment, or of waging war or of migrating elsewhere.
Greedy people are ever discontented and they yield themselves to the intrigues of an enemy
Disaffected people rise against their master along with his enemy

The Solution to Impoverishment
When the dwindling of the people is due to want of gold and grain, it is a calamity fraught with danger to the whole of the kingdom and can be remedied with difficulty. The lack of efficient men can be made up by means of gold and grain.

The Solution to Greed
Greed (is) partial and is found among a few chief officers, and it can be got rid of or satisfied by allowing them to plunder an enemy's wealth.

The Solution to Disaffection
Disaffection or disloyalty can be got rid of by putting down the leaders; for in the absence of a leader or leaders, the people are easily governed and they will not take part in the intrigues of enemies. When a people are too nervous to endure the calamities, they first become dispersed, when their leaders are put down; and when they are kept under restraint, they endure calamities.

Quick-lesson:
Having the impoverished, the greedy and disaffected people among your own people will result in calamity. Take steps to remedy the situation.

Combing Kings

Having well considered the causes which bring about peace or war, one should combine with kings of considerable power and righteous character and march against one's enemy.

'A king of considerable power,' means one who is strong enough to put down or capture an enemy in the rear of his friend or to give sufficient help to his friend in his march.

'A king of righteous character,' means one who does what one has promised to do, irrespective of good or bad results.

Having combined with one of superior power, or with two of equal power among such kings, should the conqueror march against his enemy?

It is better to march combined with two kings of equal power; for, if combined with a king of superior power, the ally appears to move, caught hold of, by his superior, whereas in marching with two kings of equal power, the same will be the result, only, when those two kings are experts in the art of intrigue; besides it is easy to separate them; and when one of them is wicked, he can be put down by the other two and made to suffer the consequence of dissension.

Combined with one of equal power or with two of lesser power, should a king march against his enemy?

Better to march with two kings of lesser power; for the conqueror can depute them to carry out any two different works and keep them under his control. When the desired end is achieved, the inferior king will quietly retire after the satisfaction of his superior.
Till his discharge, the good conduct of an ally of usually bad character should be closely scrutinised either by suddenly coming out at a critical time from a covert position to examine his conduct, or by having his wife as a pledge for his good conduct.
Though actuated with feelings of true friendship, the conqueror has reason to fear his ally, though of equal power, when the latter attains success in his mission; having succeeded in his mission, an ally of equal power is likely to change his attitude even towards the conqueror of superior power.

An ally of superior power should not be relied upon, for prosperity changes the mind. Even with little or no share in the spoils, an ally of superior power may go back, appearing contented; but some time afterwards, he may not fail to sit on the lap of the conqueror and carry off twice the amount of share due to him.

Having been satisfied with mere victory, the leading conqueror should discharge his allies, having satisfied them with their shares he may allow himself to be conquered by them instead of attempting to conquer them (in the matter of spoils); it is thus that a king can win the good graces of his Circle of States.

Quick-lesson:

When in need of assistance, avoid a very strong enemy so as to avoid being devoured by them afterwards. Use weaker allies because they are easier to control. Be wary of allies in general, for they can never be trusted. However, sometimes, a king should know when to give up his share of things to win the favour of others.

Using Peace to Kill

The following section is from Book 7, Chapter 6 of the original text.

When, in order to destroy an enemy who has fallen into troubles and who is hasty, indolent, and not foresighted, an agreement of peace with no terms of time, space, or work is made with an enemy merely for mutual peace, and when under cover of such an agreement, the enemy is caught hold of at his weak points and is struck, it is termed peace with no definite terms.

Some Forms of Peace
- *peace with no specific end*
- *peace with binding terms*
- *the breaking of peace*
- *restoration of peace broken*

When, by the employment of friends (at the Courts of each other), the agreement of peace made is kept secure and the terms are invariably observed and strictly maintained so that no dissension may creep among the parties, it is termed peace with binding terms.

When, having proved through the agency of traitors and spies the treachery of a king, who has made an agreement of peace, the agreement is broken, it is termed the breaking of peace.

When reconciliation is made with a servant, or a friend, or any other renegade, it is termed the restoration of broken peace.

When the kings of superior, equal or inferior power make peace with the conqueror and agree to pay a greater, or equal, or less amount of profit in proportion to the army supplied, it is termed even peace; that which is of the reverse character is styled uneven peace; and when the profit is proportionally very high, it is termed deception.

Quick-lesson:
Peace is not an entity that remains the same. Peace can come in multiple forms.

The Three Forms of Battle
- *open battle*
- *treacherous battle*
- *silent battle (killing an enemy by employing spies when there is no talk of battle at all)*

Runaways
There are four persons who run away from, and return to, their master:
1. *one who had reason to run away and to return*
2. *one who had no reason either to run away or to return*
3. *one who had reason to run away, but none to return*
4. *and one who had no reason to run away, but had reason to come back*

He who runs away owing to his master's fault and returns in consideration of (his master's) good nature, or he who runs away attracted by the good nature of his master's enemy and returns finding fault with the enemy is to be reconciled as he had reason to run away and to return.

Whoever runs away owing to his own fault and returns without minding the good nature either of his old or new master is a fickle-minded person having no explanation to account for his conduct, and he should have no terms of reconciliation.

Whoever runs away owing to his master's fault and returns owing to his own defects, is a renegade who had reason to run away, but none to return: and his case is to be well considered (before he is taken back).

Whoever returns deputed by the enemy; or of his own accord, with the intention of hurting his old master, as is natural to persons of such bad character; or coming to know that his old master is attempting to put down the enemy, his new master, and apprehensive of danger to himself; or looking on the attempt of his new master to destroy his old master as cruelty, these should be examined; and if he is found to be actuated with good motives, he is to be taken back respectfully; otherwise, he should be kept at a distance.

Whoever runs away owing to his own fault and returns owing to his new master's wickedness is a renegade who had no reason to run away, but had reason to come back; such a person is to be examined.

When a king thinks that:
"This renegade supplies me with full information about my enemy's weakness, and, therefore, he deserves to remain here; his own people with me are in friendship with my friends and at enmity with my enemies and are easily excited at the sight of greedy and cruel persons or of a band of enemies,"
He may treat such a renegade as deserved.

Quick-lesson:
If a retainer, employee or a servant has left but then returns, consider the reason why they left and the reasons for why they have returned. Some reasons are acceptable, some are not and there may even be treachery.

The following section is from Book 7, Chapter 10 of the original text.

Forms of Workers
- *whoever undertakes tolerable work is a beginner of possible work*
- *whoever undertakes an unblemished work is a beginner of praiseworthy work*
- *whoever undertakes work of large profits is a beginner of a productive work*
- *whoever takes no rest before the completion of the work undertaken is a resolute worker*

Fortified Victory

Enemies being equally strong, he who acquires territory after beating a fortified enemy overreaches the other; for the capture of a fort is conducive to the protection of territory and to the destruction of wild tribes.

Which is Best?
Question:

Which is better, a small piece of land, not far, or an extensive piece of land, very far?
Answer:
A small piece of land, not far, is better, inasmuch as it can be easily acquired, protected, and defended, whereas the other is of a reverse nature.

Question:
Which is better, acquisition of land from a stupid or a wise king?
Answer:
That acquired from a stupid king is better, as it can be easily acquired and secured, and cannot be taken back, whereas that obtained from a wise king, beloved of his subjects, is of a reverse nature.

Question:
Which is easier, seizing land from those who fight on plains, or from those who fight from low grounds?
Answer:
Seizing the land from the latter is easier, inasmuch as they have to fight in time and space of adverse nature whereas the former can fight anywhere and at any time.

The Cost of War
Others say:
My teacher says that in an open war, both sides suffer by sustaining a heavy loss of men and money; and that even the king who wins a victory will appear as defeated in consequence of the loss of men and money.

Chanakya disagrees and states:
No, even at considerable loss of men and money, the destruction of an enemy is desirable.

Quick-lesson:
Here this slightly differs from Sun Tzu who states that war is not preferable due to the vast costs.

The Wise Sages
Whoever is wanting in the power of deliberation should collect wise men around himself, and associate with old men of considerable learning; thus he would attain his desired ends.

Quick-lesson:
Surround yourself with people who will promote good decisions.

Irrigation
Irrigational works are the source of crops; the results of a good shower of rain are ever attained in the case of crops below irrigational works.

Quick-lesson:
Ensure that the lands you hold are at their optimum capacity of production.

Maintain the Roads
The roads of traffic are a means to overreach an enemy; for it is through the roads of traffic that armies and spies are led (from one country to another); and that weapons, armour, chariots, and draught-animals are purchased; and that entrance and exit (in travelling) are facilitated.

Quick-lesson:
Maintenance of roadways helps facilitate trade and war.

Mines
Mines are the source of whatever is useful in battle.

Forests
Timber-forests are the source of such materials as are necessary for building forts, conveyances and chariots.

Elephants
Elephant-farms are the source of elephants.

Pasture lands
Pasture-lands are the source of cows, horses, and camels to draw chariots.

In Need of Resources

> The following section is from Book 7, Chapter 14 of the original text.

In the absence of such above sources of his own, he should acquire them from someone among his relatives and friends. If he is destitute of an army, he should, as far as possible, attract to himself the brave men of corporations, of thieves, of wild tribes, of Mlechchhas, and of spies who are capable of inflicting injuries upon enemies.

> The following section is from Book 7, Chapter 15 of the original text.

The Moth and the Flame
Others say:
My teacher says that one may rush against the enemy like a moth against a flame; success in one way or other (i.e., death or victory) is certain for one who is reckless of life.

Chanakya disagrees and states:
No, having observed the conditions conducive to peace between himself and his enemy, he may make peace; in the absence of such conditions, he may, by taking recourse to threats secure peace or a friend; or he may send a messenger to one who is likely to accept peace; or having pleased with wealth and honour the messenger sent by his enemy, he may tell the latter:
"This is the king's manufactory; this is the residence of the queen and the princes; myself and this kingdom are at your disposal, as approved of by the queen and the princes."

Having secured his enemy's protection, he should:
- *behave himself like a servant to his master by serving the protector's occasional needs*
- *forts and other defensive works*
- *acquisition of things*
- *celebration of marriages*

- *installation of the heir-apparent*
- *commercial undertakings*
- *capture of elephants*
- *construction of covert places for battle, marching against an enemy*
- *holding sports*

All these he should undertake only at the permission of his protector. He should also obtain his protector's permission before making any agreement with people settled in his country or before punishing those who may run away from his country. If the citizens and country people living in his kingdom prove disloyal or inimical to him, he may request of his protector another good country; or he may get rid of wicked people by making use of such secret means as are employed against traitors. He should not accept the offer of a good country even from a friend. Unknown his protector, he may see the protector's minister, high priest, commander of the army or heir-apparent. He should also help his protector as much as he can. On all occasions of worshipping gods and of making prayers, be should cause his people to pray for the long life of his protector; and he should always proclaim his readiness to place himself at the disposal of his protector.

Serving him who is strong and combined with others and being far away from the society of suspected persons, a conquered king should thus always behave himself towards his protector.

Quick-lesson:
If it is likely that defeat will come, secure your position under a powerful overlord and serve them well.

The Sacred Oath of Peace

> The following section is from Book 7, Chapter 17 of the original text.

In case of any apprehension of breach of honesty, [kings of old] made their agreement by swearing by:
- *fire*
- *water*
- *plough*
- *the brick of a fort-wall*
- *the shoulder of an elephant*
- *the hips of a horse*
- *the front of a chariot*
- *a weapon*
- *seeds*

- *scents*
- *juice*
- *wrought gold*
- *bullion gold*

By declaring that these things will destroy and desert him who violates the oath [peace was gained].

Women Are Trouble
In peace made with children as hostages, and in the case of giving a princess or a prince as a hostage, whoever gives a princess gains advantages; for a princess, when taken as a hostage, causes troubles to the receiver, while a prince is of reverse nature.

Many Sons Are Not Wanted
With regard to two sons, whoever hands over a highborn, brave and wise son, trained in military art, or an only son is deceived, while he who acts otherwise gains advantages. It is better to give a base-born son as an hostage than a high-born one, inasmuch as the former has neither heirship nor the right to beget heirs; it is better to give a stupid son than a wise one, inasmuch as the former is destitute of the power of deliberation; better to give a timid son than a brave one, inasmuch as the former is destitute of martial spirit; better, a son who is not trained in military art than one who is trained, inasmuch as the former is devoid of the capacity for striking an enemy; and better one of many sons than an only son, since many sons are not wanted.

Quick-lesson:
If hostages must be given, give one that can be lost.

Make More Sons
When peace is made by handing over the whole lot of sons, advantage is to be sought in capacity to beget additional sons; capacity to beget additional sons being common, he who can beget able sons will have more advantages than another king (who is not so fortunate); capacity to beget able sons being common, he by whom the birth of a son is early expected will have more advantages than another (who is not so fortunate).
In the case of an only son who is also brave, he who has lost capacity to beget any more sons should surrender himself as a hostage, but not the only son.

Steal Back Your Son
Whoever is rising in power may break the agreement of peace. Carpenters, artisans, and other spies, attending upon the prince (kept as a hostage) and doing work under the

enemy, may take away the prince at night through an underground tunnel dug for the purpose. Dancers, actors, singers, players on musical instruments, buffoons, court-bards, swimmers, previously set about the enemy, may continue under his service and may indirectly serve the prince. They should have the privilege of entering into, staying in and going out of, the palace at any time without rule. The prince may therefore get out at night disguised as any one of the above spies (Fig. 163).

Fig. 163

This explains the work of prostitutes and other women spies under the garb of wives; the prince may get out, carrying their pipes, utensils, or vessels.

The prince may be removed concealed under things, clothes, commodities, vessels, beds, seats and other articles by cooks, confectioners, servants employed to serve the king while bathing, servants employed for carrying conveyances, for spreading the bed, toilet-making, dressing, and procuring water; or taking something in pitch dark, he may get out, disguised as a servant.

He may (pretend to) be in communion with god Varuna in a reservoir (which is seen) through a tunnel or to which he is taken at night; spies under the guise of traders dealing in cooked rice and fruits may (poison those things and) distribute among the sentinels (Fig. 164).

Fig. 164

Having served the sentinels with cooked rice and beverage mixed with the juice of madana plant on occasions of making offerings to gods or of performing an ancestral ceremony or some sacrificial rite, the prince may get out; or by bribing the sentinels; or spies disguised as an officer in charge of the city, a court-bard, or a physician may set fire to a building filled with valuable articles; or sentinels or spies disguised as merchants may set fire to the store of commercial articles; or in view of avoiding the fear of pursuit, the prince may, after putting some human body in the house occupied by him, set fire to it and escape by breaking open some house-joints, or a window, or through a tunnel (Fig. 165); or having disguised himself as a carrier of glass-beads, pots, and other commodities, he may set out at night; or having entered the residence of ascetics with shaven heads or with twisted hair, he may set out at night, disguised as any one of them; or having disguised himself as one suffering from a peculiar disease or as a forest-man, he may get out; or spies may carry him away as a corpse; or disguised as a widowed wife, be may follow a corpse that is being carried away. Spies disguised as forest-people, should mislead the pursuers of the prince by pointing out another direction, and the prince himself may take a different direction.

Fig. 165

He may escape, hiding himself in the midst of carts of cart-drivers; if he is closely followed, he may lead the pursuers to an ambuscade, in the absence of an ambuscade he may leave here and there gold or morsels of poisoned food on both sides of a road and take a different road.

If he is captured, he should try to win over the pursuers by conciliation and other means, or serve them with poisoned food; and having caused another body to be put in a sacrifice performed to please god Varuna or in a fire that has broken out (the prince's father), may accuse the enemy of the murder of his son and attack the enemy.
Or taking out a concealed sword, and falling upon the sentinels, he may quickly run away together with the spies concealed before.

Quick-lesson:
Escape via a variety of means is possible. In case of trouble, survive and use bribery, poison or blades. Assistance of spies will be helpful.

Calamities

The following section is from Book 8, Chapter 1 of the original text.

Others say:
My teacher says that of the calamities [listed below]: that which is first mentioned is more serious than the one, coming later in the order of enumeration

- *the king in distress*
- *the minister in distress*
- *the people in distress*
- *distress due to bad fortifications*
- *financial distress*
- *the army in distress*
- *an ally in distress*

No, says Bháradvája, of the distress of the king and of his minister, ministerial distress is more serious [because]:

- *deliberations in council*
- *the attainment of results as anticipated while deliberating in council*
- *the accomplishment of works*
- *the business of revenue-collection and its expenditure*
- *recruiting the army*
- *the driving out of the enemy and of wild tribes*
- *the protection of the kingdom*
- *taking remedial measures against calamities*

282

- *the protection of the heir-apparent*
- *the installation of princes constitutes the duties of ministers*

In the absence of ministers; the above works are ill-done; and like a bird, deprived of its feathers, the king loses his active capacity. In such calamities, the intrigues of the enemy find a ready scope. In ministerial distress, the king's life itself comes into danger, for a minister is the mainstay of the security of the king's life.

Chanakya says:
No, it is verily the king who attends to:
- *the business of appointing ministers, priests, and other servants, including the superintendents of several departments*
- *the application of remedies against the troubles of his people, and of his kingdom*
- *the adoption of progressive measures*

when his ministers fall into troubles, he employs others; he is ever ready to bestow rewards on the worthy and inflict punishments on the wicked; when the king is well off, by his welfare and prosperity, he pleases the people; of what kind the king's character is, of the same kind will be the character of his people; for their progress or downfall, the people depend upon the king; the king is, as it were, the aggregate of the people.

Visáláksha says that of the troubles of the minister and of the people; the troubles of the people are more serious:
- *finance*
- *army*
- *raw products*
- *free labour*
- *carriage of things*
- *collection (of necessaries)*

These are all secured from the people. There will be no such things in the absence of people, next to the king and his minister.

Chanakya says:
No, activities proceed from the minister, activities such as:
- *the successful accomplishment of the works of the people*
- *security of person and property from internal and external enemies*
- *remedial measures against calamities*

- *colonization and improvement of wild tracts of land*
- *recruiting the army*
- *collection of revenue*
- *bestowal of favour*

Quick-lesson:
A leader's force is made up of its leader, his commanders and the bulk of the people. There will be misfortune if one of them should fall.

Troubles within an Army

The following section is from Book 8, Chapter 5 of the original text.

The troubles of the army are:
- *that which is disrespected*
- *that which is mortified*
- *that which is not paid for*
- *that which is diseased*
- *that which has freshly arrived*
- *that which has made a long journey*
- *that which is tired*
- *that which has sustained loss*
- *that which has been repelled*
- *that of which the front portion is destroyed*
- *that which is suffering from inclemency of weather*
- *that which has found itself in an unsuitable ground*
- *that which is displeased from disappointment*
- *that which has run away*
- *that of which the men are fond of their wives*
- *that which contains traitors*
- *that of which the prime portion is provoked*
- *that which has dissensions*
- *that which has come from a foreign state*
- *that which has served in many states*
- *that which is specially trained to a particular kind of manoeuvre and encampment*

- *that which is trained to a particular movement in a particular place*
- *that which is obstructed*
- *that which is surrounded*
- *that which has its supply of grains cut off*
- *that which has its men and stores cut off*
- *that which is kept in one's own country*
- *that which is under the protection of an all*
- *that which contains inimical persons*
- *that which is afraid of an enemy in the rear*
- *that which has lost its communication*
- *that which has lost its commander*
- *that which has lost its leader*
- *that which is blind (i.e., untrained)*

Remedies for the above troubles

Of the disrespected and the mortified among these, that which is disrespected may be taken to fight after being honoured, but not that which is suffering from its own mortification.

Of unpaid and diseased armies, the unpaid may be taken to fight after making full payment but not the diseased, which is unfit for work.

Of freshly arrived and long-travelled armies, that which has freshly arrived may be taken to fight after it has taken its position without mingling with any other new army, but not that which is tired from its long journey.

Of tired and reduced armies, the army that is tired may be taken to fight after it has refreshed itself from bathing, eating, and sleeping, but not the reduced army, i.e., the army, the leaders of which have been killed.

Of armies which have either been repelled or have their front destroyed, that which has been repelled may be taken to fight together with fresh men attached to it, but not the army which has lost many of its brave men in its frontal attack.

Of armies, either suffering from inclemency of weather or driven to an unsuitable ground, that which is suffering from inclemency of weather may be taken to fight after providing it with weapons and dress appropriate for the season, but not the army on an unfavourable ground obstructing its movements.

Of disappointed and renegade armies, that which is disappointed may be taken to fight after satisfying it but not the army which has (once) run away.

Of soldiers who are either fond of their wives or are under an enemy, those who are fond of their wives may be taken to fight after separating them from their wives; but not those who are under an enemy, and are, therefore, like internal enemies.

Of provoked and disunited armies, that, of which a part is provoked, may be taken to fight after pacifying it by conciliation and other strategic means but not the disunited army, the members of which are estranged from each other.

Of armies which have left service either in one state or in many states, that whose resignation of service in a foreign state is not due to instigation or conspiracy may be taken to fight under the leadership of spies and friends, but not the army which has resigned its service in many states and is, therefore, dangerous.

Of armies which are trained either to a particular kind of manoeuvre and encampment or to a particular movement in a particular place, that which is taught a special kind of manoeuvre and encampment may be taken to fight, but not the army whose way of making encampments and marches is only suited for a particular place.

Of obstructed and surrounded armies, that which is prevented from its movements in one direction may be taken to fight against the obstructer in another direction, but not the army whose movements are obstructed on all sides.

Of troops whose supply of grain is cut off or whose supply of men and stores is cut off, that which has lost its supply of grain may be taken to fight after providing it with grain brought from another quarter or after supplying to it moveable and immoveable food-stuffs (animal and vegetable food-stuffs) but not the army to which men and provisions cannot be supplied.

Of armies kept in one's own country or under the protection of an ally, that which is kept in one's own country can possibly be disbanded in time of danger, but not the army under the protection of an ally, as it is far removed in place and time.

Of armies either filled with traitors, or frightened by an enemy in the rear, that which is full of traitors may be taken to fight apart under the leadership of a trusted commander, but not the army which is afraid of an attack from the rear.

Of armies without communication or without leaders, that which has lost its communication with the base of operations may be taken to fight after restoring the communication and placing it under the protection of citizens and country people, but not the army which is without a leader such as the king or any other persons.

Of troops which have lost their leader or which are not trained, those that have lost their leader may be taken to fight under the leadership of a different person but not the troops which are not trained.

Quick-lesson:
Identify any issues that will weaken a section of your force and make arrangements to nullify the issue.

The Hereditary and Conscripted Army

> The following section is from Book 9, Chapter 2 of the original text.

Hereditary army is better than hired army inasmuch as the former has its existence dependent on that of its master, and is constantly drilled.

That kind of hired army which is ever near, ready to rise quickly, and obedient, is better than a corporation of soldiers.

That corporation of soldiers which is native, which has the same end in view (as the king), and which is actuated with similar feelings of rivalry, anger, and expectation of success and gain, is better than the army of a friend. Even that corporation of soldiers which is further removed in place and time is, in virtue of its having the same end in view, better than the army of a friend.

The army of an enemy under the leadership of an Arya is better than the army of wild tribes. Both of them (the army of an enemy and of wild tribes) are anxious for plunder. In the absence of plunder and under troubles, they prove as dangerous as a lurking snake.

> The word Arya is a Sanskrit word meaning "noble" and is an honorific title given to those of a honourable and upright character. It is also associated with the Brahmin and Kshatriya class which are considered noble social orders. From this word, we get the English word "Aryan".

Quick-lesson:
While it is situation dependent, a permanent army has benefits over a recruited one.

Opposing armies
The army which possesses:
- *elephants*
- *machines*
- *sakatagarbha – unknown*
- *lances*
- *barbed darts*
- *kharvataka – unknown*
- *bamboo sticks*
- *iron sticks*

This is the army to oppose an army of elephants.

The same possessed of:
- *stones*
- *clubs*
- *armour*
- *hooks*
- *spears*

With the above in plenty, this is the army to oppose an army of chariots.

Continued:
- *The same is the army to oppose cavalry*
- *Men, clad in armour, can oppose elephants*
- *Horses can oppose men, clad in armour*

Men, clad in armour, chariots, men possessing defensive weapons, and infantry can oppose an army consisting of all the four constituents:
1. *elephants*
2. *chariots*
3. *cavalry*
4. *infantry*

Thus considering the strength of the constituents of one's own quadripartite army, one should recruit men to it so as to oppose an enemy's army successfully.

Danger, Danger
The various kinds of dangers are:

> The following section is from Book 9, Chapter 5 of the original text.

- *that which is of external origin and of internal abetment*
- *that which is of internal origin and of external abetment*
- *that which is of external origin and of external abetment*
- *and that which is of internal origin and of internal abetment*

Quick-lesson:
Threats can come internally or externally and can also be quelled internally or externally.

Rumour
When foreigners are abetting, the king should employ the policy of dissension and coercion.
Spies under the guise of friends may inform foreigners:
"Mind, this man is desirous of deceiving you with the help of his own spies who are disguised as traitors."

Spies under the garb of traitors may mix with traitors and separate them from foreigners, or foreigners from local traitors.

Fiery spies may make friendship with traitors and kill them with weapons or poison; or having invited the plotting foreigners, they may murder the latter.

> The following section is from Book 9, Chapter 6 of the original text.

Quick-lesson:
Disrupt any allegiance between your own men and outsiders by the use of spies.

The Five Gifts
Gifts are of five kinds:
1. *abandonment of what is to be paid*
2. *continuance of what is being given*
3. *repayment of what is received*
4. *payment of one's own wealth*
5. *help for a voluntary raid on the property of others*

Without a Fiery Spy
Spies under concealment may, without the help of a fiery spy, murder by means of weapons, poison or other things a fortified enemy who is of mean character or who is under troubles; any one of hidden spies may do the work when it is found easy; or a fiery spy alone may do the work by means of weapons, poison or fire; for a fiery spy can do what others require all the necessary aids to do.

Quick-lesson:
Normal spies may sometimes murder without the aid of a trained assassin.

Flesh and Water
- *When the country is full of local enemies, they may be got rid of by making them drink poisonous (liquids).*
- *An obstinate (clever) enemy may be destroyed by spies or by means of (poisoned) flesh given to him in good faith.*

Quick-lesson:
Resort to poisoning both water and food to kill those who are in the way.

ROUNDUP

The selection chosen above does do justice to the original text but it is of course not the text in its entirety and is not even a full account of all of the aspects of warfare found in Chanakya's teachings. It is, however, a great gateway into those teachings and to the world of ancient Indian warfare. It must be understood that this collection has been picked from a vast array of skill-sets and, therefore, for a complete understanding, we advise that the full translation should be read, including those books which offer their commentaries on the more political aspects of the manual. The selection chosen here is, of course, the exciting and the remarkable, the strange and the perplexing, giving the teachings a mysterious and thrusting edge of interest. While some aspects are direct and applicable, some are outlandish, mystical and obscure. The potions, poisons, concoctions and substances are deserved of a full chemical analysis and should be the topic of a future university student and, until that time, should not be fully dismissed as historical madness and as of yet should not be considered as truth. The assassination skills are ingenious and the spy work not only predates most records of espionage but is also fully developed and more detailed than most, with the exception of some Chinese scrolls and the shinobi scrolls of Japan which are as detailed if not more so (see author's other titles). The tactics given offer an open window into this ancient world, allowing us to see the weapons and defences used, giving a 'smell' of an atmosphere of war in which countless people had died and gone unnamed, allowing them to have a 'face' at last. This leaves our generation and the generations to come to help spread the word of the *Arthashastra* and Chanakya's teachings, allowing them to continue down the ages, inspiring each new generation to dig deeper into their story.

THE COLLECTED QUICK-LESSONS

The Quick-lessons found in this text are a breakdown of the individual lessons found in the selection of the original text and have been listed here to give an overview of the core lessons found in our selection of Chanakya's manual.

Lessons for War
Have intelligent people search the land for plots and rebellions.

Land is given to a trusted person, land which yields profit, the profit is then used to feed and provide for spies who venture out into the lands around to gather information and discover who is against the ruler.

Take those who have fallen on hard times (but not through their own fault) and provide for them so that they can become spies.

Any merchant who has fallen on hard times (but not through their own fault) shall be given land so that they can continue their trade but with the aim of espionage.

Bogus holy men are set up with a residence; word of their austere living should be made public. The pilgrims who come to see the holy man will bring information to the spy as they gather. In secret, the bogus holy man eats anything they wish.

Once set in position, informants bring information to the bogus holy man, who then appears to predict the truth of a target's situation. Upon making a prediction, agents of the ruler bring the outcome about. Through this, movement and aims in society can be monitored. Powerful people will trust in this 'holy man' and secrets will come fourth. Thus, gather information on a person, predict a future for that person, have the ruler bring about such a predicted future. As a result, the 'holy man' will have a solid reputation and will become a centre point for gathering where news will be gathered.

Using people of all backgrounds and professions to gather intelligence will give a king eyes and ears everywhere. Those with the ability to calculate likely future events are most ideal.

The five institutes of espionage are:
1. The Fraudulent Disciple
2. The Recluse
3. The Cultivator

    4. The Trader/merchant
    5. The Priest

Orphanages are to be funded and trained up as agents.

Fire-brand spies are considered as assassins and 'dare-devil commandos'.

Assassination via poison is a suitable method for heartless persons.

Destitute but beautiful and intelligent women should be used as spies.

Send out 'nuns' and women who live religious lives to gather information.

The gathering of information needs a central hub. The separate parts should not know of the existence of the other sections. This is done to validate the information which is streaming in from different channels. Have a network of spies that reaches out to the edges of the 'world' and have the information sent back to the central hub.

Spies who gather bad intelligence must face dire consequences. Often spies may simply forecast their own ideas of a situation, instead of actually doing the reconnaissance themselves, leading to a supply of bad information.

Those in the employ of the enemy who are also spies shall receive income from both the enemy and the lord who has retained them as spies.

Keeping a spy's family as hostage will encourage their loyalty.

Set up outposts in strategic places to gather information on traffic in the land.

Spies sent by the enemy must be sought out and discovered.

Secrecy in espionage was a serious matter. The *Bansenshukai* shinobi manual and the shinobi teachings of a warrior known as Chikamatsu Shigenori both build on teachings from Chinese classics, stating that any spy who gives away any information, shall be, along with the person who is informed of any plan, put to death. This is used as a deterrent, stopping spies from leaking any information out, especially to those close to them.

Weapon care is a high priority, and all weapons must be understood and maintained, down to the smallest details.

Keep an accurate record of the origin, history and current location of 'vehicles'.

Make sure each individual can maintain their equipment with the resources given to them.

Animals must be kept in good living conditions for them to remain healthy animals.

A good horse must be raised and maintained well and given the correct duties in accordance with its temperament.

Carriages can move 48, 72 or 96 miles per day and riding horses can move 40, 64 and 80 miles per day.

Good horses should be cared for by both natural and supernatural means. People failing in their duty shall be fined accordingly.

Constant monitoring of troop training will lead to a better trained army.

Project the outcome of any action of war beforehand and ascertain if it is a positive move or not. If not, do not make a move.

Know the difference between *enthusiasm for power* and *power*.

Master the following three; they are in order of importance:
1. skill for intrigue
2. power
3. enthusiasm

Land that is best suited to the army, aides that army.

The time that is best suited to an army, aides that army.

Know the different seasons and fight accordingly because each has their advantages and disadvantages.

Do not simply attack an enemy because they appear to be in period of internal trouble. The truth of their situation may not be fully apparent. Only march to war when you are prepared, especially when you are prepared and the enemy are in trouble.

A military vehicle should be suited to the environment.

The stages of a route and the waypoints of any military operation must be properly planned.

Know the difference between what should be a short campaign and what will be a long one.

When moving an army, keep to the following:
1. Plan a route
2. Know what resources are along the route
3. Know the distances
4. Carry extra food in case of emergencies
5. If food cannot be carried, use the troops to carry it. If the troops cannot carry it, position it in storage areas

Have a structured set up to ensure security and order.

Water crossing has to be done by individuals and by masses of troops. The above cover both, from bridges for the masses down to floatation devices such as rafts and gourds. Interestingly, the baskets covered with skins also appear in the ninja manual, *Bansenshukai*.

Do not cross bodies of water without a clear exit strategy.

At any point where an army is at more of a risk than other times, insert extra effort into defending the troops, whether on the move on in camp.

Set up scouts at points where an enemy army will pass. It is performed in this manner because the army have to break up into single file, thus the scouts can easily count the troop numbers, troop types, weapons and size of the baggage train.

Deception before a strike gives an advantage. False retreats, feints and unexpected attacks all tip the balance and give favour to an army using such tactics. Notice the use of leather and cotton to silence the enemy on night attacks and the concept of attacking when facing the sun.

Men who die in battle will ascend to the place where preachers and men of the cloth spend their lives trying to be. The general is saying here: *"Fight for me and gain entrance to heaven"*. Likewise, the general is also saying: *"Do not fight for me and go to hell"*.

Surround the leader with loyal men. Hide him in the ranks of normal men and have his doppelganger assume his place. From here the leader can command while the other becomes a target.

Supply the army with a feeling of ease before a battle to gain a confident feel in the forces and be clear on rewards to be given for specific actions.

To come to terms and give peace should only be done in certain circumstances, likewise, to destroy a broken enemy should only be done at certain times. An army may be broken up but if it faces utter destruction it will gain resolve and the fight will be hard. Totally destroy an army when success is guaranteed, but if not, then bring about peace on your own terms.

Have the right men do the right job and train for all conditions.

Know the ground ahead and establish if vehicles can move along such terrain.

Fast moving vehicles are needed on the battlefield.

Use heavy and powerful equipment if feasible.

The 'four constituents' are:
1. infantry
2. cavalry
3. chariots
4. elephants

Think of the following:
- A spearman is a soldier with a bayonet-fixed rifle
- The elephant is a heavy tank

- A chariot is a lightly armoured weapon-mounted jeep

The enemy should be outnumbered and outgunned.

A commander should not risk letting inferior troops lead the way. He must have his best men do what they do best.

When the enemy is not formed with strength or has internal issues. Send the best men.

Have mobile troops understand manoeuvres and precision movement.

Brihaspati – the guru of the gods. He is the lord of prayer and rituals, and is also identified with the planet Jupiter in Indian astrology. Chanakya refers to his school of thought in his text.

Cunning is superior to strength.

A weak leader should use espionage and covert death squads against his powerful enemy to compensate his lack of conventional power.

A love potion should be substituted for poison. In the second situation, a maid servant is placed in the employment of another and when she has gained trust, she administers poison instead of a love potion or medicine.

Face reading is an ancient skill where a person's features would divine their future. The spy should give a false reading to benefit the situation.

Spread rumours to force the enemy to do something they would not normally do so as to take advantage of it.

Bring people together under the guise of false orders from the enemy commander or lord. Then have them killed as if the enemy lord had killed them. The enemy should be demonised by making them appear villainous and bloodthirsty.

Instil paranoia into the enemy king and stir trouble between them and their aides, advisors and troops.

Bribes should be given to the correct people. Choose those who will turn for a price and who have key positions or those who feel resentment towards their lord.

When in a difficult situation, use wealth to secure aid and safety.

The enemy of the enemy is a friend. Buy their friendship as well as pass on vital intelligence to them about the common enemy.

Drink and food will be closely monitored. Therefore, gain trust with good wine and food, then at the right time move to poison the enemy.

Become a trusted supplier to the enemy and poison them.

Discreetly poison the food-stuffs of innocent traders, after which other spies can purchase those food-stuffs and then sell them on to unaware enemies.

If you know the enemy will attack have something to tempt them placed nearby so that their aim is changed.

Destruction upon the enemy can be given in various forms:
- by fire
- by wild animals
- by venomous animals
- by causing panic in animals

Leave troops to destroy enemy:
- supplies
- reserves
- escape

Do not give up at the sight of overwhelming forces. There is a way out. Think laterally and use the power of others, deception and geography to your advantage.

If a powerful enemy is in a position superior to yours, appease them with land and gifts that are either, trouble to hold or easy to take back.

The abstract is also a gift. The absence of fear is the gift of safety.

A conqueror should convince others their intelligence is gathered via supernatural means. This will demonstrate their power, thereby boosting the morale of his side and demoralising the opposition.

Create fake miracles. Some examples from the text:
1. using a tunnel, the fake god comes up in the middle of a fire, on to an alter or talks from within a hollow statue
2. using rafts, fake gods can be brought up from water
3. using flammable and floating liquids, fire can be seen to 'magically' spread over water at the command of the fake prophet balanced on a raft

A conqueror should convince others that he is a middleman between deities and humans. This 'prophet-hood' will win him support and power.

Religious propaganda is to be used to bring about love for a lord, fear in an enemy and awe in the population. A commander of guile should construct situations which appear to show the gods giving favour to their army.

Set the enemy mind at ease with promises of fair treatment upon surrender or defeat.

Know what actions or situations will sway the mind of a king. Provide for him an opportunity that even a king would not decline. In this manner and the ones below, the movements and placement of the king can be directed – at which point he can be snatched.

Create a situation where a leader would venture out of his normal security circle so as to kill or take him.

Spies must cause people to believe divine punishment is coming to their leaders.

Create the illusion and appearance of that which people fear on the edge of their fortification to cause panic to spread.

Create an area where hidden assassins can move freely. Entice a leader to enter this area and kill him.

A spy, knowing the positioning or the whereabouts of a leader, waits in hiding. Then upon killing the enemy uses the ensuing panic to make an escape.

A fortress with numerous security measures will make it formidable and ensure a king's safety.

One must prepare their base to the fullest so there is no chance of penetration by enemy forces. Weapons and tools to repel the enemy must be made ready.

The easiest way to get past enemy lines is to fake defection to the enemy side. Once in, lure the enemy into a trap.

Spreading suspicion and disunity among an enemy is advantageous, especially when the enemy starts killing their own.

A leader can kill or capture an enemy by luring them through a variety of ways, including unity, gifts, alliances and agreements. Bring an enemy into the allied force and then destroy them.

A leader can help their friend by deceiving the enemy of their ally. They make an agreement with the enemy of their ally, but during the agreement, switch sides

A leader should separate two inseparable allies by stirring rivalry among them. He should have them believe that one of them will turn on the other.

A leader should use their men to infiltrate the opposition and cause chaos from within. This skill directly resembles Sun Tzu's *The Art of War* and the Doomed Spy. The Japanese shinobi-trained Chikamatsu Shigenori and the shinobi, Fujibayashi Yasutake, give examples of using your own men by making it appear that they have been driven from the land and relieved of their position. At which point the enemy takes them in, to gain information. However, as they are still loyal, they spread disinformation.

Having sent an agent to make friends with the enemy forces, the agent allows the enemy to catch out spies or thieves – which again is a classic doomed spy tactic – and after having gained the trust of the enemy, inform them of a large raid. Then during the night, an allied force pretends to be the army returning from the fray, when they are admitted to the fortress, they kill the people within.

Once the enemy's stronghold has been infiltrated, the spirit of defeatism should be spread among the enemy forces to the point that it causes the enemy's downfall. Here, forces take up residence inside the enemy's castle long before the allied force attacks. These hidden agents smuggle weapons and tools. Then when the call of attack is given, they will take the fort gates in the surprise.

Before any hint of war is given, have men and supplies take up residence and position within an enemy fort. This will allow allied forces to remain on the inside.

Drugging an enemy makes it easy work to kill and loot.

- Reduce the power of an enemy that is to be sieged
- Keep the peace in a territory conquered
- End rebellion by lifting tax and giving gifts
- Tax a conquered enemy heavily before abandoning the land
- Destroy stores and crops if needs be

A leader should crush an enemy who is suffering hardships because they will be at their weakest. Victory will be swift.

The conqueror must be in a state of substantial and of preparation. The enemy must be in a state of insubstantial and unpreparedness

One whose own fortification is up-to-date, should tamper with the enemy's fortification in order to disturb its security and overpower the enemy.

The use of fire is an effective means to cause havoc among an enemy. Various means to apply fire should be prepared and utilised. Shinobi literature states that these types of small balls can be held in the hand as lights, thrown into dark corridors to illuminate places or thrown into a thatch.

Do not destroy those things that can be kept whole.

Fire can be extinguished if it is not set at an opportune time.

A king should feign friendship with an enemy in order to lower the enemy's guard so that killing or stealing from them will be no difficult task.

An enemy can be lured out and trapped if they can be convinced that the dangers posed against them have ceased.

Fill the enemy's stores with poison by deceptive means.

Spies should aid external destruction by causing internal damage.

Arrange an agreement between yourself and an intended enemy. Construct a plan to kill a mutual enemy of you both but use this as a ruse so that when your 'ally' comes out of their defences, they can be killed.

Once victory has been secured with surety, be benevolent to the defeated and enjoy victory.

A leader can conquer the world in three ways:
1. neutralising a middle king
2. gain support from the enemy's people,
3. neutralising friends and enemy's alike with strategy and might

To keep captured land, govern with grace and correctness.

One overlooked aim of the spy is to sow discontent among the enemy. This can be done in two main ways.
1. the spy may infiltrate themselves among the high ranking officers of the enemy, causing arguments between them
2. multiple spies moving around the lower echelons of the population of a target area, spreading stories and false rumours about certain people so that the news of their treachery spreads throughout, effecting the trust given to them by the lord

Remove anyone who is not loyal or obedient.

A spy can kill a rebellious minister by getting a jealous member of the minister's own family to carry out the task. Once the brother is successful, they should be demonised so that they are also removed.

Spies can eliminate targets by causing family strife.

By causing internal strife, a spy can cause deaths without suspicion. To 'frame' an unwanted minister, a leader may murder the minister's next of kin so that it appears that the minister has killed the next of kin to secure his own position. Upon which a leader can lawfully execute the minister.

A spy should turn son against father by misinforming them and tempting them with a position of power that they have a 'right' to. However, the son will not achieve what he desires as he too will be demonised and then eliminated.

Poison an enemy through making a connection with their family.

A leader wishing to eradicate an unwanted minister may send them on a fake mission and then have spies kill them upon the road.

A leader may need to keep excellent spies. Therefore, after use, give them the death sentence but replace them with common folk at the execution – allowing them to live on and continue their espionage.

Bring the target close, embroil them in a sex scandal and have rid of them.

Create a situation where it appears that a leader's target has tried to kill the leader. Then have them executed as a punishment.

Make the death of a target look like it resulted due to a misadventure during something they have a passion for.

Convince the target of an illness by adopting the guise of a trusted person (such as a doctor) then poison them with the cure.

A leader may send out someone they wish dead to undertake a fake task. Next, send out a second group to enter into conflict with the first, spies will take the opportunity to kill the target during the upcoming fight, making people believe that the target was killed due to a confrontation which has no connection to the leader.

Order a raid on a property, then push the blame and punishment for this on another person.

Poison a dinner party and force blame onto others.

Anger and cause two people to fight over the same woman and a leader may not have to get his hands dirty to have one of them killed.

If a rebellious minister is put down but their son is loyal to the leader, leave them in authority.

A spy or assassin should use hidden compartments to conceal themselves. They should also disguise themselves as people that are expected to be there and to use a person's lust against them.

Spies must be able to disguise themselves, to act out a role and to adopt a persona. The shinobi of Japan centred their arts of disguise and the adoption of persona, taking on the mantle of other identities and becoming that person.

Give the men high-energy foods to help them keep hunger at bay.

Use chemical warfare to make the enemy sick.

Luminescence at night can be used for various activities.

Use fireproof pastes so that men can move through burning places and awe spectators.

Have a set pay for set positions so that the men have clarity.

Spies must be utilised to the full and information must find its way back to a central hub.

Discover who is in league with whom. Do not be unaware of any hidden relationships.

While on a mission as an envoy, discover important facts about the enemy, to defend against others and to be the eyes and ears of the king.

Keep those who are proved loyal about the leader.

When food or eating utensils appear different to how they should, consider that poison has been administered.

If a person who is committing an act of treason does not have the correct amount of 'nerve', a change in their behaviour can give them away.

Shooting areas should be designated and cleared of dangers. Shooting practice may be done here.

Spy on your own leaders.

Mark the equipment kept in the arsenal so that it can be identified.

Prevent the general populace from bearing arms to ensure superiority.

Send out people among your own men to get a true feeling for their qualities.

If war does not give enough prospects for profit, then remain at peace for war is costly. The two forms of policy:
- Double policy – being at peace with one but going to war with another; the only costs are the costs you yourself amass
- Alliance – to be allied with another means that costs may be dictated by their plans.

Sometimes it is best to be at war without allies instead of being allied with someone who may cost you more.

If there is an enemy close by, chose a more powerful ally or sue for peace.

If a leader is lacking in power but the enemy suddenly falls from theirs, use this opportunity to ascend.

When an enemy's lands are in turmoil then attack after a declaration of war has been given.

When commencing a campaign of war, make sure to correctly predict and account for the actions of other states around you.

Have a definite contract about the splitting of war booty. If the amount is known then a fixed split can be decided upon, if it is not known then the split should be in relation to amount of forces each leader gives.

While an opportunity for war may seem positive, you may be vastly wrong about the reaction of the people of the 'knock on effects' that a war may have. Make sure to correctly predict the reaction of the people that you are to conquer.

If a leader has constant improper conduct, the long reaching consequences will be that the people will support the enemy in a time of war so that such an improper ruler is overthrown.

Having the impoverished, the greedy and disaffected people among your own people will result in calamity. Take steps to remedy the situation.

When in need of assistance, avoid a very strong enemy so as to avoid being devoured by them afterwards. Use weaker allies because they are easier to control. Be wary of allies in general, for they can never be trusted. However, sometimes, a king should know when to give up his share of things to win the favour of others.

Peace is not an entity that remains the same. Peace can come in multiple forms.

If a retainer, employee or a servant has left but then returns, consider the reason why they left and the reasons for why they have returned. Some reasons are acceptable, some are not and there may even be treachery.

Surround yourself with people who will promote good decision.

Ensure that the lands you hold are at their optimum capacity of production.

Maintenance of roadways helps facilitate trade and war.

If it is likely that defeat will come, secure your position under a powerful overlord and serve them well.

If hostages must be given, give one that can be lost.

A leader's force is made up of its leader, his commanders and the bulk of the people. There will be misfortune if one of them should fall.

Identify any issues that will weaken a section of your force and make arrangements to nullify the issue.

While it is situation dependent, a permanent army has benefits over a recruited one.

Threat can come internally or externally and can also be quelled internally or externally.

Disrupt any allegiance between your own men and outsiders by the use of spies.

Normal spies may sometimes murder without the aid of a trained assassin.

Resort to poisoning both water and food to kill those who are in the way.

GLOSSARY (SANSKRIT-ENGLISH)

Achala – Immovable. The name of a battle formation
Agninidhána – Fire pots
Agnisamyógas – Explosives
Ákásayuddha – Fighting from heights
Ákranda – Powerful ally
Angavidya – Palmistry, the practice of predicting a person's future by interpreting their hand lines
Antara-chakra – Augury, the practice of interpreting omens
Apratihata – An elephant-repelling protective device
Apratihata – Invincible. The name of a battle formation
Ardhabáhu – Half-sized crushing-pillar
Arishta – Auspicious. The name of a battle formation
Arka – Calotropis gigantea, which can be used to make bow-strings
Atharvaveda – One of the four *Vedas*, Hinduism's oldest and holiest books. Written in Sanskrit, the focus of this *Veda* is charms, prayers and spells. Chanakya mentions this *Veda* in his text
Asahya – Irresistible. The name of a battle formation
Asiyashti – A sword with a long, thin blade
Ásphátima – Catapult, a ballistic device for launching projectiles
Audaka – Water-fortification
Audhghátima – A siege engine used to ram the gates and walls of forts
Ávápa – Surplus, the excess of an army

Bahumukha – Tower from which archers can shoot arrows at the enemy
Bali – Animal sacrifice
Báhirikas – Outsider, foreigner
Bhed – The strategy of dividing an enemy
Bhikshuki – A female ascetic beggar. A guise which a spy could assume
Bhindivála – Broad-tipped rod
Bhoga – Snake-like battle formation
Bhrita – Hired troops
Brahmin – Priest class of the Hindu social order

Chakra – Flat metal ring with a sharp edge that is thrown at an enemy
Charma – Shield made from leather

Dand – The strategy of punishing an enemy
Danda – Staff-like. The name of a battle formation
Dandásana – Rod arrow, a type of arrow used by archers
Devadanda – Log/beam that is dropped upon enemy soldiers
Dhaam – The strategy of bribing an enemy
Dhanus – Bows made of *sringa* (bone or horn)
Dharma – Righteousness, religion
Dharmanika – Inflatable leather bag used as a protectant
Divyastra – Divine missiles. Each missile is associated with a particular Hindu deity and is summoned and powered by special mantras. Each missile has a different capability such as causing tornadoes to blow back enemy soldiers, etc.
Dridhaka – Firm. The name of a battle formation
Druna – Bows made of *dáru* (a kind of wood)
Dúta – Envoy

Gada – Large, blunt metal club with heavy round/pear-shaped head
Gavedhu – Coix barbata used for bow-strings
Ghashasya – Face of the fish. The name of a battle formation
Grihapaitika – Spy under the guise of a householder
Gudhalekhya – cipher-writing, used by spies to communicate covertly
Guru – Teacher/master

Háláhala – A lethal poison
Halamukháni – Ploughshare
Hastikarna – Large body shield
Hastinakha – Turrets, small tower that projects vertically from a fort wall
Hastiváraka – Pronged-pole
Hastiyuddha – Elephant vs. elephant warfare
Hátaka – Several-pointed lance

Jamadagnya – A device that shoots arrows

Kanaya – Double-ended trident
Kanchuka – A soldier's coat extending as far as the knee joints
Kándachchhedana – Large axe
Kanthatrána – A protective cover for a soldier's neck
Kápatika-chhátra – A fraudulent disciple. A spy who can skilfully profile people
Kármuka – Bows made of palmyra

Karpana – Javelin, lightweight spear that is thrown at an enemy
Kaváta – Wooden board/door for protection against assault
Khadyota – Fire-fly, an ingredient for a mixture used for night-vision
Khanakayuddha – Fighting under the cover of entrenchment
Khanitra – Pick axe used for military purposes
Kitika – Cane and leather shield
Kodanda – Bows made of *chápa* (a kind of bamboo)
Kosha – Treasury
Kshatriya – Warrior class of the Hindu social order
Kshatriyasrení – The corporations of warriors
Kuddála – Spade designed used for military purposes
Kumára – A prince
Kunta – Lance, used by mounted soldiers
Kúrpása – Armour that protects the soldier's torso
Kuthára – Hatchet designed for combat

Loha – Metals

Manavaka – A sorcerer
Mandala – Circle-like. The name of a battle formation
Mandalágra – A sword with a straight blade
Mantra – A sacred utterance, invocation, incantation
Mantrayuddha – Treacherous fight
Manu – The Hindu progenitor of humanity. The *Manusmriti* (Laws of Manu) is a text containing laws attributed to him. Chanakya refers to Manu's school of thought in his text. The origin of the English word 'man' is related to the Sanskrit name, Manu
Mauhúrtika – An astrologer
Maula – Hereditary troops
Máyágata – Sorcery, the use of magic/illusions
Mlechchha – A term describing people who are non-Vedic, foreign, barbaric
Mudgara – A metal war hammer or wooden war mallet
Múrva – Sansevieria roxburghiana, which can be used to make bow-strings
Musala – Large, heavy wooden war pestle
Musrinthi – Cudgel

Naga – Serpent beings with various powers including the ability to shapeshift
Nágodariká – Gloves that protect a soldier's hands during combat
Nárácha – Iron arrow

Náyaka – Leader
Nistrimsa – A long sword with a curved blade

Om – Also Aum, it is considered the primordial sound of creation. Many mantras begin with this sacred syllable

Padika – Commander
Pánchálika – Plank that is studded with nails/spikes
Parasu – Battle axe
Parjanyaka – A device which extinguishes fire
Párshnigráha – Rear-enemy
Párvata – Mountainous fortification
Patta – A soldier's coat without cover for the arms
Pattasa – Double-ended trident and axe
Prachchhandaka – Mystics
Prása – A dart that is barbed
Pratirodhaka – Spies under the guise of robbers
Pratyávápa – Absence of surplus, the deficiency in infantry
Purohita – A priest

Rakshasa – A demon
Rasada – A spy who specialises in poisons
Rigveda – One of the four *Vedas*, Hinduism's oldest and holiest books. Written in Sanskrit, this *Veda* is the oldest of them and its focus is mantras. Chanakya mentions this *Veda* in his text
Ritvig – Sacrificial priest
Rochaní – Mill-stone

Saam – The strategy of appeasing an enemy
Sakti – Dart
Saláka – Arrow with a shaft made from wood
Samgháti – A device which hurls fire at the enemy
Samstháh – Institutes of espionage
Samaveda – One of the four *Vedas*, Hinduism's oldest and holiest books. Written in Sanskrit, the focus of this *Veda* is melodies. Chanakya mentions this *Veda* in his text
Sána – Hemp, which can be used to make bow-strings
Sandhi – Agreement of peace
Sángrámika – Chariots designed for battle

Sanjaya – Victory
Sara – Arrow with a shaft made from reed
Sarvatobhadra – A wheeled device that hurls stones at the enemy
Sataghni – Wheeled spiked-pillar that is rolled/hurled into the enemy
Satri – Class-mate or a colleague spy
Sattra – Ambush, attacking an unsuspecting enemy from a concealed position
Senápati – Commander-in-chief
Shikha – Lock of hair on the back of the shaven head of male Orthodox Hindus
Shudra – Labour class of the Hindu social order
Sirastrána – A helmet to protect the head from injury during combat
Sísa – Lead, a soft and malleable metal. An ingredient used in making an inflammable powder
Snáyu – Sinew, which can be used to make bow-strings
Spriktala – Club with the head studded with protruding spikes
Súkarika – Padded leather bags that protect turrets of forts
Súla – Spike-tipped rod
Syena – Eagle-like. The name of a battle formation

Tálamúla – Large flat shield
Tálavrinta – A device that blows dust into the direction of enemy soldiers
Tantra – Magical/spiritual practices
Tápasa – An austerities-practicing recluse. A guise which a spy could assume
Tejanachúrna – Ignition powder
Tíkshna – Fire-brand/furious. A dedicated assassin
Tomara – An arrow-tipped weapon
Trapu – Zinc, a liquid metal. An ingredient used in making inflammable powder
Trásika – Long sharp rod
Trishúla – Trident, a three-pronged spear

Udásthita – Recluse. A guise which a spy could assume
Upasthána – Drill
Úrdhvabáhu – Heavy crushing-pillar

Vaidehaka – Merchant. A guise which a spy could assume
Vaishya – Merchant and artisan class of the Hindu social order
Valáhakánta – Metal-tipped weapon that repels elephants
Vanadurga – Forest fortification
Varáhakarna – Pole with a boar ear-shaped spearhead

Váravána – A coat extending as far as the heels
Venu – Arrow with a shaft made from bamboo
Veti – Wooden cover
Vijaya – Conqueror. Also victory
Vikrama – Valour
Visalavijaya – Vast victory. The name of a battle formation
Visvásagháti – Log or beam that is dropped upon enemies
Vyúha – Battle formations consisting of chariots, elephants, cavalry and/or infantry arranged in a variety of ways

Yajurveda – One of the four *Vedas*, Hinduism's oldest and holiest books. Written in Sanskrit, the focus of this *Veda* is sacrificial rites. Chanakya mentions this *Veda* in his text
Yánaka – A log-throwing device
Yantra – Instrument/machine. Also symbols and geometric patterns
Yashti – Short staff
Yátra – Journey
Yuddha – War

BIBLIOGRAPHY

Agarwal, S.K. *Towards Improving Governance*. (New Delhi: Academic Foundation, 2008).

Arya, Ravi Prakash. *Dhanurveda: The Vedic Military Science*. (New Delhi: Indian Foundation for Vedic Science, 2008).

Aulakh, Ajit Singh. *Guru Gobind Singh Ji*. (Amritsar: Chattar Singh Jiwan Singh, 1999).

Barclay, Shelly. "Who are the Janjaweed." August, 2010. http://www.worldissues360.com/index.php/who-are-the-janjaweed-11318/ (accessed April, 2014).

Bhosle, Varsha. "First Blood." *Rediff*. 1997. http://www.rediff.com/news/may/23varsha.htm (accessed September, 2013).

Cummins, Antony & Minami, Yoshie. *Iga and Koka Ninja Skills: The Secret Shinobi Scrolls of Chikamatsu Shigenori*. (Gloucestershire: The History Press Ltd., 2014).

"Demonstrations and Public Order." Metropolitan Police. http://content.met.police.uk/Article/Demonstrations-and-Public-Order/1400007129835/mountedbranchofficerduties (accessed September, 2013).

Fraas, Arthur Mitchell. "A Rocket Cat? Early Modern Explosives Treatises at Penn." *Unique at Penn*. 5 February, 2013. http://uniqueatpenn.wordpress.com/2013/02/05/a-rocket-cat-early-modern-explosives-treatises-at-penn/ (accessed June, 2014).

"Guru Gobind Singh Sahib." Shiromani Gurdwara Parbandhak Committee. http://www.sgpc.net/gurus/gurugobind.asp (accessed September, 2013).

Hymns of the Atharva-Veda. Sacred Books of the East, Volume 42, translated into English by Maurice Bloomfield (Oxford University Press, 1897).

Indo-Asian News Service. "Scientists Look Back for the Future." *The Tribune*. November 3 2002. http://www.tribuneindia.com/2002/20021104/nation.htm (accessed January, 2013).

Kashyap, Siddhartha D. "Chanakya'neeti' to be studied at defence institute." *The Times of India.* http://timesofindia.indiatimes.com/city/pune/chanakyaneeti-to-be-studied-at-defence-institute/articleshow/18602258.cms (accessed May, 2014).

Kautilya, *Arthashastra*, translated into English by R. Shamasastry (Bangalore: Government Press, 1915).

Kautilya. *The Arthashastra,* edited by L.N. Rangarajan (Penguin Books India, 1992).

Krishnamachariar, M. and Srinivasachariar, M. *History of Classical Sanskrit Literature.* (Madras: Tirumalai-Tirupati Devasthanams Press, 1937).

Machiavelli, Niccolo. *The Prince*. Volume 36 of Harvard classics, translated into English by Ninian Hill Thomson (P. F. Collier & Son, 1910).

Madrigal, Alexis C. "Do Not Try to Recreate This 16th-Century German Cat Bomb at Home." *The Atlantic*. 23 January, 2013. http://www.theatlantic.com/technology/archive/2013/01/do-not-try-to-recreate-this-16th-century-german-cat-bomb-at-home/272458/ (accessed June, 2014).

Manu. *The Laws of Manu*. Sacred Books of the East, Volume 25, translated into English by George Buhler, (Oxford: Clarendon Press, 1886).

Oppert, Gustav. *On The Weapons, Army Organisation, and Political Maxims of the Ancient Hindus, with Special Reference to Gunpowder and Firearms.* (Madras: Higginbotham, 1880).

Plutarch. *The Parallel Lives.* The Life of Alexander. http://penelope.uchicago.edu/Thayer/E/Roman/Texts/Plutarch/Lives/Alexander*/9.html (accessed July, 2014).

Rahman, Shaikh Azizur. "India Defence Looks to Ancient Text." *BBC News*. 14 May, 2002. http://news.bbc.co.uk/1/hi/world/south_asia/1986595.stm (accessed January, 2013).

Sagoo, Harjit Singh, "Indian martial culture." *Boevie Iskusstva*. May, 2013.

Sah N.K., Singh S.N., Sahdev S., Banerji S., Jha V., Khan Z., Hasnain S.E. "Indian herb 'Sanjeevani' (Selaginella bryopteris) can promote growth and protect against heat shock and apoptotic activities of ultra violet and oxidative stress." *Journal of Biosciences.* September, 2005. http://www.ias.ac.in/jbiosci/sep2005/499.pdf (accessed June, 2014).

Singh, Charanjit Ajit. "A Spiritual Throne." *Faith Initiative*. 2005. http://www.faithinitiative.co.uk/article.php?issue=1123632028 (accessed May, 2014).

Singh, Gobind. Sri Dasam Granth Sahib. http://www.sridasam.org/dasam?c=t Project initiative, coding and website by Jasjeet Singh Thind. (accessed July, 2013).

Singh, Nidar. "Asking... Niddar Singh." Interview by Harjit Singh Sagoo. *Martial Arts Illustrated.* May, 2009.

Srinivasaraju, Sugata. "Year Of The Guru." *Outlook India*. 27 July, 2009. http://www.outlookindia.com/printarticle.aspx?250522 (accessed April, 2014).

Subramanian, V. K. *Maxims of Chanakya.* (New Delhi: Abhinav Publications, 2003).

Subramanyam, Harivansh. "When a Guru Confronted a Serial Killer." *True Crime.* September, 2011.

Thornton, Edward. *Illustrations of the History and Practices of the Thugs.* (London, W. H. Allen and Co., 1837).

Tzu, Sun. *The Art of War*, translated into English by Lionel Giles, M.A. (1910).

Vyasa. *The Mahabharata of Krishna-Dwaipayana Vyasa*, translated into English by Kisari Mohan Ganguli (Calcutta: Bharat Press, 1883-1896).

Wang, Hengwei. *"Chinese History Lecture: Volume II Warring States."* (Beijing: Zhonghua Book Company, 2005/2006).

PHOTO AND IMAGE CREDITS

Rani Kaur: photos of Harjit Singh Sagoo for human silhouette images

Guru Piumal Edirisinghe: Angampora photo

Gurumustuk Singh: Baba Deep Singh fresco photo

Prasanna Revan: Kushti photo

Kaur Khalsa Gatka Group, Dharamkot: Gatka photo

Ranjeet Singh: Bagh nakh and Kara images

Varun Kapur: Indian fort photo

Amrit Pal Singh 'Amrit': Nihang warriors photo

www.tripura4u.com: Hindu weapon-worship photo

Arthur Mitchell Fraas, University of Pennsylvania Libraries: Cat and bird rockets illustration

Abdul Qadir Memon: Taxila site photo

Linda De Volder: Rama on Indonesian Hindu temple photo – https://www.flickr.com/photos/lindadevolder/4603487395/in/set-72157623220682876

Sri E.S. Narayanan Embranthiri: Kalaripayattu photo

Kiranjot Singh Malhotra: Ashtbhuja photo

Harjit Singh Sagoo: Silhouette images and line drawings of gods, humans, animals, demons, buildings, war machines, military vehicles and weapons

ABOUT THE AUTHORS

Harjit Singh Sagoo is a published multi-genre writer, illustrator and researcher of reality-based combat. He has been published in Martial Arts Illustrated – his series: 'Asking the Masters' (England), Black Belt magazine (USA), Blitz (Australia), Asana International Yoga Journal (India), Samurai Bushido (Italy), Kung Fu Era (Singapore), Animal Voice (Northern Ireland), Iran Daily (Iran), Positive Life (Republic of Ireland), Outwords (Canada), El Budoka 2.0 (Spain) and Boevie Iskusstva (Ukraine). Other publications include The Horror Zine, Totally Taekwondo, Fish Rap Live! and Kung Fu Tai Chi magazine. Under the pseudonym, Harivansh Subramanyam, he has published articles in Combat magazine, True Crime, Beacon Online, Fighters Only, and others. He has also done illustrations which have appeared in The Colonel, www.alittlebitfunny.com and The Medium. Also among these is a piece of artwork that was selected and featured as 'for sale' on robertenglund.com.

Harjit's first book, *A Crash Course in Surviving Gangsters, Serial Killers, Contract Killers and Terrorists*, was published in 2015. His reality-based system is an amalgamation of various Asian and Western fighting arts, including Indian Gatka. For the original 2013 PDF versions of his book, he received Letters of Appreciation from the Danish Armed Forces; the Hungarian National Police HQ; the Office of Hon. Rob Nicholson, Canada's then Minister of Defence; the Humanist Association for Leadership, Equity and Accountability (HALEA) and others. Techniques from his manual were implemented into the combat training curriculum of the Danish Armed Forces. Nearly 100 copies of the printed version of his book were received by Ukraine's Ministry of Defence for personnel within the Ukrainian Armed Forces, including special units.

ANTONY CUMMINS

Antony Cummins is an author and historical researcher. He is the founder of the Historical Ninjutsu Research Team and is responsible for the translation of multiple medieval ninja manuals and samurai scrolls into English. His books include: *Book of Ninja, Book of Samurai, True Path of the Ninja, Secrets Traditions of the Shinobi, Iga and Koka Ninja Skills, Samurai and Ninja, In Search of the Ninja* and *Samurai War Stories*. Alongside this Antony has featured in the documentaries: *Ninja Shadow Warriors, Samurai Headhunters, Samurai Warrior Queens, The Ninja* and *47 Ronin* among others. He is also the rejuvenating force behind the rebirth of the samurai school Natori-Ryu and has been appointed as Ambassador for Tourism for Wakayama, Japan. For more information see www.natori.co.uk

Printed in Great Britain
by Amazon